THE PRICE OF FOOTBALL

THE PRICE OF FOOTBALL

Understanding Football Club Finance

KIERAN MAGUIRE

agenda
publishing

First edition published in 2020 by Agenda Publishing
Reprinted 2020 (twice)

Agenda Publishing Limited
The Core
Bath Lane
Newcastle Helix
Newcastle upon Tyne
NE4 5TF
www.agendapub.com

ISBN 978-1-911116-89-9 (hardcover)
ISBN 978-1-911116-90-5 (paperback)

British Library Cataloguing-in-Publication Data
A catalogue record for this book is available from the British Library

Typeset by Newgen Publishing UK
Printed and bound in the UK by TJ International

CONTENTS

CONTENTS

1

INTRODUCTION

In an ideal world this book would not need to be written as there would be no interest or demand for it. Football is the world's most universal sport, on both a domestic and international stage and all the discussion from fans and others should be about goals, saves, formations, VAR, red and yellow cards, managerial decisions and shouting obscenities at Mike Dean (other referees are also available).

But at what cost can we ignore the financial impact of the sport? For football fans, many of the top ten moments in their lives will be football related yet ask them what they dislike most about the game and you will most likely hear that "money has ruined it". Transfer fees, footballers' wages, clubs being bought and sold on a whim as rich men's toys, arguments over the objectives and application of financial fair play – all this and more has, in the eyes of many, turned a much loved, emotionally-fuelled sport into a cold, callous business.

The idea for this book arose by accident. I was on the BBC 1 Breakfast couch, having been asked to fill in the gaps between Carol Kirkwood's regular weather forecasts, and was talking about the latest television deal for the Premier League; the publisher of Agenda, Steven Gerrard (no, not that one) was eating his Weetabix watching the television at the time and thought that football finance would be a good idea for a book.

The central focus of this book is the influence of money and finance on the game. It seeks to discuss the big questions that spring to mind and simplify in layman's terms wherever possible some key finance related issues. Questions such as what are the sources of income, both internal and external, for a club? How do you show those sources in the accounts? How do you deal with benefactors, new stadia, players coming to and leaving the club? What happens in the accounts if that multi-million-pound centre forward, signed a year ago, turns out to be rubbish? (This may be of particular use to any fan who has had Andy Carroll play for their favourite team in the last few years).

While there will be facts and figures along the way, this book is not intended to turn the reader into accountants (tricky), or even to like them (impossible). It is intended to give an overview of what happens in terms of the financial implications of all the transactions that are regularly discussed in the media, in club press releases and for those of you who may be studying a football finance module as part of your education.

Football is the greatest game in the world. It makes you hug complete strangers on a Saturday afternoon and encourages grown men and women to sing, and for those reasons alone it is to be cherished. This book won't make you want to hug a football club finance director, although each to their own of course, but hopefully it will help you understand better just what he or she is talking about and whether you should take their comments at face value or with scepticism.

According to FIFA, the governing body of football, there were 265 million registered football players when last surveyed, albeit about a decade ago. Since then FIFA seem to have been preoccupied by other issues and researching the popularity of the sport has not been as high on their agenda. Of this 265 million, only a small fraction of these players participate in the game on a professional level, in terms of being paid money to play for an individual team. To fund the costs of running a football team, wages, maintenance, infrastructure and so on, a club must generate income. This book aims to identify the main sources of income, the typical costs that are incurred, and how clubs are bought, sold and valued.

Football started as an amateur sport, and the first rules were created in England in the nineteenth century. Initially there were a variety of rules, depending on the geographical location of the club in the country. The game in the first half of the nineteenth century was played most frequently between public schools, as well as between villages and towns. Games could take up to three days to complete. Given that most teams did not travel far to play their opponents there were few problems in agreeing to the rules as local ones took precedence. Confusion only started to arise when universities started playing football as there would be players from different public schools at universities trying to play by their own local rules, so it was essential that an agreed format for the game was created.

Cambridge University took it upon themselves to devise a set of rules to avoid confusion and these became popular in the south of England. Northerners preferred to play by their own rules so followed another collection set up by the then Sheffield Football Club. In 1863 the Football Association was formed in London and established a set of rules which contained elements of each of the Cambridge and Sheffield variants. And finally in 1877 the London Football Association and Sheffield Football Association agreed upon a common set of laws, which have formed the template for the evolution of the game ever since.

The first international match took place in 1872 between Scotland and England. The attendance was 4,000, but spectators were willing to pay 1 shilling (5 pence) to watch the game, giving total gate receipts of £200. There was a realization that football was not just a sport, but also entertainment for the masses, and perhaps a potential business too. The world's first professional football club was Notts County. Clubs initially organized their own fixtures against opposing teams in what was a glorified set of exhibition matches. However, to be successful they needed players who were available, talented, fit and healthy, which given the working conditions and poverty of the Victorian era was no easy task. It was impractical for footballers to take time off work to practise and play in matches. Football needed to transform from an amateur to a professional sport if clubs wanted to attract large crowds to pay to watch games.

The codification of the game led to the creation of tournaments. The Football Association Challenge Cup (more commonly known as the FA Cup) was the world's first organized tournament, kicking off in 1871. The competition was initially marred by some clubs withdrawing from the competition being unable to pay wages or transport costs to fulfil fixtures, but nevertheless it went from strength to strength. As attendances at matches increased and the game became more popular, the first league competition commenced in 1888, again in England. It consisted of one division, 12 clubs (all from the north and the midlands; southern teams were still mainly amateur at this time with gentlemen players). Since then the game has moved on with rapid pace to become the global phenomenon it is today. There are presently 211 countries affiliated to FIFA, as well as many non-recognized states and islands who play in their own tournaments not sanctioned by FIFA.

The growth of the game has coincided with an increase in its finances. By 2018 the 20 largest global club sides (in terms of income) generated revenue, according to the Deloitte Money League, of £8.3 billion and FIFA itself had cash and financial assets of nearly $3 billion. In the chapters that follow we will look at the extent to which finance impacts upon the game, in terms of funding, income, wages, ticket prices and infrastructure. As football clubs have become multi-million-pound operations they need to present their monetary information in a professional manner too, which means they need to prepare financial reports. And this is where we shall begin.

PART I
FOOTBALL CLUB FINANCIAL REPORTS

2

THE BALANCE SHEET

The first step towards understanding football finances is being able to decipher a set of club accounts. This can be an overwhelming task as they may consist of many pages of technical jargon and so are best broken down into their key components. There are three main financial statements published by all businesses, including football clubs, typically contained in what is usually referred to as an annual report, and consist of:

1. The balance sheet, which shows the financial position of the club in terms of what it owns in the form of assets and what it owes to both outside parties (liabilities) and owners (equity, also referred to as capital);
2. The profit or loss account (sometimes called the income statement), which deals with revenues, costs and profit; and
3. The cash flow statement, which shows where cash has come from and how it has been spent. The most common mistake made by those unfamiliar with finance is to assume that cash and profit are the same, which is not the case in practice.

Most football clubs in the UK are limited liability companies, which are legally obliged to submit their financial statements to the government agency Companies House. The great thing for anyone interested in the finances of the club they support is that this information is freely available to access and download from the Companies House website. Rules vary in other countries as to the extent of financial information in the public domain according to local legislation. The amount of detail shown in the accounts sent to Companies House varies according to the size of the club. There are supporting footnotes that must be prepared as well as the main financial statements. The extent of these is again dependent upon the size of the club's finances. Manchester United's annual report for the year ended 30 June 2019 consisted of 1,434 pages when it filed its accounts with the US authorities, whereas those of Mansfield Town Football Club Limited, currently in League Two of the English Football League, were just three pages from start to finish.

These accounts and their supporting notes tell a financial story of the club, which can often explain some of the strategic and operational decisions made by the directors and management team in terms of player trading, commercial partnership deals, stadium and infrastructure development, overseas tours and other issues which are so regularly commented upon in the sport and business media. Being able to declutter the accounts and identify key trends, risks, opportunities and threats is a useful skill for anyone wanting to analyse any business's finances, not just those of a football club, even if the aim is to just gain a greater insight into the club that a fan supports. The numbers help tell the story, and we all like stories in relation to our club, or perhaps relating to our rivals provided they paint a negative picture of the team we love to hate.

The best place to start when analysing a club's accounts is to become familiar with the balance sheet. The balance sheet is a financial photograph of a club on a single date that correlates with the end of the club's financial year. A balance sheet (also known as a statement of financial position) shows the relationship between three financial elements, and is expressed by the equation:

assets = equity + liabilities

The equation can also be reconfigured in the balance sheet as assets − liabilities = equity. It makes no difference to a club's financial security or profitability which method it uses to present the balance sheet.

The balance sheet shown in Figure 2.1 is from the annual report of Celtic plc at 30 June 2018. It shows that the club had total assets of £149.8 million at that date. Those assets are broken down into subcategories.

Non-current assets (also known as fixed assets) are ones that are going to be used by the club for at least one year. These include property, plant and equipment – the stadium, training facilities, offices, etc. – at a figure of £58 million. Players are classified as "intangible" assets and have an accounting value (which in no way relates to their market value, especially if you consider the transfer of Moussa Dembele by Celtic a couple of months later) of £21 million. In addition, Celtic had "trade receivables" (debtors) of £4.4 million for goods and services supplied by the club to customers but the club does not expect to receive payment for at least a year. This is likely to be in relation to instalments on transfer fees on players sold by the club.

Current assets are ones which are cash or expected to be converted into cash in less than a year. Again, there are trade receivables, which here are £21.2 million, representing the amount Celtic contractually is entitled to receive from customers (mainly other clubs for transfers) over the next 12 months. Other current assets include stocks of merchandise and over £42 million of cash.

The balance sheets show that the equation of "assets = liabilities + equity" holds true, however this does not mean that the club is either profitable or financially secure as all balance sheets should balance regardless of the strength of the club's finances. There are no rules as to when a club should produce its balance sheet, although clubs are encouraged to tie them into the industry year. In practice, most clubs prepare their balance sheets to

Table 2.1 Consolidated balance sheet at 30 June 2018, Celtic

	2018 £000	2017 £000
Assets		
Non-current assets		
Property, plant and equipment	58,265	56,332
Intangible assets	20,963	13,927
Trade receivables	4,397	–
	83,625	70,259
Inventories	2,407	2,414
Trade and other receivables	21,261	12,284
Cash and cash equivalents	42,563	24,505
	66,231	39,203
Total assets	149,856	109,462
Equity		
Issued share capital	27,132	27,107
Share premium	14,720	14,657
Other reserve	21,222	21,222
Accumulated profits/ (losses)	9,860	(5,563)
Total equity	72,934	57,423
Non-current liabilities		
Borrowings	6,250	6,450
Debt element of Convertible Cumulative Preference Shares	4,208	4,232
Trade and other payables	10,302	5,940
Provisions	2,309	1,543
Deferred income	86	115
	23,155	18,280
Current liabilities		
Trade and other payables	27,005	10,435
Current borrowings	300	304
Provisions	2,442	658
Deferred income	24,020	22,362
	53,767	33,759
Total liabilities	76,922	52,039
Total equity and liabilities	149,856	109,462

Source: Celtic Plc annual report ending 30 June 2018

coincide with the end of the football season. Therefore, nearly all major European clubs have a balance sheet dated 31 May, 30 June or 31 July. Remember that the balance sheet is a financial photograph, so these dates tend to be when the finances of the club are looking at their most impressive. The club will have received income from season ticket sales for the following season, for example, which will have increased its cash balance. Many transfers for the following season may not have been signed by the financial year-end if it is May or June, so these financial commitments will not be reflected in the balance sheet.

What is an asset?

Most people would simply say that an asset is something that a person or business owns. And in most cases that is correct, but the accounting definition is a little more complex than that. To satisfy the definition of a football club asset the item must satisfy three conditions:

1. *It must be controlled by the football club.* Control means the club has all or almost all the risks and rewards of ownership. The main risks are the likes of damage, maintenance, obsolescence, theft and poor performance. For a football club, therefore, this could be something as simple as a lawnmower used to cut the grass on the pitch, or a centre forward signed for £40 million who hasn't scored for 12 months. The main rewards of owning something are freedom of use in relation to the asset, preventing anyone else from using it (very important in terms of football player registrations) and protection from future price rises.
2. *It is expected to generate economic benefits for the club.* Economic benefits can either be generating income or cost savings. For a club, football players for whom they have registration certificates are the biggest generators of income, as these players attract spectators, broadcast companies and sponsors. Other assets include the stadium, training facilities used to develop players, and many other items used to ensure the day-to-day running of the club.
3. *It is due to a past event.* There is usually a contract signed on a particular date that would prove this.

If a club bought, for example, a new computer system on 1 January 2018, it would be classified as an asset because:

- The club can use the computer for whatever purpose it chooses, such as player health monitoring, finance, player matchday statistical analysis, ticketing and so on. The club also has the risks in relation to the computer, such as theft, a virus, another club hacking the password and using the sensitive information contained on the computer, and so on.
- The club benefits from using the computer, either from improving player skills when used in training, or part of the club's financial operations, communications, etc.
- The computer was bought at some time in the past.

You will see that not all assets appear in the balance sheet. If you consider the brand value of a big football club such as FC Barcelona or Manchester United, there is no doubting that it has a significant monetary amount, but there is no such asset in the accounts. It is for this reason that most balance sheets understate the market value of a club as they fail to include all the assets.

For an asset to appear in the balance sheet, there is an additional test, and this is a critical one for a football club. The asset must have a *known* monetary value. This usually means that the club must have purchased the asset, at an agreed price, for it to appear in the balance sheet. Although Manchester United claim in their press releases to have 1.1 billion fans worldwide, it is not possible to work out a value for that huge fanbase, as United did not pay for the fans to support the club. Therefore, under the accounting rules, there is no value shown for the Manchester United fanbase, its logo or its brand.

The football industry is fairly unique in that its most important assets, the players, are sometimes shown on the balance sheet, but sometimes not shown too and the rules, whilst at first appearing illogical, are applied consistently from club to club.

Types of asset

Non-current vs current assets

Accountants split assets into different categories. A "non-current asset" (also known as a "fixed asset") is one that benefits the club for more than one year. This would include football stadia, motor vehicles, equipment used by the ground staff and purchased football player registrations if the player has signed a contract for more than one year.

In contrast a "current asset" is one that is expected to be converted into cash in less than one year, or cash itself. The main categories of current assets are inventories of football merchandise, moneys owed by other clubs for transfers and other parties (usually called debtors or receivables), prepaid expenses (where the club may, for example, have paid a deposit on a player before signing him, or paid rent in advance on some property), cash and bank balances.

If the club is owed money for transfer fees from other clubs, this could have elements of both a current and a non-current asset, depending on when the fees are due from the buying club.

In Table 2.2, at 31 May 2018 Manchester City had player transfer debtors of £53.6 million due within one year and a further £26.5 million due in more than one year, to give total transfer debtors of £80.1 million. With transfer deals being for such large sums at the elite level in today's market, it is common for payments to be paid in instalments, over a period of many years. This is often linked to the length of contract signed by the player himself. This information is useful to anyone trying to work out a club's future cash position, as the split between current and non-current assets can be taken into consideration when producing budgets and forecasts of the future cash position.

Table 2.2 Notes to the financial statements, Annual Report 2017/18, Manchester City

14. DEBTORS

	2018 £000	2017 £000
Amounts falling due within one year		
Trade debtors	**134,487**	129,659
Debtors arising from player transfers	**53,585**	29,955
Amounts owed by group undertakings (Note 23)	**16,541**	74,145
Amounts owed by related party undertakings (Note 23)	**486**	367
Other debtors	**43**	40
Prepayments and accrued income	**46,702**	36,521
	251,644	270,687
Amounts tailing due after more than one year		
Debtors arising from player transfers	**26,465**	23,194
Other debtors	**450**	157
	26,915	23,351
Total debtors	**278,759**	294,038

Source: Manchester City Football Club Limited annual report

Tangible assets vs intangible assets

A further division of assets then arises, splitting them between tangibles and intangible categories.

A "tangible asset" has physical substance, so you can see it, touch it, or perhaps from a football perspective, kick it. Tangible assets of a football club therefore include things such as stadia, offices, computers, vehicles, equipment and similar items. Tangible assets are usually grouped together under the heading "property, plant and equipment" or "fixed assets" in the balance sheet. The cost of the tangible asset is then spread over the period of time the club expects to use it in its business. This spreading of the asset cost is called "depreciation" and is shown as an expense in the profit or loss account. Often it is uncertain how long an individual asset will be used by the club, so an estimate of the life is made when the asset is purchased.

The extract in Table 2.3 is from the accounts of Wolverhampton Wanderers. The stadium development, for example, is depreciated at 2 per cent per year, which equates to an expected life of 50 years. The club therefore reduces the value of the stadium by 2 per cent each year and this is also shown as a running cost when calculating profits. Motor vehicles, in contrast, are depreciated by 20 per cent per year which gives them an accounting life of five years. This makes commercial sense as a car is likely to be used by the club for a much shorter period of time than a stadium. The land on which the stadium is built is not depreciated because it does not wear out over time, unlike cars, computers, lawnmowers, etc. Land has an infinite useful life and so spreading its cost over an infinite number gives a zero depreciation figure.

Table 2.3 Tangible fixed assets, Wolverhampton Wanderers

Tangible fixed assets are stated at cost, net of depreciation and any provision for impairment. Depreciation is provided on all tangible assets at rates calculated to write off the cost less estimated market residual value of each asset, on a straight-line basis over its expected useful life as below:

Land	*Not depreciated*
Stadium development	2%
Training facilities	2–20%
Car park	2%
Plant and equipment	10%
Motor vehicles	20%
Fixtures and fittings	12.5%

Source: W. W. (1990) Ltd annual report, year ended 31 May 2018

An "intangible asset" is similar to a tangible asset but has a key distinguishing feature in that it has no physical substance, but nevertheless a club has a legal right that allows it to transfer an intangible asset to another club or business. These can include items such as patent rights, trademarks, goodwill and licences. The most significant intangible asset seen in a football club balance sheet is football player registration transfers. These represent the sum paid to acquire a player's registration from another club. When a transfer takes place, the transfer fee is for the right to register the player exclusively for a single club. It is the piece of paper giving this right to which the fee relates, not the individual player. By signing for club A from club B on a contract, the player commits himself to play for his new club for an agreed period of time and no other club. It is this exclusivity of employment right that has value.

Philippe Coutinho signed for Liverpool in 2013 on a long-term contract and then signed a five-year contract extension in January 2017. This meant that he could not play for another football club until 2022 unless Liverpool agreed to release him from this contract. Therefore, when Barcelona tried to recruit him in January 2018 to play for their team, they had to agree a compensation fee with Liverpool for releasing Coutinho from his contract four years early. This compensation fee was agreed at a fee rumoured to be £142 million. Coutinho then signed a five-and-a-half-year contract with Barcelona, as this gives the La Liga club the protection of exclusivity in relation to the player during this period, unless another club persuades Barcelona to release him with a satisfactory fee.

Liabilities and equity

Before a club builds a stadium, signs a player, pays wages, or even gets around to cutting the grass on the new pitch, it must have funding to pay for these assets. This funding comes from two sources, which are shown on the other side of the balance sheet, in the form of liabilities and/or equity.

What is a liability?

A liability is an amount due from the club to someone other than those who own the club. This could be a trade supplier, such as an electricity company, another football club for a transfer fee outstanding, the government for tax payments that are due, or even an individual person to whom the club owes money, such as the window cleaner. For a liability to be shown in the balance sheet of a football club the following conditions must apply:

- There is an obligation/commitment to the other party (such as another club, a player, a supplier, tax authority). This obligation will normally have arisen by the club signing a contract or taking delivery of goods from someone else. The obligation will usually be legal in nature.
- The commitment can only be settled by an outflow of economic benefits. This is accounting speak for the club having to give an asset, usually cash, or perhaps a player in a swap deal, or a service, to the other party.
- It is due to a past event.

For example, in July 2018 Juventus signed Cristiano Ronaldo from Real Madrid for €112 million on a four-year contract. The fee payable by Juventus was in instalments. This creates a liability in the balance sheet of Juventus because:

- Juventus had a contractual obligation to Real due to the latter agreeing to transfer Ronaldo's registration;
- Juventus could only settle the obligation by paying Real €112 million and at Juventus's next balance sheet date part of the fee was still outstanding;
- The obligation arose due to a past event, when the transfer of Ronaldo's registration from Real to Juventus took place.

Types of liability

Non-current vs current liabilities

A "non-current liability" is one for which payment is not due for at least twelve months. For a football club such liabilities tend to be loans, often taken out to fund infrastructure expansion and other major projects. "Current liabilities" are where the payment is due in less than twelve months. These can include amounts due to suppliers, taxes, player and staff bonuses, overdrafts and short-term financing agreements, although it is important

Table 2.4 Creditors, 2017 and 2018, West Ham United

16. Creditors		
	Group	
	2018 £000	2017 £000
Amounts falling due within one year		
Bank and other loans (notes 17 & 19)	10,000	30,000
Trade Creditors	4,661	2,904
Taxation and social security	8,705	12,295
Creditors arising from player transfers	32,500	31,050
Other creditors	1,308	1,392
Season ticket and other receipts in advance	17,962	17,972
Unsecured shareholder loan (note 17)	9,500	–
Accruals	13,805	21,697
	98,441	117,310
Amounts falling due after more than one year		
Debenture loans (notes 18)	611	611
Loans from shareholders (note 17)	45,000	45,000
Creditors arising from player transfers	24,490	24,889
Other creditors	2,774	1,502
Season ticket and other receipts in advance	890	816
	73,765	72,818

Source: W H Holding Ltd annual report, year ended 31 May 2018

to note that the club's bank balance can be either a current asset (if positive) or a current liability (if negative).

Sums owing for players can appear as either non-current or current liabilities, depending on when the contracted sums are due to the selling club. In the present transfer market, with so many deals taking place in instalments, this can also include significant sums due to other football clubs too.

Table 2.4 shows West Ham United's liabilities at 31 May 2018. The club's parent company, WH Holding Limited, owed a total of £57 million to other clubs at this date, of which nearly £25 million was due in instalments in over one year.

It is very rare for a club to show the individual sums owing in respect of player transfers. Juventus SA has the best disclosures of any club who publishes their financial details, as can be seen from the balance sheet below, and set a standard to which perhaps other clubs should aspire. Juventus owed over €85 million to overseas clubs for player transfers at 30 June 2018 (see Table 2.5) and a further €92 million to other Italian clubs (not shown).

Table 2.5 Juventus player transfers, amounts owing at 30 June 2018 (€ '000s)

Bayern Munchen AG	28,075	20,000	48,075
Chelsea F.C. Plc	6,666	6,667	13,333
Paris Saint-Germain F.C.	7,125	4,750	11,875
Arsenal F.C. Pic	6,000	–	6,000
Envigado F.C. SA	1,400	–	1,400
Gremio Football Porto-Alegrense	452	452	904
Shakhtar Donetsk	398	398	796
RCD Espanyol de Barcelona SAD	175	350	525
C.A. Boca Juniors	499	–	499
Confederacao Brasileira de Futebol	150	150	300
SASP ESTAC Club de Football	151	101	252
Club Sportivo Luqueno	200	–	200
PSV NV	199	–	199
SASP AS Saint Etienne SA	112	74	186
MKS Agrykola	180	–	180
Olympique de Marseille SASP	127	–	127
EL Equipo del Pieblo S.A. – Independiente de Medellin	52	53	105
Club Olympique Vincennois	56	38	94
SASP Clermont Foot Auvergne	85	–	85
U.S.C.L. Creteil-Lusilanos	70	13	83
Atletico Uraba	34	33	67
Embajadores F.C.	33	33	66
Leones F.C.	33	33	66
Federation Francaise de Football	38	25	63
Bretigny Foot C.S.	43	–	43
F.C. Lorient Bretagne Sud SASP	40	–	40
SA En Avant de Guingamp SASP	39	–	39
Brentford F.C. Ltd	16	–	16
Croatian Football Federation	14	–	14
GNK Dinamo Zagreb	5	–	5
NK Zagreb	5	–	5
Fundacio P. Escola F. Calella	3	1	4
Club Artesaro de Colonia Suiza	2	–	2
U.E. Vilassar de Mar	1	1	2
Legia Warszawa SA	1	–	1
N.E.C. BV	1	–	1
NK Livada Zeljeznicar	1	–	1
AEK Athens	1	–	1
Total foreign	**52,482**	**33,172**	**85,654**

Source: Juventus SA

Financing vs operating liabilities

Most analysts split liabilities between two types, financing and operating, although they will not be described as such in the balance sheet of the club.

A "financing liability" is an amount due to a bank or other financial institution. Financing liabilities can be dangerous for any business, let alone a football club. Banks and other lenders typically have conditions attached to the sums they advance to businesses, such that if repayments are missed, the bank has the right to impose penalties, or even worse, petition for some form of corporate bankruptcy to recover the amount outstanding. Many banks will lend only to clubs in the form of secured loans, which is similar to a mortgage for anyone who is buying a house. If you get into mortgage arrears, then the bank potentially can take possession of the house and sell it to pay back the sum owed. When it comes to football clubs, lenders may secure lending on a variety of potential assets and cash flows. It is most common to see the loan linked to property, future payments from television deals, outstanding transfer fees owing to the club, and season ticket sales income.

Middlesbrough Football and Athletic Company (1986) Ltd annual report 2018 shows a mortgage loan, in which Middlesbrough Football Club borrowed money from Macquarie Bank Ltd, and this appears to be relatively typical. Middlesbrough wanted cash to provide the the manager with funds to trade players in the January 2018 transfer window. However, when reading the small print of the loan agreement the lender linked the sum advanced to the €13.5 million that was being paid by the Italian club Atalanta in respect of a transfer earlier in the year in respect of Marten De Roon, who Middlesbrough had ironically signed only 13 months previously ... from Atalanta. At the transfer date Middlesbrough declined to reveal the transfer fee due to a privacy clause so documentation such as the loan agreement is often needed to provide further information of a club's dealings. However, the loan agreement with Macquarie did set out the terms of the transfer deal, with a fee of €13.5 million being paid in six instalments.

As well as borrowing money from Macquarie for De Roon, Middlesbrough borrowed a further €6 million secured on the transfer of Uruguayan player Gaston Ramirez on the same date with a similar arrangement. Ramirez is famous throughout Middlesbrough for setting up the goal that secured the club's promotion to the Premier League in May 2016, as well as having the world's smallest pair of shinpads.

When analysing financial statements of a club, it is important to identify financial liabilities to calculate "net debt", which is "financial liabilities less cash and cash equivalents". Financial liabilities can take many forms and are described using many different technical terms, including loans, notes payable, finance leases, overdrafts and revolving credit facilities.

Football clubs are different from many other large businesses in that some of their loans may come from club owners, and these loans may be at more favourable terms than from banks.

The extract (Table 2.6) from Brighton & Hove Albion's accounts for 2018 shows that the club owed more than £222 million to owner Tony Bloom. Bloom, a maths graduate, professional poker player, racehorse owner, betting consultant and property developer, also happens to be a lifelong fan of the club. Loans from owners are typically different from bank loans as they are often interest free (as in the case of the Bloom loan to

Table 2.6 Related party transactions, Brighton & Hove Albion

28. Related party transactions

Directors loan
At 30 June 2018, an amount owed to AG Bloom by the Group amounted to £222,716,000 (2017 – £190,684,000). These loans are interest free, unsecured and repayable on demand and included in other creditors above

Source: Brighton and Hove Albion Holdings Ltd annual report 2018

Brighton) and the repayment date may be extended if the club does not have the ability to meet the original agreed repayment schedule.

An "operating liability" is a sum due to anyone other than a financial institution. For football clubs at the highest levels the most significant operating liability will be sums due to other clubs in respect of player transfers. When analysing the balance sheet of a club it is beneficial to separate out financial from operating liabilities, as this allows an analyst to better see the level of financial commitment the club has to lenders. How to treat owner loans is difficult; it could be argued that they are financial, operational, or even part of … equity.

What is equity?

Equity (sometimes called capital) is the amount the club owes to its owners. There are two main types of equity: invested and reinvested equity. "Invested equity" represents the sums paid into the club by owners in return for shares. To start a club, or indeed any other business, it needs cash. This cash is used to build the stadium and buy other items of plant and machinery, acquire players, pay wages, set up marketing campaigns, train staff and many other start-up costs, all before the club has generated any income from selling tickets and rights. Most shares carry voting rights. Owning or controlling a majority of the voting rights of a club allows a person or an institution, depending on the circumstances, to control the club. Some shares carry more voting rights than others, so it is essential to review the nature of the shares of a club to see if anyone has more than 50 per cent of the votes and can therefore exercise control.

Table 2.7 shows that Manchester United have two types of equity shares. The Class A shares carry one vote each and the Class B shares carry ten votes each. This allows the Class B shareholders, who are the Glazer family and their family trusts, to control nearly 97 per cent of the votes despite the Class B shares only representing 75 per cent of the total shares issued.

Shares owned by investors typically differ from loans because a loan has a fixed repayment date and involves fixed dates for interest payments. In contrast most shares of a

Table 2.7 share capital, Manchester United

21 Share capital

	Number of shares (thousands)	Ordinary shares £'000
At 1 July 2016	164,025	52
Employee share-based compensation awards–issue of shares	170	1
At 30 June 2017	164,195	53
Employee share-based compensation awards–issue of shares	331	
At 30 June 2018	164,526	53

The company has two classes of ordinary shares outstanding: Class A ordinary shares and Class B ordinary shares, each with a par value of $0.0005 per share. The rights of the holders of Class A ordinary shares and Class B ordinary shares are identical, except with respect to voting and conversions. Each Class A ordinary share is entitled to one vote per share and is not convertible into any other shares. Each Class B ordinary share is entitled to 10 votes per share is convertible into one Class A ordinary share at any time. ...

Source: Manchester United plc annual report 2018

club are called "irredeemable", which means that the club has no obligation to repay the shareholders of the club for their original investment. If shareholders want to generate some cash from their investment, they typically have to sell their shares to another person or business. The downside of selling the shares is that in doing so they will also be relinquishing some of their control of the club, especially if their shareholding falls below 50 per cent of the total number of votes.

"Reinvested equity" represents the profit made by the club since it started trading as a company. Reinvested profits are often called "retained earnings" or "accumulated profits" in the balance sheet. If the club has regularly lost money, then the retained earnings balance will appear as a negative figure in the balance sheet. If the club wants to distribute some of these profits to shareholders, it can do this via a dividend payment. The dividends are deducted from retained earnings directly and do not appear as an expense in the profit or loss account.

In practice it is very rare for a football club to pay a dividend. Most clubs have not made sufficient profits on a regular basis to be able to afford to pay back their owners. In addition, most owners would rather reinvest any profits back into the playing side of the club rather than use the cash for personal benefits. The one club that has consistently paid dividends in recent years is Manchester United. This is because United's shares are, uniquely, traded on the New York Stock Exchange and the club has many thousands of investors, many of whom are not fans and see the club purely in financial terms. In the year ended 30 June 2019 the club paid out £23.3 million in dividends from £18.9 million of profits made that year, effectively having to use profits from previous years to fund the dividend payment. Some fans might think that this money would be better spent improving the playing squad, improving facilities at the stadium, or lowering ticket prices.

Recording transactions in the club balance sheet

Every time a financial transaction takes place, it impacts upon the balance sheet in at least two places. This is why accountants call it "double entry". The golden rules of recording transactions are as follows:

Asset UP =	(another) asset DOWN or, liability UP or, equity UP
Asset DOWN =	(another) asset UP or, liability DOWN or, equity DOWN

To take a simple example, think of a club buying a player for £2 million:

- The company could buy the player for cash and if so, increase player registrations (assets) by £2 million and decrease cash (assets) by £2 million;
- Alternatively, if the club bought the player and agreed to pay for him at a later date, the club would increase player registrations (assets) by £2 million and increase trade payables (liabilities) by £2 million;
- Or, the final option would be to issue shares to the owners to fund the purchase, and increase cash (asset) by £2 million which could then be used to buy the player registration (assets) and increase share capital (equity) by £2 million.

The creation of a balance sheet is sufficient if you want to assess the club's assets and funding, but it doesn't show the detail of how much money is generated by the club on a day-to-day basis or its running costs, for that we need a profit or loss account.

3
THE PROFIT OR LOSS ACCOUNT

A profit or loss account (also called an income statement, or statement of profit or losses, or statement of comprehensive income) summarizes the trading transactions of a business over a period of time. The profit or loss account deals with two main elements: income and costs. If total income exceeds total costs the difference is called a profit. If total income is less than total costs the difference is a loss. Most football clubs produce a profit or loss account covering a 12-month period, sometimes it might be slightly shorter or longer if they have altered their balance sheet date.

The profit or loss account in Table 3.1 covers the greatest year, to date, in the history of Leicester City Football Club. In 2015/16 Leicester won the English Premier League, despite having a fraction of the income of more established clubs. Whilst the fans of Leicester had perhaps some of the greatest days of their lives watching their team lift the Premier League trophy, the club also made a profit of over £20 million. This seems a lot of money, but the following year, when Leicester finished only twelfth in the Premier League, the club made a profit of over £80 million. This was mainly due to the club's participation in the UEFA Champions' League. The club accountants, stoics that they are, may have been happier with the club's performance in 2016/17 and the record income and profits generated that year. Leicester's lower profits in 2015/16, despite the club's on-field success, suggests than an understanding of the profit or loss account, its components and how it is calculated, is a useful tool for anyone wanting to understand football finance.

It is important to be aware that clubs who have their shares listed on a stock exchange (like Manchester United, mentioned earlier), may have to produce more regular financial information to satisfy local legislation and stock exchange rules. These are called interim accounts and may cover a period of three, six or nine months.

Table 3.2 shows Juventus's income statement for the six months to December 2017. It shows both the financial performance for the six months to December 2017 as well as comparative data for the previous year. This allows an analyst to see financial information and trends earlier in the financial year than would otherwise be the case, which is useful when budgeting, valuing the club when buying or selling its shares, or forecasting future financial results.

Table 3.1 Profit and loss account for the year ended 31 May 2017, Leicester City

	Note	2017 £'000	2016 £'000
Turnover	2	**233,013**	128,715
Cost of sales		**(158,289)**	(108,641)
Gross profit		**74,724**	20,074
Administrative expenses		**(15,810)**	(9,548)
Stadium expenses		**(3,946)**	(3,444)
Other operating income		**830**	597
Profit on disposal of fixed assets		**112**	–
Profit on disposal of player registrations		**38,830**	10,793
Operating profit before interest and taxation	3	**94,740**	18,472
Interest receivable and similar income	4	**443**	166
Interest payable and similar expenses	4	**(2,696)**	(2,273)
Net interest payable	4	**(2,253)**	(2,107)
Profit before taxation		**92,487**	16,365
Tax on profit	6	**(12,479)**	3,697
Profit for the financial year		**80,008**	20,062

Source: Leicester City Football Club Ltd

Income

All businesses, including football clubs, earn income from the sale of goods and services. However, the proceeds from player sales are not included as part of income. The purpose of a club is not to buy and sell players. Although gains and losses on player sales are shown in the profit or loss account, they are often separated out elsewhere in the profit or loss account, to emphasize the volatile nature of such transactions and remind readers that the main business of the club is selling seats, shirts and broadcast rights, rather than football players.

In the extract from Stoke City's profit or loss account in Table 3.3, the club made a loss of £52.5 million in the year ended 31 May 2018 before considering player sales. Player disposals managed to reduce these losses as they generated a profit of £22.3 million, mainly from the sale of Marko Arnautovic to West Ham. The reason why player sales are shown separately is that such profits tend to vary from year to year and are unpredictable, far more so than match ticket sales or money from shirt sponsorship. In 2016/17 Stoke were less successful in terms of player trading and made a profit of only £3.7 million from player sales such as Marc Wilson. By showing gains on player sales separately, it allows analysts to see the difference between sustainable/recurring profits arising from the day-to-day activities of the club and the impact made from less regular transactions such as selling players at a profit. We will look at player trading and why clubs so often report profits on player sales, in more depth in Chapter 5.

Table 3.2 Juventus income statement for the six months period to 31 December 2017

INCOME STATEMENT

2016/2017	Amounts in euro	Note	1 half-year 2017/2018	1 half-year 2016/2017	Change
57,835,297	Ticket sales	34	**30,282,897**	27,743,898	2,538,999
232,773,784	Television and radio rights and media revenues	35	**109,406,975**	107,239,991	2,166,984
74,718,794	Revenues from sponsorship and advertising	36	**43,318,193**	36,446,421	6,871,772
19,198,979	Revenues from sales of products and licences	37	**14,657,176**	9,208,343	5,448,833
151,149,536	Revenues from players' registration rights	38	**76,843,656**	121,764,381	(44,920,725)
27,034,664	Other revenues	39	**16,081,698**	12,739,664	3,342,034
562,711,054	**Total revenues**		**290,590,596**	315,142,698	(24,552,102)
(2,979,934)	Purchase of materials, supplies and other consumables	40	**(3,148,123)**	(2,417,324)	(730,798)
(8,290,140)	Purchases of products for sale	41	**(5,886,780)**	(3,799,988)	(2,086,793)
(66,578,563)	External services	42	**(40,361,693)**	(28,279,064)	(12,082,629)
(235,344,554)	Players' wages and technical staff costs	43	**(104,868,836)**	(97,183,708)	(7,685,129)
(26,481,657)	Other personnel	44	**(9,557,093)**	(9,250,271)	(306,822)
(50,492,316)	Expenses from players' registration rights	45	**(10,738,802)**	(37,202,332)	26,463,530
(10,524,690)	Other expenses	46	**(4,117,836)**	(4,122,171)	4,335
(400,691,854)	**Total operating costs**		**(178,679,164)**	(182,254,858)	3,575,694
(82,949,776)	Amortisation and write downs of players' registration rights	47	**(53,582,555)**	(40,069,479)	(13,513,076)
(9,934,144)	Depreciation/amortisation of other tangible and intangible assets		**(6,000,741)**	(4,993,441)	(1,007,300)
(2,107,849)	Provisions, write-downs and release of funds	48	**(1,278,375)**	(3,131,662)	1,853,287
350,000	Other non-recurring revenues and costs		**–**	332,350	(332,350)
67,377,431	**Operating income**		**51,049,760**	85,025,607	(33,975,847)
4,273,061	Financial income	49	**2,182,730**	2,136,333	46,397
(11,969,140)	Financial expenses	50	**(6,401,050)**	(6,063,605)	(337,445)
(1,266,633)	Group's share of results of associates and joint ventures	51	**(542,737)**	(1,760,621)	1,217,884
58,414,719	**Risultato prima delle imposte**		**46,288,703**	79,337,714	(33,049,011)
(11,363,921)	Current taxes	52	**(3,522,117)**	(4,750,840)	1,228,723
(4,482,874)	Deferred taxes	52	**541,408**	(2,580,452)	3,121,86
42,567,924	**Profit for period**		**43,307,994**	72,006,424	(28,698,430)

Source: Juventus SA

Table 3.3 Statement of total income and retained earnings for year ended 31 May 2018, Stoke City

	Notes	Operations excluding player trading £000	2018		2017 £000
			Player trading (note 6) £000	Total £000	
TURNOVER	2	**127,192**	–	**127,192**	135,954
Operating expenses		**(123,789)**	**(55,903)**	**(179,692)**	(134,798)
		3,403	**(55,903)**	**(52,500)**	1,156
Profit on disposal of players' registrations	6	–	**22,230**	**22,230**	3,728
Profit on disposal of fixed assets		**79**	–	**79**	20
OPERATING (LOSS)/PROFIT	4	**3,482**	**(33,673)**	**(30,191)**	4,904
Interest receivable and similar income	3	**52**	–	**52**	41
(LOSS)/PROFIT BEFORE TAXATION	2–6	**3,534**	**(33,673)**	**(30,139)**	4,945
Taxation	7	**(1,777)**	–	**(1,777)**	(1,371)
(LOSS)/PROFIT AFTER TAX AND (LOSS)/PROFIT FOR THE FINANCIAL YEAR		**1,757**	**(33,673)**	**(31,916)**	**3,574**
RETAINED EARNINGS AT 1 JUNE				**(55,213)**	(58,787)
RETAINED EARNINGS AT 31 MAY				**(87,129)**	(55,213)

Source: Stoke City Football Club Ltd

Football clubs generate income from three main sources: matchday receipts, broadcasting rights and commercial transactions. The amount of income generated from each source depends on many factors. Manchester United, for example, had total income over four and a half times that of West Bromwich Albion in 2017/18 (see Figure 3.1). A more detailed breakdown, obtained by looking at the footnotes to the accounts, is revealed in Figure 3.2.

Why the huge difference? An initial observation is that Manchester United have greater appeal to television viewers as they have so many fans, so generate more broadcasting income as they appear on television more often. Manchester United is a global brand, which makes them attractive to companies who want to sell their products globally. This

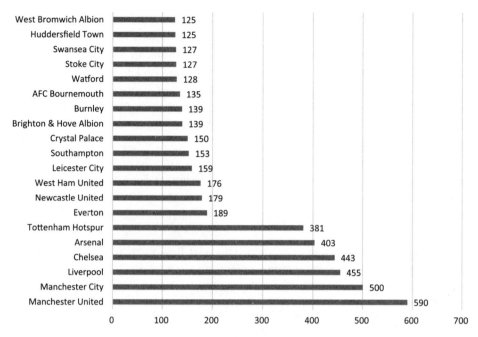

Figure 3.1 Premier League club revenues, 2017/18 (£ millions)

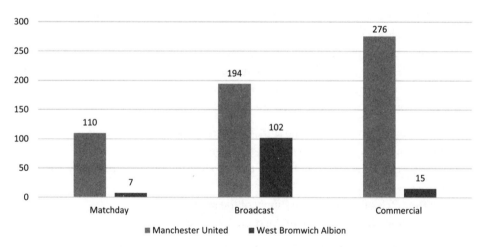

Figure 3.2 Revenue sources for Manchester United and West Bromwich Albion, 2017/18 (£ millions)

allows United to sign huge deals with such organizations, who are aware that United claim to have more than a billion fans worldwide. United's shirt sponsorship deal with Chevrolet is estimated to be worth £57 million per season. In addition Adidas have signed a £750 million ten-year contract to supply the club with kit and official merchandise. Finally, Manchester United's stadium at Old Trafford (capacity 76,000) is much larger than West Bromwich Albion's The Hawthorns (capacity 26,000) and so this boosts matchday income, as well as making Old Trafford a more viable venue for other events outside of the football season such as concerts.

There is a slight problem in the profit or loss account when deciding in which financial year to show income (also called revenue, sales, or turnover). For example, if a club with a 30 June 2018 financial year-end, sells a season ticket in March 2018 for the forthcoming 2018/19 season, which starts in August 2018, into which financial year should it show the income?

There are rules (accountants call these Financial Reporting Standards) on nearly every key item in company accounts and income is no exception. Income should only be recognized in the profit or loss account after applying a five-step test:

1. There must be a contract between the club and the customer;
2. The club has an obligation to the customer;
3. There is an agreed price;
4. The price is allocated to the obligation;
5. Revenue/income is recognized as the club delivers the obligation.

This may appear over-complicated, but in practice applying the rules for most sales is relatively straightforward.

The main types of goods sold by clubs are merchandise and catering related. Because these transactions are usually retail goods in nature, income is recognized when the customer, usually a fan, makes the purchase. For example, a fan wants to buy a replica shirt at the club store for £50, the five steps are applied as follows:

1. The fan makes an offer to buy the shirt, by offering £50, and the club accepts the offer, by taking the cash. This is the contract between the two parties;
2. Having accepted the £50 from the fan, the club has an obligation to supply the shirt;
3. The price is agreed at £50;
4. All of the £50 is allocated to the supply of the shirt;
5. The club shows £50 of income in the profit or loss account.

The transaction will be shown in the club accounts by increasing current assets (cash) by £50 and increasing equity (profit or loss account sales) by the same amount. The club will make a profit on the transaction if the shirt cost the club less than the sales price. So, if the club buys the shirt from the kit manufacturer for £20, it makes a profit of £30 on the sale. If the fan pays for the shirt at a later date (which would be very unusual) then instead of increasing cash, the club would recognize a trade receivable (debtor) in the balance sheet but would still increase income by the agreed sales price of £50. This is because the club has satisfied the obligation to supply the shirt and has an agreed price. The timing of the payment is an irrelevance when it comes to determining income in most transactions.

For many clubs the vast majority of their revenue relates to services rather than goods. These take the form of match ticket or season ticket sales, broadcasting rights and commercial deals with business partners. Recognising income here is more complex, but the principles of the five-step model should be applied to determine the correct treatment. The main difference with services is that income is recognized over the time period in which the club delivers the service. This can be instantaneous (such as when a fan buys a ticket at the turnstiles), or over a longer timeframe (such as a season ticket, or a commercial deal is signed with a business partner). For example, Fulchester Rovers agrees a four-year shirt sponsorship deal on 1 January 20X8 with a commercial partner, Grimethorpe Construction, for £10 million. Fulchester Rovers financial year-end is 30 June each year. The shirt sponsorship commences on 1 July 20X8, in time for the release of the new kit for 20X8/X9 season. Grimethorpe pays the full £10 million to Fulchester on 1 January 20X8. How should Fulchester treat the contract in the accounts? We again apply the five-step model.

1. There is a contract between Fulchester and Grimethorpe from 1 January 20X8;
2. Fulchester has a four-year obligation to advertise Grimethorpe on its shirts;
3. The agreed price is £10 million;
4. The obligation commences on 1 July 20X8, so income is recognized from that date;
5. Fulchester recognizes no income in its accounts during the year ended 30 June 20X8 because it has not met any obligations.

Fulchester will then recognize £2.5 million a year in the profit or loss account for four years commencing 30 June 20X9 (as shown in Table 3.4). This is because the obligation is delivered over a period of time. On 1 January 20X8 Fulchester will increase current assets (cash) by £10 million but cannot yet show any income. Fulchester therefore creates a liability, which accountants call deferred revenue, in the balance sheet. This is because in theory if it fails to advertise Grimethorpe Construction on its shirts from 1 July 20X8 it would have to return the money to the sponsor. At the initial balance sheet date (30 June 20X8) the deferred revenue liability would be split between current liabilities (1/4 × £10 million = £2.5 million) and non-current liabilities (3/4 × £10 million = £7.5 million). In the year ended 30 June 20X9 and the three subsequent years Fulchester would recognize income of £2.5 million in the profit or loss account and reduce liabilities by the same amount.

Table 3.4 Fulchester Rovers, profit or loss account

| | Year ended 30 June | | | | |
	20X8 £'m	20X9 £'m	20Y0 £'m	20Y1 £'m	20Y2 £'m
Profit and loss account Income	Nil	2.5	2.5	2.5	2.5
Balance Sheet **Non-current liabilities** Deferred income	7.5	5.0	2.5	0	0
Current liabilities Deferred income	2.5	2.5	2.5	2.5	0

Table 3.5 Consolidated balance sheet at 30 June 2018, Rangers

18. DEFERRED INCOME

	2018 £'000	2017 £'000
Group		
Deferred income less than one year	20,746	17,881
Deferred income more than one year	488	488
Total deferred income	**21,234**	**18,369**

Deferred income less than one year comprises season tickets, sponsorship, hospitality and other elements of income that have been received in advance and will be recognized as revenue in the 2018/19 financial year. Deferred income more than one year relates to income received in advance from catering service contracts. *Source*: Rangers International Football Club PLC, Annual Report 2018.

Let's now return to the issue of a season ticket sale in March 2018 for the season commencing in August 2018. This too would initially be classified as deferred income, as the club does not actually start to deliver the obligation until August 2018 onwards. Season tickets sold in advance can be a significant sum for a club. This is because loyal and often very superstitious fans often want to secure their usual "lucky" seats as early as possible for the following season as well as ensuring they sit with friends who sit near them.

Table 3.5 shows that Rangers at 30 June 2018 had over £21 million within deferred income. This was a significant increase from the previous year. The main driver of the increase was the number of season ticket sales increasing from 43,253 to 44,658 as well as increased prices charged for executive boxes and hospitality packages purchased in advance.

Deferred revenue from season ticket sales is important to clubs for two reasons. Firstly, the cash received, usually before the end of the previous football season, allows the club to pay wages and other bills during the summer period when there is no football being played and therefore no income being generated from matches. Secondly, deferred revenue is interest-free funding for the club. The club would otherwise potentially have to

Table 3.6 Consolidated proft and loss account for year ended 31 May 2018, Liverpool

	Note	2018 £000	2017 £000
Turnover	2	**455,089**	364,508
Cost of sales		**(42,495)**	(37,628)
Gross profit		**412,594**	326,880
Administrative expenses	3	**(405,319)**	(320,197)
Operating profit		**7,275**	6,683
Profit on disposal of players' registrations		**123,854**	38,263
Interest receivable and similar income	6	**1,578**	1,392
Interest payable and similar charges	7	**(7,572)**	(6,746)
Profit on ordinary activities before taxation'		**125,135**	39,592

Source: Liverpool Football Club and Athletic Grounds Limited annual report 2018

borrow from a bank or other lender, incurring interest charges which would decrease profit. This would reduce the amount of money the manager has to spend on the playing budget.

Costs/expenses

Expenses are the costs incurred in running a football club on a day-to-day basis. They are often grouped together into different categories and headings. There is no agreed way in which these headings appear, which can at times make comparisons between clubs difficult, but there are also some common costs which are always disclosed in the footnotes.

Some clubs show a "cost of sales" figure, which includes all the costs incurred by the club in selling any goods. Income less cost of sales is called gross profit. But gross profit is a relatively meaningless term for a football club as they mainly sell services, in the form of tickets to watch matches, sponsorship deals and broadcasting rights rather than actual physical goods. The lack of consistency in how such information is presented means that gross profit should not be used as a comparative measure between clubs, for example, some clubs, such as Liverpool, simply include the cost of merchandise and catering products under cost of sales. Their stated gross profit figure of £412.6 million is fairly meaningless (see Table 3.6) and contrasts with that of Leicester City who include player wages in cost of sales. Leicester showed a gross loss of £21 million in the year ended 31 May 2018 but that is not a like for like comparison with Liverpool due to differing ways the two clubs present the data.

For this reason, most clubs do not show a cost of sales figures and instead show a figure called "operating costs", which includes all the day-to-day costs of running the club: the likes of wages, rent, insurance, player amortisation and ground maintenance. Some of these costs are then shown in more detail in the footnotes to the accounts. Operating profit is therefore calculated as income less operating costs. If the figure is negative it is called an operating loss. Operating profit is a figure that is far more comparable between clubs than gross profit, this is because all day-to-day costs are deducted in arriving at operating profit regardless of whether they present costs within cost of sales or operating expenses. The level of detail provided in the profit or loss account is ultimately determined by the board of directors of the club, although there are a few figures that must be shown by statutory rules.

Table 3.7 shows the many different types of running expense that FC Barcelona provide on the face of their income statement. This is good in some ways, as the significance of individual expense types can be instantly seen but at the same time does give a very cluttered approach. Many clubs therefore streamline the income statement and put more detail in the footnotes.

Brighton & Hove Albion, in Table 3.8, combine all running costs into one heading called operating expenses. To analyse the operating expenses in more detail we need to examine the footnotes to the figures.

Some clubs do separate out certain player costs on the face of their profit or loss account to make it easier to see the impact of player trading. The main elements of player trading are profits and losses from player sales and amortisation of player registration contracts.

Table 3.9 is an extract from Everton's profit or loss account. It shows in a separate column the amortisation charge for players purchased (we will look at this in more depth later) of £66.9 million, and the profit on player sales, mainly due to Everton selling Romelu Lukaku to Manchester United for £75 million plus other sales for lower sums such as Ross Barkley to Chelsea.

Sometimes a club may include a heading called "exceptional items" on the face of the profit or loss account. Exceptional items typically refer to transactions that a club does not expect to incur on a regular basis. These might include payments to managers who have been dismissed (which for some clubs *is* a regular occurrence and hardly exceptional), asset sale profits, promotion bonuses or legal settlements. Exceptional items are often shown separately on the face of the profit or loss account to highlight to readers that profits are distorted by these transactions.

Table 3.10 shows Chelsea's profit or loss account for the year ended 30 June 2016, where there is a figure for exceptional items of £75.3 million. Further investigation in the footnotes reveals that Chelsea had decided to change kit manufacturers from Adidas to Nike and the cost to the club of buying themselves out of the original contract with Adidas was £67 million. The original contract with Adidas still had six years remaining, but the offer from Nike was so lucrative that Chelsea calculated that they would be better off financially by cancelling the Adidas deal and paying the resultant contractual penalty. In addition, Chelsea dismissed their manager, Jose Mourinho and some of his management team in December 2015. The compensation paid to Mourinho and his entourage

Table 3.7 Income statement for year ended 30 June 2018, Barcelona FC

(Thousands of Euros)

	Notes	SEASON 2017/18	SEASON 2016/17
CONTINUING OPERATIONS			
Revenue	Note 17.1	**686,471**	**638,189(*)**
Revenue from competitions		104,001	92,954
Revenue from season ticket holders and membership card holders		60,008	50,383
Revenue from TV broadcasts and TV rights		187,383	177,959
Revenue from marketing and advertising		335,079	316,393
Work performed by the entity and capitalized		**1,209**	1,116
Cost of sales		**(7,871)**	**(6,966)**
Consumption of sports equipment		(5,365)	(3,994)
Other consumables		(2506)	(2,972)
Other operating income	Note 17.2	**3,828**	**10,029(*)**
Ancillary income		3,300	9,660
Grants related to income		528	369
Employee benefits expense	Note 17.3	**(529,121)**	**(163,423)**
Wages and salaries of sports personnel		(480,947)	(334,106)
Wages and salaries at non-sports personnel		(35,520)	(32,035)
Social security costs, et al,		(12,654)	(11,793)
Other operating expenses		**(190,289)**	**(163,423)**
External services	Note 17.4	(122,690)	(104,452)
Taxes		(4,772)	(3,509)
Loses on, impairment of and change in trade provisions	Note 10.3	(1,746)	(1,494)
Impairment loses on trade receivables		(1,946)	(1,582)
Reversal of implement losses on trade receivables		200	88
Away matches		(9,191)	(8,596)
Player acquisition expenses		(848)	(2,138)
Other current management expenses		(51,042)	(43,234)
Depreciation and amortization		**(132,441)**	**(80,224)**
Amortization of player acquisition rights	Note 5	(118,676)	(67,045)
Other depreciation and amortization	Notes 6 and 7	(13,765)	(13,179)
Grants related to non-finanical assets and other grants	Note 11.2	108	109
Overprovisions		**2,965**	–
Impairment losses and grains (losses) on		**205,362**	**(12,193)**
disposal of non-current assets			
Impairment losses and losses	Note 5	(2,500)	(33,907)
Impairment losses on intangible sporting assets		(12,042)	(8,564)
Reversal of impairment losses on intangible sporting assets		9,542)	3,609
Impairment losses on investment property		–	(28,952)
Gains (losses) on disposals	Note 5 and 7	207,862	21,714
Losses on property plant and equipment		(42)	–
Gains on property plant and equipment		128	–
Losses on intangible sporting assets		(1,413)	(4,364)
Gains on intangible sporting assets		209,189	26,078

(continued)

Table 3.7 (Cont.)

(Thousands of Euros)

	Notes	SEASON 2017/18	SEASON 2016/17
Charge for the year and utilization of provisions and others	Note 17.5	**(8,198)**	**22,290**
Charge for the year and other non-recurring expenses		(8,463)	(6,663)
Utilization of provisions and other non-recurring income		265	28,953
OPERATING PROFIT/(LOSS)		**32,023**	**30,999**
Finance income		**715**	**4,873**
From marketable securities and other financial instruments		715	4,873
– Of third parties		715	4,873
Finance costs		**(10,100)**	**(1,996)**
Third-party borrowings		(10,100)	(1,996)
Exchange gains (losses)		**(352)**	**(174)**
Exchange gains		345	200
Exchange losses		(697)	(374)
Impairment and grains (losses) on disposal of financial instruments		**(2,138)**	**(2,311)**
FINANCE COST		**(11,875)**	**392**
PROFIT/(LOSS) BEFORE TAX		**20,148**	**31,385**
Income tax	Note 14.4	(7,218)	(13,251)
PROFIT/(LOSS) FOR THE YEAR		**12,930**	**18,134**

Source: FC Barcelona annual report 2018

Table 3.8 Consolidated statement of comprehensive income, year ended 30 June 2018, Brighton & Hove Albion

	Note	2018			2017
		Operations excluding player rading £'000	Player trading £'000	Total £'000	Total £'000
Turnover	3	139,432	–	139,432	29,208
Operating expenses		(110,640)	(19,311)	(129,951)	(59,332)
Exceptional operating expenses		–	–	–	(9,082)
Profit on player trading		–	3,367	3,367	313
Operating profit/(loss) before interest and taxation	5	28,792	(15,944)	12,848	(38,893)
Interest receivable and similar income	8	21	–	21	7
Interest payable and similar charges	9	–	(785)	(785)	–
Profit/(loss) before taxation		28,813	(16,729)	12,084	(38,886)
Tax on profit	10	(808)	–	(808)	–
Profit/(loss) after taxation		28,005	(16,729)	11,276	(38,886)

Source: Brighton & Hove Albion Holdings Ltd annual report 2018

Table 3.9 Consolidated profit or loss account year ended 31 May 2018, Everton

	Notes	2018			2017		
		Operations excluding player and management trading £'000	Player and management trading £'000	Total £'000	Operations excluding player and management trading £'000	Player and management trading £'000	Total £'000
Turnover	1,2	**189,159**	–	**189,159**	**171,330**	–	**171,330**
Operating expenses	3	(186,276)	(66,933)	(253,20	(146,334)	(37,296)	(183,63
Operating expenses – exceptional costs	3	(25,787)	(8,175)	(33,962)	–	–	–
		(212,063)	(75,108)	(287,171)	(146,334)	(37,298)	(183,632)
Operating (loss) / profit	4	**(22,904)**	**(75,108)**	**(98,012)**	**24,996**	**(37,298)**	**(12,302)**
Profit on player trading		–	87,786	87,786	–	51,945	51,945
Profit on disposal of tangible fixed assets		–	–	–	7	–	7
(Loss) / profit before interest and taxation		**(22,904)**	**12,678**	**(10,226)**	**25,003**	**14,647**	**39,650**

Source: Everton Football Club Company Annual Report 2018

Table 3.10 Group profit or loss account year ended 30 June 2016, Chelsea FC

	Notes	Operations excluding player trading 30 June 2016 £000	Player amortisation and trading 30 June 2016 £000	Total 30 June 2016 £000
Turnover	3	329,122	–	329,122
Cost of sales		(249,377)	–	(249,377)
Gross profit		79,745	–	79,745
Administrative expenses		(54,887)	(70,877)	(125,764)
Exceptional item	4	(75,315)	–	(75,315)
Operating loss		(50,457)	(70,877)	(121,334)
Interest receivable and similar income	9	171	2,885	3,056
Interest payable and similar charges	10	(10)	(450)	(460)
Profit on disposal of player registrations		–	49,000	49,000
Fair value gains on investment properties		100	–	100
Loss on disposal of tangible fixed assets		(23)	–	(23)
Loss on disposal of investments		(128)	–	(128)
Loss before taxation	5	(50,347)	(19,442)	(69,789)

Source: Chelsea FC Plc Annual Report 2016

was £8.3 million. Mourinho had already received £18 million from Chelsea for being sacked in 2005 and subsequently £19 million in a similar payout from Manchester United in 2018.

Under maverick Italian owner Massimo Cellino, Leeds United had disputes with their kit supplier, which resulted in a write down of the values of inventories, as well as disputes with former employees, broadcasting companies and the Football League. The total estimated cost of these disputes was £3.54 million, which reduced profits by the same amount. In their accounts (see Table 3.11) Leeds United showed these exceptional items *below* the operating loss heading, whereas Chelsea presented exceptional items *above* the operating loss heading. Such inconsistencies need to be carefully monitored when comparing the results of clubs. Some clubs might choose to not include exceptional items on the face of the profit or loss account at all. It is therefore essential to scrutinize the footnotes to the accounts for any unusual payments.

In Aston Villa's financial statements for 2015/16 (Table 3.12) there was an expense of more than £79 million for exceptional items listed in the profit or loss account but no detail, so it was necessary to look at the footnotes to identify the breakdown. Villa were relegated in 2015/16 and the club's owners looked at the value of their major assets, the stadium and playing squad, and concluded that both were overvalued in the accounts. The owners therefore reduced the value of the playing squad by £34.8 million and that of long-term tangible assets by £44.8 million, to reflect fairer values. Under accounting rules, it is acceptable to undervalue assets, but not overvalue them. These write downs

Table 3.11 Consolidated statement of comprehensive income year ended 30 June 2016, Leeds United

	Note	*2016*
		£
Turnover	4	30,149,475
Cost of sales		(5,405,959)
Gross profit		24,743,516
Administrative expenses		(32,358,816)
Other operating income		469,408
Operating loss	5	(7,145,892)
Gain on disposal of players' registrations		2,781,812
Exceptional stock write down		(1,154,533)
Exceptional costs of commercial disputes	9	(2,386,062)
interest payable and similar charges	10	(966,259)
Loss on ordinary activities before taxation		(8,870,934)

Source: Leeds United Football Club Ltd Annual report 2016

Table 3.12 Loss before taxation, 2015/16 Aston Villa

The Group's operating loss for the year has been arrived at after charging/(crediting):

	2017	*2016*
	£'000	*£'000*
Depreciation of owned tangible fixed assets	**2,944**	3,735
Loss/(profit) on disposal of tangible fixed assets	**5**	(15)
Amortisation of players' registrations	**23,737**	16,017
Deferred grant income	**(140)**	(140)
Stock recognized as an expense	**2,981**	4,756
Staff costs excluding exceptional items (note 5)	**61,473**	93,014
Impairment of trade debtors	–	–
Community development expenditure	**2,016**	2,224
Youth development expenditure	**5,875**	5,043
Auditors' remuneration for audit services:		
– audit of the parent Company's individual and consolidated financial statements	**15**	10
– audit of the Company's subsidiaries	**60**	49
– audit–related assurance services	**16**	45
– non-audit services	**23**	29
Exceptional items:		
Impairment of intangible assets (included in 'administrative expenses')	–	34,842
Impairment of tangible assets (included in 'administrative expenses')	–	44,802

Source: Reform Acquisitions Ltd Annual Report 2016

Table 3.13 Income statement year ended 30 June 2019, Hull City Tigers

	Notes	2019 £	2018 £
Turnover	2	11,155,410	12,300,164
Cost of sales		(27,395,368)	(38,626,813)
Gross loss		(16,239,958)	(26,326,649)
Amortisation and impairment of players		(12,960,093)	(12,252,362)
Administrative expenses		(7,918,337)	(9,357,129)
Operating loss	3	(37,118,388)	(47,936,140)
Profit on the disposal of players		4,624,141	30,858,817
Profit/(loss) on sale of fixed assets		7,764	(7,095)
Parachute payments		37,219,169	43,379,799
Interest receivable		611,453	555,984
Interest payable	5	(2,382,885)	(3,139,964)
Profit on ordinary activities before taxation		2,961,254	23,711,401

Source: Hull City Tigers Ltd Annual Report 2019

Table 3.14 Statement of comprehensive income year ended 30 June 2017, Bournemouth

	Note	11 month period ended 30 June 2017 £000	Year ended 31 July 2016 £000
Turnover	4	**136,456**	87,875
Other operating income	5	**2,241**	740
(Loss)/profit on disposal of players' registrations	6	**(1,195)**	10,692
Staff costs	8	**(71,534)**	(59,557)
Depreciation and other amounts written off tangible and intangible fixed assets	6	**(20,760)**	(14,223)
Other operating expenses		**(29,087)**	(20,535)
Operating profit	6	**16,121**	4,992
Interest receivable and similar income	10	**322**	76
Interest payable and similar expenses	11	**(1,794)**	(1,673)
Profit before tax		**14,649**	3,395

Source: AFC Bournemouth Ltd Annual Report 2018

are considered to be exceptional because Aston Villa would not expect to incur such costs every year.

Football clubs buy and sell players on a regular basis. The calculations of how to determine a gain or loss on a player sale will be discussed later. Whilst player trading is a regular feature of a club, the gains and losses on player sales can vary significantly from year to year and are, as we've seen, usually shown separately on the face of the profit or loss account. As can be seen from Figures 3.13 and 3.14 Hull City and AFC Bournemouth report the impact of player sales on profits but there is a difference in the presentation of the gains between the two clubs. Bournemouth show their gains just below turnover and before operating profit, whereas Hull City show the gains below operating profit. This makes comparison of operating profit somewhat difficult between clubs. For this reason most analysts comparing football club accounts set them out in a common format on a spreadsheet, allowing easier comparison of the movements in key numbers.

Finance/Interest

If a club has borrowed money from banks and other financial institutions, it will have to pay interest on the borrowings. As we've seen, sometimes the club owners will lend the club money, and frequently they will not charge the club interest on those loans, but this is not always the case. Finance/interest costs are shown separately underneath operating profit to emphasize that different forms of funding come at different costs and are independent of the day-to-day running of the club. Finance costs are usually a function of the sum borrowed and the interest rate charged.

Manchester United were acquired by the Glazer family during 2005 for approximately £790 million. A substantial amount of this sum paid was financed by bank borrowings. Prior to the acquisition Manchester United had more cash than borrowings, and so generated interest income rather than interest payments. Initially the lending banks were wary about the ability of the club to meet scheduled repayments. This resulted in some lenders charging punitive interest rates on some of the loans, which peaked at 16.25 per cent, the type of rate usually associated with a credit card for an individual. As United's income has risen over the years the risk of defaulting on the interest payments has diminished, which has

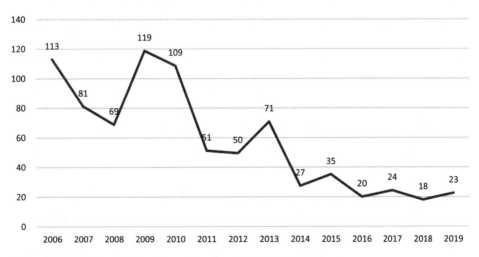

Figure 3.3 Manchester United interest payments, 2006–19 (£ millions)

allowed the club to rearrange some of the loans at lower interest rates and this is reflected in the decrease in the annual interest charges in recent years. Even taking into consideration the revised loans at lower interest rates Manchester United have paid approximately £809 million in bank interest since the Glazer takeover until June 2019 (see Figure 3.3). This compares to a net spend on players of £1,040 million during the same period, the majority of which has been in the last few years. Many United fans will argue that the club have been hamstrung in the transfer market, especially in the early years under the Glazers' ownership, due to the huge sums of money being paid out to the banks.

Profit

The profit made after deducting finance costs and exceptional items from operating profit is called pre-tax profit. This is potentially then taxed by the government. However, it is profits that are taxed, not revenues. Whereas government coffers benefits from ticket sales and player transfers, as they are subject to VAT, and from player wages (income tax and national insurance payments) historically football clubs have been loss-making businesses, and so have not paid much tax on their business activities. However recent significant increases in broadcasting and commercial income have converted many clubs from loss-making to profit-making entities. Calculating tax on club profits is a complex issue, far outside the scope of this book. Clubs may appear to pay a tax rate that is higher or lower than the rate quoted by the government due to adjustments made by the tax authorities (see Table 3.15).

One common explanation for the variety of tax rates effectively payable is that if a club has historically made losses, it can offset some of these against profits it makes in future years. For example, as shown in Table 3.16, Fulchester Rovers made losses of £25 million a year for the three years ending 30 June 20X6. The club then made a profit of £40 million a year in the year ended 30 June 20X7 and £45 million in the year ended 30 June 20X8. The tax rate is 20%. In this example Fulchester pay no tax in the first three years as the club made losses. In 20X7, although the club makes a profit of £40 million, it can offset this sum from the £75 million of losses made in the period 20X4–20X6 and so has no taxable profit in 20X7. In the year to June 20X8 Fulchester can offset the remaining losses of £35 million against the pre-tax profit made that year of £45 million to give a taxable profit of £10 million, on which tax of £2 million will then be charged.

The profit made after deducting tax is called net profit. This profit belongs to the club owners. This is why the owners are often called the risk-taker in relation to the business, as they are entitled to the residual figures after everyone else (suppliers with operating costs, players with wages, banks with interest costs, government with taxes) have taken their agreed share of club revenues. Net profit can be positive or negative (in which case it is a net loss).

Table 3.15 Pre-tax profits and tax expenses for Premier League clubs, 2017/18

	Profit £'m	Tax £'m	Tax Rate
Spurs	139	26	19%
Liverpool	125	19	15%
Manchester United	26	17	67%
Arsenal	70	14	19%
Burnley	45	9	19%
Southampton	35	6	18%
Chelsea	67	5	8%
Newcastle	23	4	19%
Stoke	(30)	2	(6%)
Brighton	12	1	7%
West Ham	18	0	2%
Leicester	2	0	5%
Everton	(13)	0	(0%)
Manchester City	10	0	0%
Bournemouth	(11)	(0)	3%
Swansea	(3)	(0)	10%
Watford	(32)	(1)	3%
West Brom	(8)	(2)	22%
Crystal Palace	(38)	(2)	6%
Huddersfield	30	(5)	(16%)

Table 3.16 Fulchester Rovers' tax charge

Fulchester Rovers' Tax Charge	Year ended 30 June				
	20X4 £'m	20X5 £'m	20X6 £'m	20X7 £'m	20X8 £'m
Profit/(loss) before tax	(25)	(25)	(25)	40	45
Cumulative profit/(loss)	(25)	(50)	(75)	(35)	10
Taxable profit/(loss)	0	0	0	0	10
Tax charge at 20% of taxable profit	0	0	0	0	2

Figure 3.4 shows that the Championship is the most problematic division in English football as 18 out of its 24 clubs made a net loss in 2017/18, which overall totalled £292 million. Norwich and Hull made the highest profits in the division, but if we drill deeper into their accounts we see that this was mainly due to both clubs receiving parachute payments following their recent relegation from the Premier League. Had this not taken place then both clubs would have made eight figure losses. This shows why anyone attempting any form of analysis has to carefully review the supporting data behind the quoted headline figures. In the five years to the end of 2017/18 the cumulative losses in the Championship exceeded £1.1 billion, meaning that clubs, despite the benefits of parachute payments and player sales, are consistently losing money and there appeared to be no desire or ability to reduce these losses.

A profit or loss account contains income and expenses for the period between two balance sheet dates. The net profit or loss made by the club is added to the reinvested

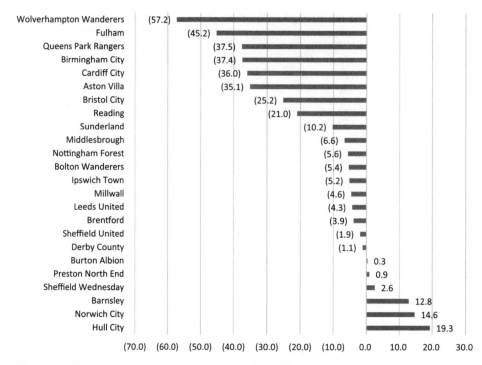

Figure 3.4 Championship net profit/losses 2017/18 (£ millions)

equity total in the balance sheet. The club can then pay some of the profits back from owners in the form of dividends, or more likely, reinvest those profits to help the club be more successful on the pitch in future years.

Total profits (or losses) made by the club at the end of the year are therefore:

Profits at start of year	£X
Plus	
profits made in the year per the P&L account	£X
Less	
Any dividends paid to shareholders	(£X)
Profits at end of year (shown in balance sheet)	£X

Table 3.17 is taken from Manchester City's 2018 annual report. It shows that City made a small profit of £10.4 million in 2018, and £1.1 million in 2017. It also highlights that City had racked up losses of £626.2 million in preceding years as owner Sheik Mansour, who bought the club in August 2008, underwrote huge spending to bring the club to a par

Table 3.17 Statement of changes in equity, Manchester City

	Share capital £000	Share premium £000	Profit and loss account £000
As at 1 June 2016	1,258,346	45,008	(626,238)
Profit for the year	–	–	1,038
As at 30 June 2017	1,258,346	45.008	(625,150)
Shares issued in the year	58,000	–	–
Profit for the year	–	–	10,438
As at 30 June 2018	**1,316,346**	**40,008**	**(614,712)**

Source: Manchester City Football Club Ltd 2018 Annual Report

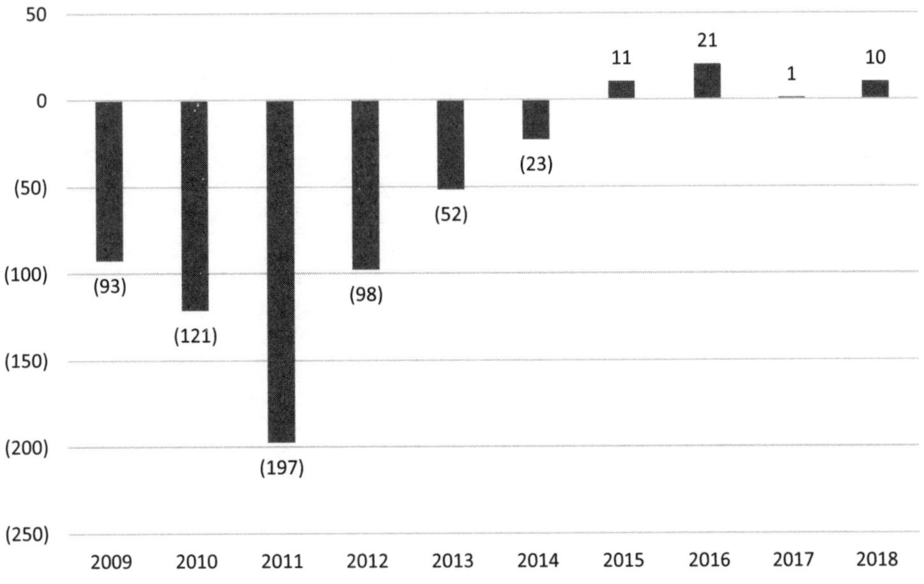

Figure 3.5 Manchester City profit or loss account (£ millions)

with other large Premier League clubs. Of City's total historic losses of £615 million at 30 June 2018, £574 million of them have arisen under Mansour (see Figure 3.5). Manchester City supporters will point out that the club has now made profits for the four years since 2014/15. This is true, but the sums involved are dwarfed by the extent of the earlier losses.

The rules in relation to transactions that were used when preparing the balance sheet still apply. The key issue here is to remember that trading transactions affect the profit or loss account, and that will also impact on the equity total in the balance sheet. The profit or loss account shows the difference between the revenue generated from trading by the club over the course of a season and the day-to-day running costs. This generates a profit or loss dependent upon a variety of factors, some controllable by the club, some independent of the club, some relate to footballing matters on the pitch but equally many arise regardless of match events.

All the above is fine, but profits don't pay the bills, for that we need cash, and therefore clubs also produce something called a cash flow statement.

4

THE CASH FLOW STATEMENT

The cash flow statement summarises the cash in and out of a club over a period of time, which matches the period covered in the profit or loss account. It explains how the cash figure has changed from one balance sheet date to the next. Cash flow statements are no different to a bank statement for an individual. They highlight the sources from which the club generates cash, and the choices management made when spending it over the year.

The rules on how to present a cash flow statement vary from country to country. Under the most common rules cash flows are split into three main categories: operating, investing and financing.

Table 4.1 higlights how Borussia Dortmund had €51.7 million at 1 July 2016 and how this increased to €59.5 million in the two years to 30 June 2018. The cash flow statement is a very good "why" document that explains to the reader the reasons behind the overall increase or decrease in cash over the period.

Cash from operations

This represents the cash generated by the club in terms of its day-to-day activities, which include selling tickets and merchandise, paying wages and suppliers. In a normal business one would expect this to be a positive number, but for football clubs this is not always the case, especially if the club has a big wage bill compared to the income it generates. The cash from operations figure is calculated by adjusting the club's profit for the year for:

- Non-cash expenses such as depreciation, player amortisation and gains on player sales;
- Converting sales and purchases in the profit or loss account to cash received from customers and paid to suppliers.

Table 4.2 provides some extra detail on the operating cash inflow total of £29.4 million for Leicester City in 2018. It starts with the net profit of £1.5 million. Included in that total are some non-cash expenses such as depreciation, gains on player sales and amortisation.

Table 4.1 Consolidated statement of cash flows, Borussia Dortmund

	EUR '000	
	2017/2018	*2016/2017*
Profit before income taxes	+31,751	+9,119
Depreciation, amortisation and write-downs of non-current assets	+90,556	+63,415
Gain/loss on disposals of non-current assets	+182	+34*
Other non-cash expenses/income	+40,589	+12,295*
Interest income	−552	−678
Interest expense	+4,888	+2,245
Net income/loss from investments in associates	−13	−28
Changes in other assets not classified as from investing or financing activities	+5,014	+16,026*
Changes in other liabilities not classified as from investing or financing activities	−8,657	+15,462
Interest received	+13	+2
Interest paid	−3,681	−2,004
Income taxes paid	−1,723	−5,476
Cash flows from operating activities	**+158,367**	**+110,412**
Payments for investments in intangible assets	−123,562	−96,526
Proceeds from disposals of intangible assets	0	0*
Payments for investments in property, plant and equipment	−7,471	−8,192
Proceeds from disposals of property plant and equipment	+276	+ 53
Proceeds from financial assets	+38	+52
Payments for investments in financial assets	−13	−20
Cash flows from investing activities	**−130,732**	**−104,633**
Acquisition of minority interests	0	−45
Payment for settlement of derivatives	−1,654	0
Dividend payments	−5,519	−5,519
Repayment of liabilities under finance leases	−10,295	−2,640
Cash flows from financing activities	**−17,468**	**−8,204**
Change in cash and cash equivalents	+ 0,167	−2,425
Cash and cash equivalents at the beginning of the period	+49,297	+51,722
Cash and cash equivalents at the end of the period	**+59,464**	**+49,297**

Source: Borussia Dortmund GmbH & Co. KgaA

These are accounting adjustments rather than cash amounts and so are adjusted for by reversing their treatment from the profit or loss account.

Cash flows from investing activities

This summarises the cash coming into and out of the club in relation to investment decisions made by the board of directors and management team. The main cash flows here are in respect of:

Table 4.2 Notes to cash flow statement, year ended 31 May 2018, Leicester City
a) Reconciliation of profit for the financial year to cash generated from operating activities

	2018 £'000	2017 £'000
Profit for the financial year	1,494	80,008
Tax on profit	85	12,479
Net interest payable	2,674	2,253
Operating profit before interest and taxation	4,253	94,740
Amortisation and impairment charge	48,807	29,701
Depreciation charge	3,147	2,926
Profit on disposal of tangible and intangible fixed assets	(38,185)	(38,942)
Decrease / (Increase) in inventories	1,010	(898)
Decrease / (Increase) in debtors	16,407	(20,588)
Decrease in creditors	(2,904)	(7,351)
Settlement of provisions	(3,100)	–
Cash generated from operating activities	29,435	59,588

Source: Leicester City Football Club Limited

+ Player signings (purchase of intangible assets);
+ Player sales (proceeds of sale of intangible assets);
+ New plant and equipment purchases (purchase of tangible assets/property, plant and equipment).

The figure would usually be negative in respect of property plant and equipment. This is because the club buys machinery, vehicles, computers, etc. when new, and sells them or scraps them when no longer required for far lower prices. The figures in respect of player transactions are more volatile as can be seen from Southampton's cash flow statement for the year ended 30 June 2017 (Table 4.3).

In recent years Southampton have gained a reputation for being a "selling club" with the likes of Gareth Bale, Theo Walcott, Luke Shaw, Adam Lallana, Sadio Mane and Virgil Van Dijk leaving the club. In the year ended 30 June 2017 (on the right-hand side of the extract from the accounts) Southampton had a positive investing cash flow of

Table 4.3 Cash flows from investing activities, Southampton

Cash flows from investing activities		
Purchase of tangible fixed assets	(4,822)	(3,564)
Purchase of intangible fixed assets	(65,900)	(70,395)
Proceeds from sale of intangible fixed assets	79,884	75,485
Proceeds from sale of tangible fixed assets	398	1
Interest receivable	173	69
Net cash generated from investing activities	9,733	1,596

Source: Southampton Football Club

Table 4.4 Cash flows from financing activities, Manchester United

Cash flows from financing activities			
Repayment of borrowings	**(3,750)**	(419)	(395)
Dividends paid	**(23,326)**	(21,982)	(23,295)
Net cash outflow from financing activities	**(27,076)**	(22,401)	(23,690)

Source: Manchester United

£1.6 million. This is because the club signed players for significant sums but this was exceeded by the sales proceeds of those leaving. In 2018 (on the left) this cash surplus increased to £9.7 million. Southampton fans may have thought that these figures should be different based on the quoted prices for players bought and sold, but some of the sales were on credit, and the club did not receive the cash until the buying clubs paid the full sums at a later date.

Cash from financing activities

As we've seen, clubs are dependent upon two types of finance: debt and equity. The financing section of the cash flow statement shows the cash received and paid to these stakeholders in the club. In respect of equity shareholders, the cash flows are usually new shares issued by the club to raise finance. In theory, the club could also pay a dividend to shareholders, but the vast majority either make losses or reinvest all profits back into the business. If a club has shares which are traded on a stock exchange, such as Manchester United, there is a greater probability of dividends being paid.

Table 4.4 from Manchester United's accounts covers the three years (from right to left) 2017–19. United were not in a position to pay a dividend to shareholders until 2016, due to having significant demands on their cash in earlier years but were able to give over £20 million to shareholders as a dividend payment thereafter. In respect of debt finance the club could either borrow or repay loans during the year. Manchester United renegotiated their loans in 2015, allowing them to borrow from fresh lenders and repay some existing debts which charged a higher rate of interest.

The total cash flows from operating, investing and financing activities are combined to give a total cash flow movement for the period between the two balance sheet dates. This movement is added to the opening cash balance and reconciles to the closing cash balance in the balance sheet.

How to create a cash flow statement

Cash flow statements are easier to prepare than many people think. Ultimately cash can only either go in or out of a business. The statement looks complicated because of the way it is presented and removing some non-cash items from the profit or loss account and balance sheet. Let's use an example from Fulchester Rovers financial statements:

Income statement for year ended 31 December 20X9

	£'000
Revenue	200,000
Wages	90,000
Amortisation	25,000
Depreciation	10,000
Other operating costs	40,000
Net profit	35,000

Balance sheet at 31 December 20X9

	20X9 £'000	20X8 £'000
Property and plant	60,000	45,000
Player registrations	110,000	98,000
Cash	42,000	26,000
Total assets	212,000	169,000
Share capital	35,000	30,000
Retained earnings	67,000	40,000
Loans	80,000	60,000
Trade creditors	30,000	39,000
Total equity and liabilities	212,000	169,000

Step 1. Start with the profit figure in the profit or loss account and adjust for all non-cash expenses (such as depreciation and player amortisation).

Operating cash flows

Net profit	35,000
Amortisation	25,000
Depreciation	10,000

Step 2. Work down the balance sheet line by line and apply the following golden rules of cash:

Asset UP = Cash DOWN
Liabilities and Equity UP = Cash UP
Asset DOWN = Cash UP

Liabilities and Equity DOWN = Cash DOWN

Movement in share capital (35,000 − 30,000)	5,000
Movement in loans (80,000 − 60,000)	20,000
Movement in trade creditors (30,000 − 39,000)	(9,000)

Step 3. For some items (such as property and plant, player registrations and retained earnings in the balance sheet) it may be necessary to prepare a more detailed working to calculate missing figures. For this example assume there are no player sales.

Property and plant purchases (60,000 + 10,000 − 45,000)	(25,000)
Player purchases (110,000 + 25,000 − 98,000)	(37,000)
Dividends paid from retained earnings (40,000 + 35,000 − 67,000)	(8,000)

Step 4. Add together the totals of operating, investing and financing activities to determine an overall movement in cash flows.

Operating cash flows	
Net profit	35,000
Amortisation	25,000
Depreciation	10,000
Movement in trade creditors	(9,000)
Total movement in operating cash flows	**61,000**
Investing cash flows	
Property and plant purchases	(25,000)
Player purchases	(37,000)
Total movement in investing cash flows	**(62,000)**
Financing cash flows	
Share capital issue proceeds	5,000
Borrowings from loans	20,000
Dividends paid	(8,000)
Total movement in financing cash flows	**17,000**
Total movement in cash flows (61,000 − 62,000 +17,000)	**16,000**

Step 5. Add the overall movement in cash flows to the opening cash figure and this should reconcile to the closing cash figure.

Total movement in cash flows	**16,000**
Plus: Opening cash	26,000
Closing cash	42,000

Cash management, as for any business, is a critical issue to a football club. Clubs fail because they have insufficient cash to pay their financial commitments and the history of the game is littered with winding-up orders, administrations and emergency sales due to poor cash management. An ability to budget and manage cash well is essential to all businesses and the football industry is no exception. Some of the biggest cash flows are in relation to player transactions and the methods used to account for them in the financial statements, as we shall see in the next chapter, need special explanation.

PART II

THE PRICE OF FOOTBALL

5

PLAYERS (AND AGENTS)

Footballers' wages and transfer fees generate huge amounts of media attention as well as moans and groans on message boards, social media and in pubs across the country as fans debate and justify the transfer fees and wages relating to the likes of Neymar, Cristiano Ronaldo and Virgil Van Dijk. Football players are employees, just like those in any other industry, or business. The players might not see themselves as such, but in reality, they are no different to mechanics, insurance sellers or healthcare workers. However, what is unusual about players is that they sign contracts of employment for a fixed time period, usually measured in years. This commits the player to play exclusively for a club for the duration of the contracted period. The club holds the player's registration certificate with the national football association and under UEFA and FIFA regulations the player cannot move to a new football club without the registration certificate being transferred.

If the player's registration is held by another club, then a potential employer may have to pay compensation for the player's registration certificate. This is called a transfer fee. The fee may be negotiated by the two clubs or set out in the employment contract. This could be as simple as a buying club asking the existing one for their player valuation of the player and agreeing to pay that sum. If the buying club does not want to pay the quoted price they might make a lower offer, and see if it is accepted or rejected. There then may be a series of offers until a final fee is agreed. When Philippe Coutinho moved from Liverpool to Barcelona in January 2018 the Catalan club initially offered £92 million for the player, this was rejected and followed by a series of higher bids until a final fee of £142 million was accepted by Liverpool.

The transfer fee can be paid as a single amount or spread over a period of time and paid in instalments, some of which may be performance related. The clubs are not obliged to disclose the sums involved or the dates of payments, but a combination of agents with loose tongues, dogged journalists trying to get the full details of a player move and sometimes documents lodged at government regulators can often piece together the full story.

How does a club value a player?

A player's value is similar to that of any other unique good or service, such as an original painting, sculpture or piece of land. When Newcastle United fans used to sing "One Alan Shearer, there's only one Alan Shearer" after the club signed him from Blackburn Rovers for a then world record fee of £15 million in 1996, they were reflecting an economic reality.

Determining a fee for an individual player is based on supply and demand, the clubs' available financial resources, contract length and sometimes a release clause.

Supply and demand

The first lesson of any economics course will talk about the forces of supply and demand. Millions of people play football as a recreation or hobby, but there are very few who can be reasonably expected to score 20 or more goals in La Liga or the Premier League, win 60 per cent or more of tackles, thread balls through the eye of a needle, or pull off match-saving saves. This means that the supply of players at the elite level is very scarce, and scarcity for anything (diamonds, Picasso originals, Ming vases, properties overlooking the Golden Gate bridge, etc.) usually drives up the price as demand exceeds supply.

The buying club may be desperate for a player for a particular position on the pitch, and this can increase demand. Historically, despite the statistical importance of goalkeepers and defenders it is forward players that have commanded premium prices, but this has changed in the last couple of years as greater analysis has highlighted the importance of clean sheets to final league tables. If there are many clubs all seeking a player with the same skills, then how will the selling club choose a buyer? Market forces would suggest that the selling club can play off interested buyers against each other until there is only one interested party remaining: the player's registration is effectively auctioned to the highest bidder. If there are few players who can be expected to deliver the standard of technical ability and positional awareness required by a demanding team manager, then the selling club is in a strong negotiating position to negotiate a high transfer fee for the player. Table 5.1 lists the ten largest transfer fees paid (at October 2019) and shows that scarcity applies mainly to either strikers or attacking midfield players. Some fees are estimated (quoted by media sources), as clubs are not legally obliged to disclose them.

Available financial resources

The buying club needs to have the financial resources to pay the transfer fee. The buyers shown in Table 5.1 are all in the global top dozen income-generating clubs. The

Table 5.1 Ten largest player transfer fees

Name	Clubs	Date	Fee	Position
Neymar	Barcelona to PSG	2017	£198m	Striker
Kylian Mbappe	Monaco to PSG	2018	£130m	Striker
Joao Felix	Benfica to Athletico Madrid	2019	£112m	Striker
Philippe Coutinho	Liverpool to Barcelona	2018	£108m	Attacking midfield
Antoine Griezmann	Athletico Madrid to Barcelona	2019	£108m	Striker
Ousmane Delbele	Dortmund to Barcelona	2017	£94m	Striker
Cristiano Ronaldo	Real Madrid to Juventus	2018	£90m	Striker
Paul Pogba	Juventus to Manchester United	2016	£90 million	Midfield
Gareth Bale	Tottenham to Real Madrid	2013	£85 million	Midfield
Eden Hazard	Chelsea to Real Madrid	2019	£85 million	Striker

Source: Goal.com (and others)

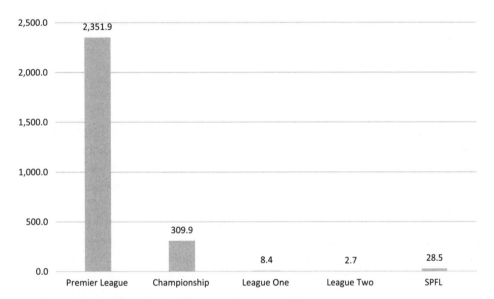

Figure 5.1 Player signings by EFL division 2017/18 (£ millions)

impact of buying power also is an issue domestically. An analysis of the relative buying power of the four English professional divisions and the Scottish Premiership shows for 2017/18 that for every £1,000 spent by League Two clubs signing players, clubs in League One spent £3,110, the Championship £114,770, and the English Premier League £871,060. In the Scottish Premiership it was £10,570.

Figure 5.1 shows that the total sum spent on new signings in the Premier League in 2017/18 was £2.35 billion. This contrasts with League Two, where only £2.7 million was spent in the whole division, and 11 out of 24 clubs did not make a signing for a fee. Over time clubs' buying power has increased due to the attraction of football to both domestic

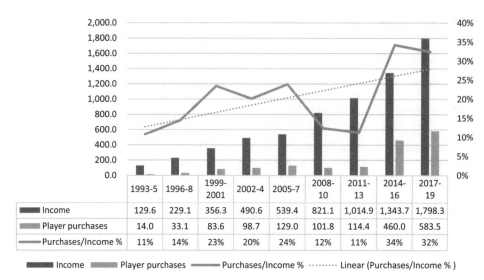

	1993-5	1996-8	1999-2001	2002-4	2005-7	2008-10	2011-13	2014-16	2017-19
Income	129.6	229.1	356.3	490.6	539.4	821.1	1,014.9	1,343.7	1,798.3
Player purchases	14.0	33.1	83.6	98.7	129.0	101.8	114.4	460.0	583.5
Purchases/Income %	11%	14%	23%	20%	24%	12%	11%	34%	32%

Income Player purchases Purchases/Income % ········ Linear (Purchases/Income %)

Figure 5.2 Income, player signings, 1992–2017, Manchester United
Source: Manchester United Annual Reports 1992–2018

and international broadcasters, and this has been reflected in turn in the price paid by broadcasters to secure those rights. This has allowed clubs to increase not only the fees paid to sign players, but the prospect of future significant broadcast revenue growth has encouraged clubs to invest a greater proportion of their income for buying players.

Figure 5.2 indicates that, whilst player signings on a year by year basis are erratic for Manchester United, the long-term trend is for the club to spend a greater proportion of income signing new players, provided the club can be confident that it will have sufficient funds in the future to pay any instalments in relation to the transfer. Being able to pay future instalments and wage commitments is highly achievable for a club like Manchester United, who have a very low probability of being relegated from the Premier League, although Liverpool and Manchester City fans live in hope (United's record since the formation of the Premier League in 1992/3 is champions on 13 occasions, and a lowest finish of seventh).

Contract length

When a footballer's registration certificate approaches its finishing date, the player is allowed to sign another contract with the existing club, or they can move to a new employer if one is available. Under a European Court of Justice decision in 1995, known as the Bosman ruling, no transfer fee is payable if the contract has expired and the player is aged 23 or older. John-Marc Bosman was a Belgian footballer contracted to RFC Liège.

When his playing contract expired the club offered him a pay cut because he was no longer in the first team but would not allow him to join another club. Bosman took his case to court and was successful. Players such as Zlatan Ibrahimovic moving from PSG to Manchester United and Aaron Ramsey from Arsenal to Juventus have changed clubs based on the Bosman ruling.

The outstanding length of contract can therefore play a part in the fee payable. Buying clubs will not be willing to pay large sums of money if a player is in the last year of his contract, when there's the possibility of being able to sign him for nothing a few months later. Everton agreed to sell Ross Barkley to Chelsea for £35 million in August 2017, when the player had just under a year left on his contract. Barkley had declined a new contract offer from Everton, who feared losing the player a year later for nothing. Barkley rejected the transfer opportunity in August 2017 but signed for Chelsea in January 2018 for £15 million. With only six months of his contract remaining, Everton reluctantly accepted this lower offer.

This shows the danger in clubs not securing players on long contracts if the player is very talented and worth a significant amount in the market. Long contracts can prevent clubs losing their best players for low fees, but this comes at a cost. If the player suffers a loss of form or turns out to be less talented than the buying club initially considered him to be then the club has to pay his wages for the whole of the contract period. Nikola Žigić signed for (at the time) Premier League Birmingham City for an estimated £6 million from Valencia in May 2010 on a four-year contract, for an alleged £50,000 a week. Birmingham's belief was that Žigić would score the goals that ensured Premier League survival, but he only hit the back of the net five times in the Premier League in 2010/11 and the club was relegated to the Championship.

Many clubs have clauses in player contracts in case relegation arises, but Birmingham failed to do this with Žigić. The player then played out the remainder of his contract in the Championship, where Birmingham, even with parachute payments, struggled to survive financially. Whilst fans can get very irate at this, and there is evidence of the likes of Jamie O'Hara at Wolves and Jack Rodwell at Sunderland being on the receiving end of much abuse for sitting out their contracts, no one forced the club to offer a high level of wages to the player. Had the player turned out to be a star performer then there is every chance he would have been sold at a significant profit by the club who take the risk and earn the reward in relation to offering long-term contracts to players.

Release clause

When a player signs a contract with a club, there may be a sum inserted into the contract that states an amount which, if bid by another club, allows the player to discuss a move elsewhere. This is referred to as a release clause. Clubs normally insert high release fees to act as a deterrent to potential suitors snatching away their prize assets. In August

2017 Neymar was transferred from FC Barcelona to Paris St Germain for €222 million. This sum was based on Neymar's release clause when he signed a five-year contract with Barcelona in October 2016. The clause was agreed by Neymar's representatives in 2016 and was a sign of intent from Barcelona that they wanted the player to remain at the Nou Camp for a long time. At the time of signing the contract Barcelona were confident that no club would ever bid the amount of the release fee, but they were shown to be wrong. Consequently, when Barcelona signed Philippe Coutinho for £142 million in January 2018, the Catalan club inserted a release fee of £355 million to try to prevent any other clubs trying to sign him.

How to show football player transactions in the accounts

Transfer fees

Football player transfer fees are treated as intangible assets in the club balance sheet. This is because the registration of the player satisfies the asset definition previously discussed.

- The registration contract means the player is controlled by the football club. This is evidenced as the club has the main benefits of the player, which is the exclusive use of his football services for the life of the contract, and the risks, such as loss of form or injury;
- The player generates economic benefits for the club. The player generates income as he contributes towards the club's performance on the pitch, and therefore helps ensure fans watch the team, commercial partners can use the player to advertise their products, and broadcasters pay to screen matches featuring star players;
- It is due to a past event, which is the transfer of the registration certificate from the selling club.

This does create an inconsistency in the balance sheet, as many players are developed by clubs through their youth schemes and so no transfer fee is paid. Big name players such as Lionel Messi of Barcelona, Steven Gerrard of Liverpool, Francesco Totti of AS Roma and Paul Scholes at Manchester United are all examples of highly skilled and appreciated players, but none appeared in the balance sheets of their respective clubs. This is because they were identified at an early age by football scouts and signed schoolboy contracts at a zero fee. These players do not therefore appear in the balance sheet, which means that the cost of the playing squad usually significantly understates the market value as a whole. This should be borne in mind by anyone considering buying a club, as the balance sheet total for players is usually much lower than the market value.

In the accounts of the buying club, the transfer fee shown usually includes all the external costs incurred in acquiring the player's signature. Therefore, agent and lawyer fees relating to the transfer and similar costs are added to the fee received by the buying club.

Amortisation

Once a player has signed for a club, the registration/transfer fee is shown as an expense in the profit or loss account spread over the contract period. This amortisation cost might not be shown on the face of the profit or loss account but can always be found by reviewing the footnotes that accompany the club's annual accounts.

Table 5.2 is taken from Juventus's financial report for 2017/18. It shows an amortisation charge for that period of £107.9 million, compared to £82.9 million for the previous year. This reflects that in 2017/18 Juventus invested heavily in players such as Federico Bernardeschi, Juan Cuadrado, Blaise Matuidi and Medhi Benatia. These signings increased the amortisation charge due to the fees paid for their transfers. When Neymar signed for PSG from Barcelona in the summer of 2017 for €222 million on a five-year contract, this meant there will be an amortisation expense of €44.4 million (€222m/5) a year for the next five years in PSG's profit or loss account.

Table 5.2 Income statement, 2017/18, Juventus

Amounts in euros	Note	2017/2018 Financial year	2016/2017 Financial year	Change
Ticket sales	32	**56,410,423**	57,835,297	(1,424,874)
Television and radio rights and media revenues	33	**200,169,142**	232,773,784	(32,604,642)
Revenues from sponsorship and advertising	34	**86,896,999**	74,718,794	12,178,205
Revenues from sales of products and licences	35	**27,796,591**	19,198,979	8,597,612
Revenues from players' registration rights	36	**102,401,466**	151,149,536	(48,748,070)
Other revenues	37	**30,995,269**	27,034,664	3,960,605
Total revenues		**504,669,890**	562,711,054	(58,041,164)
Purchase of materials, supplies and other consumables	38	**(3,464,062)**	(2,979,934)	(484,128)
Purchases of products for sale	39	**(11,469,144)**	(8,290,140)	(3,179,004)
External services	40	**(76,943,169)**	(66,578,563)	(10,364,606)
Players' wages and technical staff costs	41	**(233,319,806)**	(235,344,554)	2,024,748
Other personnel	42	**(25,683,238)**	(26,481,657)	798,419
Expenses from players' registration rights	43	**(20,107,143)**	(50,492,316)	30,385,173
Other expenses	44	**(12,273,621)**	(10,524,690)	(1,748,931)
Total operating costs		**(383,260,183)**	(400,691,854)	17,431,671
Amortisation and write-downs of players' registration rights	45	**(107,954,427)**	(82,949,776)	(25,004,651)
Amortisation of other tangible and intangible assets	46	**(12,525,527)**	(9,934,144)	(2,591,383)
Provisions, write-downs and release of funds	47	**(2,363,811)**	(2,107,849)	(255,962)
Other non-current revenues and expenses		–	350,000	(350,000)
Operating income		**(1,434,058)**	67,377,431	(68,811,489)

Source: Juventus SA

In addition to being an expense in the profit or loss account, the amortisation charge for the year is deducted from the original cost of the transfer registration in the balance sheet. The following table shows how Neymar's contract will appear in the balance sheet, assuming he continues to play for PSG for five years. The figures are accounting values and do not reflect Neymar's transfer value in the open market:

Year ended 30 June	€ millions
2018	177.6 (222 − 44.4)
2019	133.2 (222 − (2 × 44.4))
2020	88.8 (222 − (3 × 44.4))
2021	44.4 (222 − (4 × 44.4))
2022	0 (222 − (5 × 44.4))

The cost of all the players signed for fees, less the total amortisation expense since signing, is called the net book value (or carrying amount) of player registrations.

Table 5.3 is a note to Arsenal's balance sheet for 2017/18. It shows that Arsenal bought new players for £165.8 million in the season and sold players who originally cost the club £118.4 million. The amortisation charge for the year of £85.8 million will also be included in expenses in the profit or loss account and will decrease profits by this sum too. The amortisation expense in the profit or loss account is not a cash expense, and so is added back to profit in the cash flow statement.

Table 5.3 Intangible assets, 2017/18 Arsenal 11. Intangible assets

	£'000
Cost of player registrations	
At 1 June 2017	432,603
Additions	165,831
Disposals	(118,423)
At 31 May 2018	480,011
Amortisation of player registrations	
At 1 June 2018	250,574
Charge for the year	85,812
Impairment	5,948
Disposals	(100,568)
At 31 May 2018	241,766
Net book value	
At 31 May 2018	238,245
At 31 May 2017	182,029

Source: Arsenal FC

Contract extensions

A player may be offered a contract extension by a club. This is usually when the player is highly valued as it ties the player to the club for an extra period of time. The contract extension may accompany a pay raise for the player to incentivize him to agree to the extension period. When this happens the amortisation expense decreases. This is because amortisation is based on the balance sheet value of the player spread over the remaining length of the contract. If the contract length is effectively increased, then the annual cost falls. For example, using the Neymar example above, let's assume he is offered a three-year contract extension by PSG on 1 July 2020. Based on the original figures, Neymar would be measured in the balance sheet at €88.8 million at 1 July 2020. If his contract is extended, then he will then have five years remaining from that date on his contract, and the annual amortisation fee will decrease to €17.8 million (€88.8 million over five years) compared to the original $44.4 million.

Impairments

When a player is signed, there is always a risk that he may perform more poorly than anticipated. Every club has made errors in their recruitment policy over the years and fans of all clubs can very quickly name them. At the end of the financial year, under accounting rules, clubs are obliged to look at each player and decide if they believe their market value is less than that shown in the balance sheet. Should that be the case, then an impairment arises, and the player's value is written down to his expected market sale price. The impairment is shown as an expense in the profit or loss account and reduces profit, as well as the value of player registrations in the balance sheet. For example, Fulchester Rovers sign a striker, Mario Luigi, on 1 July 20X6 for £50 million on a five-year contract. Mario only scores two goals in the 20X6/20X7 season. Mario's value in the balance sheet at 30 June 20X7, which is Fulchester Rovers' financial year end, is £40 million (£50 million cost less (1/5 × £50 million) amortisation. At the end of the 20X7 season Fulchester Rovers' director of football considers that Mario is only worth £22 million at 30 June 20X7. An impairment expense of £18 million (£40m – £22m) is charged to the profit or loss account and the intangible asset in relation to player registrations in the balance sheet is reduced by the same sum.

The impairment expense is shown separately in the footnotes to the accounts. The rationale behind showing it separately is that clubs do not anticipate impairments arising every year, and so this sum can be separated out if trying to determine the club's recurring profits.

Table 5.4 is taken from Liverpool's accounts for 2015/16. The club concluded that a player was overvalued in its financial statements as his performances did not meet

Table 5.4 Administrative expenses, 2015/16, Liverpool FC

Administrative expenses

Included in administrative expenses are the following:

	2016 £000
Amortisation of players' registrations	64,537
Redundancy and associated costs	15,669
Impairment loss on player registrations	7,878
Depreciation of tangible fixed assets	3,978
Operating lease rentals	2,397
Amortisation of goodwill	1,272
Auditors remuneration	90
Loss/(gain) on disposal of tangible fixed assets	19
Stadium development related (credits)	–

Source: Liverpool Football Club and Athletic Grounds Ltd Annual Report

expectations. They therefore reduced the value of his registration by £7.9 million. The player's name is not mentioned, probably to avoid embarrassment to the individual concerned, but the smart money is that it relates to Mario Balotelli, whom Liverpool signed from Milan on a three-year contract in 2014. After a poor first season at Anfield, where he scored only one league goal, he was then sent back to Milan on loan, where he also scored only one league goal during 2015/16. Upon his return to Liverpool, it looks as if the club took the view that he was overvalued in the accounts and wrote his value down to zero at the end of May 2016, before allowing him to leave on a free transfer to Nice in August 2016.

The impairment also has an impact on the balance sheet value of player registrations. In Liverpool's note to the 2015/16 balance sheet (Table 5.5) the impairment charge of £7.9 million seen earlier in the profit or loss account is effectively added to the amortisation figure for the year, and both are subtracted from the cost of buying player registrations to arrive at the net book value at the end of the year.

Impairments can be reversed but very rarely. If a player recovers from an injury that was previously thought to be career threatening or wins back the confidence of the manager and is restored to the first team squad, then a negative expense is shown in the profit or loss account, and the same adjustment is made in the balance sheet too to increase the net book value of player registrations.

Table 5.6 shows that Manchester United reversed an impairment in 2016/17 in relation to a player who fell out of favour the previous season. The club had an impairment charge of £6.7 million in the 2015/16 accounts, which probably related to Bastian Schweinsteiger who they had signed by then manager Louis van Gaal from Bayern Munich on a three-year contract in July 2015. Schweinsteiger fell out of favour when Jose Mourinho took over as United's manager less than a year later. Schweinsteiger was made to train with

Table 5.5 Balance sheet notes to financial statements 31 May 2016, Liverpool FC

9 Intangible assets and goodwill

	Goodwill £000	Players' registrations £000	Total £000
Cost			
Balance at 1 June 2015 (restated)	13,994	309,933	323,927
Additions	–	101,841	101,841
Disposals	–	(51,646)	(51,646)
Balance at 31 May 2016	**13,994**	**360,128**	**374,122**
Amortisation and impairment			
Balance at 1 June 2015 (restated)	7,421	147,452	154,873
Amortisation for the year	1,272	64,537	65,809
Impairment charge	–	7,878	7,878
Disposals	–	(44,510)	(44,510)
Balance at 31 May 2016	8,693	175,357	184,050
Net book value			
At 1 June 2015 (restated)	6,573	162,481	169,054
At 31 May 2016	**5,301**	**184,771**	**190,072**

Source: Liverpool Football Club and Athletic Grounds Ltd Annual Report 31 May 2016

Table 5.6 Exceptional items, Manchester United

6 Exceptional items

	2017 £'000	2016 £'000	2015 £'000
Impairment reversal/(charge)—registrations (note 15)	4,753	(6,693)	—
Compensation paid for loss of office	—	(8,442)	—
Football League pension scheme deficit (note 30)	—	—	(1,247)
Professional adviser fees relating to public sale of Class A ordinary shares	—	—	(1,089)
	4,753	(15,135)	(2,336)

A registrations impairment charge amounting to £6,693,000 was originally made in the year ended 30 June 2016 in respect of a player who was no longer considered to be a member of the first team playing squad. This impairment was reversed during the year ended 30 June 2017 as the player was re-established as a member of the first team playing squad. The reversal was calculated to increase the carrying value of the player's registration to the value that would have been recognized had the original...

Source: Manchester United

Table 5.7 Intangible assets, balance sheet, Manchester United

	Goodwill £'000	Registrations £'000
At 1 July 2015		
Cost	421,453	465,830
Accumulated amortization	—	(227,684)
Net book amount	421,453	238,146
Year ended 30 June 2016		
Opening net book amount	421,453	238,146
Additions	—	167,089
Disposals	—	(68,965)
Amortization charge	—	(87,853)
Impairment charge (note 6)	—	(6,693)
Closing book amount	421,453	241,724
At 30 June 2016		
Cost	421,453	511,893
Accumulated amortization	—	(270,169)
Net book amount	421,453	241,724
Year ended 30 June 2017		
Opening net book amount	421,453	241,724
Additions	—	205,091
Disposals	—	(37,353)
Amortization charge	—	(123,695)
Reversal of impairment (note 6)	—	4,753
Closing book amount	421,453	290,520
At 30 June 2017		
Cost	421,453	645,433
Accumulated amortization	—	(354,913)
Net book amount	**421,453**	**290,520**

Source: Manchester United

the under-23 squad under Mourinho, and the club therefore wrote down the value of his signing in the 2015/16 accounts. Mourinho then decided a few months later that he did want Schweinsteiger back in the first team squad, and so United reversed part of the impairment. This resulted in a negative expense of £4.8 million in the profit or loss account, which increased profit by the same figure. But such reversals of impairment charges are rare in practice and most clubs would instead show a profit on the sale of the player when he is sold.

Table 5.7 shows that the reversal of the impairment of Schweinsteiger also increased the net book value of Manchester United's player registrations by £4.753 million in the balance sheet in 2017.

Player sales

When a club sells a player, his registration must be removed from the balance sheet. This is because the club no longer has use of his services, and his registration is no longer contributing future economic benefits. Therefore, the registration can no longer be treated as an intangible asset. At the sale date, both the cost and the accumulated amortisation amounts are removed from the player registration totals. This gives the players' balance sheet value (also called the net book value) at the date of disposal. The agreed player sale fee is compared to the balance sheet value, and a gain or loss on disposal is the difference between the two figures.

This causes an anomaly in the profit or loss account. The cost of buying a player is spread over a number of years in the profit or loss account via the amortisation charge, but the sale price is reflected in the accounts in the year in which the player is sold. This can make the profits shown in the profit or loss account very erratic, as the whole gain on sale is loaded into the accounts in a single year whereas the purchase price for a player is spread over the contract term.

Case study 1: Ousmane Dembele
Dembele was signed by Borussia Dortmund in the summer of 2016 for €15 million on a five-year contract from French club Rennes where he had made his senior debut and scored 25 goals in 48 appearances during the previous two seasons. In Dortmund's accounts, Dembele's player registration would appear in the balance sheet as an intangible asset. At the date he signed for the club he was initially valued at the transfer fee of €15 million. A year later, when the balance sheet was prepared for summer 2017, his registration would be valued at the original cost of €15 million less one year's amortisation of €3 million (€15m × 1/5). This gives a balance sheet value of €12 million in summer 2017.

Dortmund then sold Dembele, who had just been named Bundesliga Rookie of the Season, to Barcelona in summer 2017 for an initial fee of €110 million, making him (at the start of 2018) the third most expensive player in the world (behind Neymar and Philippe Coutinho). Dortmund will therefore show a gain of €98 million (€110 million less the net book value of €12 million) in respect of the sale of Dembele in their profit or loss account for the year ended June 2018. The nature of player sales and the prices received is erratic and can have a significant impact on profit from year to year.

Case study 2: Andy Carroll
The accounting nature relating to player sales can create figures which seem counterintuitive. Andy Carroll signed for Liverpool from his hometown club Newcastle in January 2011 for a fee of £35 million, which was the highest fee paid for an English player between two English clubs for many years. Carroll signed a five and a half year

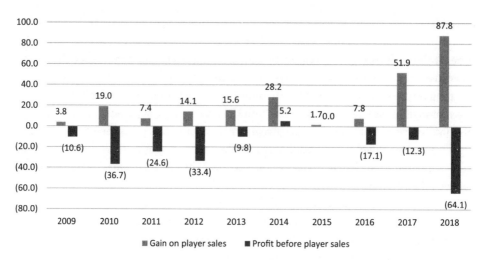

Figure 5.3 Everton losses before player sales and gains on player disposals (£ millions)

contract, which resulted in an annual impairment charge of £6.4 million. Carroll's career at Anfield was unexceptional and he was sold to West Ham two and a half years later for £15 million. A fan might therefore think that Liverpool suffered a £20 million loss on the deal. However, at the sale date to West Ham Carroll's accounting value was £19.1 million (£35m – 2.5 years x £6.4 million amortisation charge) and so an accounting loss on sale of just £4.1 million was recorded in the profit or loss account. Carroll's career at Liverpool illustrates that clubs typically show substantial profits on player sales in the accounts, but this is more to do with the accounting method used rather than comparing the difference between purchase and sales price. Carroll subsequently left West Ham in the summer of 2019 when his contract expired and signed for Newcastle for the second time for no fee.

The importance of player sales to a club cannot be underestimated. Figure 5.3 shows that Everton made losses before player sales of £155.5 million in the period 2008–17. Until the club was bought by Farhad Moshiri in February 2016 it had not had a rich benefactor and had to ensure that it did not live beyond its means. Gains on player sales over the same period were £160.5 million, allowing the club to effectively break even. This suggests to a certain extent that Everton was forced to sell players to keep the bank happy during this period, as the owners at the time did not have spare cash to invest in the club.

How to calculate the sales price of players sold?

Clubs don't show the fees of players sold separately in the accounts, but it is possible to extract the figure from elsewhere in the accounts. By adding the profit on disposal of players (from the income statement) to the net book balance sheet value of disposals of intangible assets (from the footnotes), the total sales value of players is determined. Many people make the mistake of using the cash received from player sales figure from the cash flow statement instead, but this is incorrect, as the player may have been sold on credit, and so payment will not be received for a year or more.

Case study 1: Juventus
Juventus were active in the transfer market during 2017/18, when the club once again won Serie A.

Table 5.8 Statement of cash flows, Juventus

Amounts in euros	Note	2017/2018 Financial year	2016/2017 Financial year
Income/(loss) before taxes Non-cash items:		**(10,022,550)**	58,414,719
– amortisation, depreciation and write-down	45 and 46	**120,479,954**	92,883,920
– release of provisions		**-**	9,638
– employee benefit liability and other provisions		**3,003,937**	3,751,782
– Provision for the *Long Term Incentive Plan*		**3,145,014**	6,134,680
– gains on disposal of players' registration rights	36	**(93,925,290)**	(140,309,387)
– gains on disposal of other fixed assets		**(97)**	–
– losses on disposal of players' registration rights	43	**104,182**	493,491
– losses on disposal of other fixed assets		**308**	–
– other non-recurring revenues and costs		**–**	(350,000)
– Group's share of results of associates and joint ventures		**886,073**	1,266,633
– financial income	48	**(4,260,740)**	(4,273,061)
– financial expenses	49	**11,963,159**	11,969,140
Change in trade receivables and other non financial activities		**(452,471)**	(11,478,515)
Change in trade payables and other non-financial liabilities		**(20,983,966)**	50,129,799
Income taxes paid		**(14,891,685)**	(8,908,028)
Use of the Employees' Severance indemnity Provision and other funds		**(3,049,000)**	(4,085,823)
Net cash from (used in) operating activities		**(8,003,172)**	55,648,988
Investments in players' registration rights	8	**(157,906,041)**	(252,338,708)
Increase (decrease) of payables related to players' registration rights		**(45,654,910)**	60,588,404
Disposals of players' registration rights		**114,905,139**	193,413,850
(Increase) decrease of receivables related to players' registration rights		**(18,149,044)**	(20,196,782)
increase (decrease) of payables for auxiliary expenses on players' registration rights (a)		**(12,682,572)**	20,393,190
investments in other fixed assets		**(12,408,439)**	(15,599,717)
Sale of 50% of the investment in J Medical S.r.l.		**–**	2,400,000
Purchases of investments		**(832,642)**	(1,690,040)
Disposals of other fixed assets		**58,153**	721
Interest income	48	**60,049**	114,672
Net cash from (used in) investing activities		**(132,610,306)**	(12,914,410)

Source: Juventus SA

From a first glance at their cash flow statement (Table 5.8) it looks as if Juventus sold players for €114.9 million in 2017/18, but this is incorrect as these sums only represent the cash from player sales and may include sums relating to disposals in previous years which were on credit. We therefore need to look at Juventus's income statement for clarification.

The income statement (Table 5.9) showed revenue from players' registration rights (effectively gains on player sales) of €102.4 million in 2017/18, substantially less than the figure in the cash flow statement. This is because this figure does not represent the sums receivable for player sales, merely the profit on those sales. It's the same as if you bought a house for £300,000 and then sold it for £350,000. This gives a profit on sale of £50,000, which is not the sale price in itself. We do the same with football player sales, by finding out the balance sheet value of the players sold, and for that we need to look at the footnotes to the accounts.

In Juventus's footnote to their accounts (Table 5.10) we see that the players Juventus sold in 2017/8 – called disinvestments (gross) in the note – originally cost the club €64.7 million. Further down the note it says that the net value of these player registrations was €21.1 million. The net disinvestment figure is then added to the profit on disposal from the income statement of €102.4 million to give total sale proceeds of €123.5 million (€102.4m + €21.1m). It's not a straightforward way to determine the sales value of players sold, but as clubs are reluctant to reveal the information themselves, at least informed fans can answer those questions that often are asked when querying the owners' and directors' ambitions.

Conditional fees payable

When a club signs a player, they are taking a gamble in relation to the impact he will have on the pitch. Sometimes a club will try to lessen that risk by linking the transfer fee to certain conditions. The sum ultimately payable may be dependent upon achievements such as the number of appearances the player makes, future international caps, trophies won (or perhaps relegation being avoided) and so on. These sums are called conditional fees and are split into two types: those which are payable to the selling club and those which are payable to the player. As it is not possible to predict with confidence whether or not a player will satisfy the contractual conditions that will trigger the additional payments, the notes to the accounts can act to warn of potential extra payments that the club may have to pay at a future date.

The following footnote from Manchester City's accounts shows the club had total potential extra payments of over £158 million at 31 May 2018 to players and former clubs:

Transfer fees payable

Additional transfer fees, signing on fees and loyalty bonuses of £158,916,000 (2017: £111,033,000) that will become payable upon the achievement of certain conditions contained within player and transfer contracts if they are still in the service of the Club on specific future dates are accounted for in the year in which they fall due for payment.

These sums are not shown in the accounts themselves but are disclosed in the footnotes. This is because under current accounting rules a liability – to another club or to a player – cannot be included in the accounts until the payment is probable (i.e. more than 50% likely to occur).

Table 5.9 Income statement, Juventus

Amounts in euros	Note	2017/2018 Financial year	2016/2017 Financial year	Change
Ticket sales	32	**56,410,423**	57,835,297	(1,424,874)
Television and radio rights and media revenues	33	**200,169,142**	232,773,784	(32,604,642)
Revenues from sponsorship and advertising	34	**86,896,999**	74,718,794	12,178,205
Revenues from sales of products and licences	35	**27,796,591**	19,198,979	8,597,612
Revenues from players' registration rights	36	**102,401,466**	151,149,536	(48,748,070)
Other revenues	37	**30,995,269**	27,034,664	3,960,605
Total revenues		**504,669,890**	562,711,054	(58,041,164)

Source: Juventus SA

Table 5.10 Notes to financial statements, Juventus

Amounts in thousands of euros	Professionals	Registered young players	Women	Total
Book value	525,964	3,477	–	529,441
Amortisation provision	(225,048)	(1,424)	–	(226,472)
Allowance for doubtful accounts	(945)	(64)	–	(1,009)
Balance at 30/06/2017	**299,971**	**1,989**	**–**	**301,960**
Investments	**156,409**	**1,481**	**16**	**157,906**
Disinvestments (gross)	*(64,046)*	*(690)*	*–*	*(64,736)*
Use of accumulated amortisation	*42,202*	*441*	*–*	*42,643*
Use of allowance for doubtful accounts	*945*	*64*	*–*	*1,009*
Disinvestments (net)	**(20,899)**	**(185)**	**–**	**(21,084)**
Amortisation	**(106,658)**	**(554)**	**(8)**	**(107,220)**
Depreciation	**(586)**	**(140)**	**(8)**	**(734)**
Reclassifications	**1,200**	**(1,200)**	**–**	**–**
Balance at 30/06/2018	**329,437**	**1,391**	**–**	**330,828**
Book value	619,850	2,745	16	622,611
Amortisation provision	(289,827)	(1,214)	(8)	(291,049)
Allowance for doubtful accounts	(586)	(140)	(8)	(734)
Balance at 30/06/2018	**329,437**	**1,391**	**–**	**330,828**

Source: Juventus SA

Paying by instalments

Player transfer fees have increased in value significantly over time. The first £1 million transfer was that of Trevor Francis from Birmingham City to Brian Clough's Nottingham Forest in 1979. The transfer fee was considered enormous at the time, nearly doubling the fee paid for a player between two English clubs, but Francis proved his worth by scoring the winning goal in the European Cup final the following season. By 1996 the record fee had risen to £15 million when Alan Shearer moved from Blackburn Rovers to Newcastle United. At the time of writing, the record fee remains the €222 million paid by PSG for Brazilian striker Neymar Jr. in August 2017.

Given the size of these fees it may be difficult for the buying club to pay for the player immediately, as the club may not have sufficient funds to complete the transfer, and few clubs have bank balances that are in the tens of millions. The contract to transfer the player registration will stipulate the nature of how the transfer fee will be paid. If paying in instalments then the amount unpaid will appear in the balance sheet as a trade liability, split between current (due in less than a year) and non-current (due in more than one year) amounts. Similarly, for the club that has sold the player and is receiving the fee in instalments, there will be a trade debtor (receivable) asset in the balance sheet for the outstanding sums due.

Table 5.11 is an extract from Leicester City's 2018 annual report. It shows that Leicester owed their creditors a total of £133.3 million. Of this sum, £67.8 million was in relation to player transfers, and over £21 million was not due for at least a year. When Leicester refer in the notes to the gross transfer fees payable before discounting this refers to the cash sum due to the other club for transfers. The difference between the figure in the table and the one in the narrative note is due to what is called the time value of money.

If a person was offered a million pounds today or a million pounds in a year, then they would opt to receive the money immediately. This is due to a combination of inflation, which eats away at the value of cash, and also uncertainty in relation to the future, the person who owes the money may become bankrupt within a year and be unable to pay.

If the figures were changed, so that the choice was, say, £909,091 today or £1 million in a year, then the decision may be different. The time value of money is based on the interest rate that it earns which makes the recipient indifferent whether they receive the money today or in a year (or a number of years). The sum of £909,091 earning 10 per cent interest would be worth £1 million in a year, so here we would say the time value of money is 10 per cent.

The same is true for football transfers. A selling club might be asking £20 million for a player if paid immediately. If the buyer offered three annual payments of £8 million, one paid immediately, and the others one and two years later, then the total cash cost would be £24 million but the transfer fee would be recorded as £20 million. The additional

Table 5.11 Notes to the financial statements: creditors, year ended 31 May 2018, Leicester City

11 Creditors: amounts falling due within one year

	2018 £'000	2017 £'000
Bank loans and overdrafts	32	32
Trade creditors	4,051	1,821
Transfer fees payable	46,536	31,891
Amounts owed to group undertakings:		
– subordinated loans and other amounts payable	9,820	12,267
– obligations under finance lease and hire purchase contracts	14,827	16,662
Taxation and social security	9,645	8,483
Other creditors	21,741	21,783
Accruals and deferred income	5,179	6,639
	111,831	99,578

Gross transfer fees payable before discounting are £47,817,000 (2017: £32,543,000).

The Subordinated loans and other amounts owed by group undertakings are unsecured, interest free and repayable on demand whilst the obligations under hire purchase agreements are unsecured, repayable on demand and carry interest at 8%.

Other creditors include £13,996,000 payable to employees (2017: £11,380,000).

12 Creditors: amounts falling due after more than one year

	2018 £'000	2017 £'000
Bank loans and overdrafts	119	151
Transfer fees payable	21,303	12,050
	21,422	12,201

Gross transfer fees payable before discounting are £21,590,000 (2017: £12,273,000).

Source: Leicester City

£4 million (3 × £8 million less the £20 million) would be treated as an interest cost in the profit or loss account.

Leicester signed the likes of Harry Maguire, Kelechi Iheanacho and others in 2017/18 for a total of almost £93 million. Some of the selling clubs, such as Hull and Manchester City may have been willing to accept higher fees that were spread over instalments. Similarly, Leicester were owed over £24 million at the end of 2017/18 having sold Danny Drinkwater to Chelsea for a substantial fee and part of this was being received in instalments, as evidenced by the difference in gross transfer fees receivable and the figures shown in the balance sheet debtors note (Table 5.12).

Information of this nature is very useful for anyone trying to build a model that predicts a football club's future cash flows. This may be the case when trying to value the club or identify if it has any cash flow problems on the horizon. In general, the bigger the transfer fee, the greater the likelihood of payments being made by instalments.

Table 5.12 Balance sheet: debtors, Leicester City

	2018 £'000	2017 £'000
Trade debtors	2,739	3,385
Amounts owed by group undertakings	4,773	1,862
Corporation Tax	105	185
Transfer fees receivable	24,277	10,832
Other debtors	5,761	5,430
Prepayments and accrued income	15,065	33,259
	52,720	54,953

Trade Debtors are stated after provisions for impairment of £21,000 (2017: £58,000)
Amounts owed by group undertakings are unsecured, interest free and repayable on demand.
Transfer fees receivable includes £305,000 (2017: £330,000) falling due after more than one year.
Gross transfer fees receivable before discounting are £24,448,000 (2017: £10,996,000).

Source: Leicester City

The selling club may however need cash urgently and increasingly clubs are factoring sums due from other clubs. This involves selling the agreed instalments on transfers to a bank or other financial institution for immediate cash. When the instalments are received this is then paid over to the bank along with an interest charge. For example, Watford sold Brazilian player Richarlison to Everton in July 2018 for an estimated £40 million. Everton agreed to put down a deposit fee plus instalments over the next two years. In October 2018 Watford borrowed money from Santander Bank and the loan agreement included two promissory notes for repayments in 2019 and 2020 from the outstanding instalments due from Everton. In addition, Watford would pay interest to Santander during the period that the loan was outstanding. This is a convenient method of accelerating cash flow for a club.

Signing-on fees

When a player agrees to play for a club, he may receive an upfront payment, which is commonly referred to as a signing on fee. This can be a substantial sum, especially if the player is out of contract and, under the Bosman rule, the acquiring club does not have to pay for the transfer registration. Signing on fees are usually spread over the life of the contract agreed between the club and the player. When Polish-born German striker Robert Lewandowski's contract for Borussia Dortmund expired at the end of the 2013/14 season, he then joined Bundesliga rivals Bayern Munich under the Bosman ruling. Bayern paid Lewandowski a signing on fee of an estimated £9 million. Lewandowski signed a four-year contract with Bayern, so this resulted in an annual cost of £2.25 million (£9 million/4) in the profit or loss account. From that date until the end of the 2016/17 season Lewandowski scored 92 goals in 113 appearances, so the signing on fee will be regarded as money well spent to secure his services.

Football player wages

More column inches are written about football players' wages than any other profession. A player signing a new lucrative contract will often prompt headlines and stories asking why footballers are paid so much more than nurses, teachers and others in worthy professions. It's an interesting viewpoint, but does not stand up to scrutiny. Wages are a price for labour, in this case, a football player's services, and price is determined by supply and demand factors. Simply put, the higher the demand the higher the price, and the lower the supply the higher the price too.

There are millions of people who play football every week, so why are the likes of Cristiano Ronaldo and Lionel Messi paid millions every year, and my career as a left back in the Manchester Accountants Sunday League Division 2 in the 1980s was conspicuous by no payments for my silky skills. No one is prepared to pay to watch park football between a bunch of overweight men with goalposts but no nets on a pitch that is half mud and half a dog's toilet, but millions are willing to pay to watch Real Madrid vs Barcelona, either through attending the match or a broadcasting medium. If people are prepared to pay to watch, then clubs have the means to pay their players.

Even within professional football itself, there are vast gulfs between the different divisions in which clubs play, and even between the clubs within those divisions.

Figure 5.4 is based on an analysis of club financial statements for 2017/18. The figures for League Two are probably a little high, as only eight out of 24 clubs produced wage information in their published accounts. To put the figures in context, for every £100

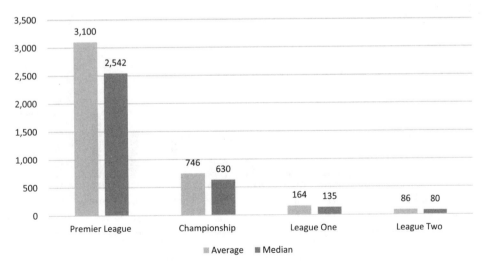

Figure 5.4 Average and median annual player salaries (£ '000)

earned by an average League Two player, his counterparts in League One earned £191, in the Championship it was £867 and for the Premier League £3,604. The reason for the large difference is down to what an individual player can offer a club: simply, the number of players who can score 20 goals a season in the Premier League is far fewer than the number who can score 20 goals in League Two.

The fundamental economic concept of supply and demand therefore applies to footballers in terms of their employment price in the form of the wages they command. Every club wants to have a player in their team of the calibre of Cristiano Ronaldo, Lionel Messi, Gianluigi Buffon or Kevin De Bruyne. But there are very few players who have such ability to make a positive impact upon a football match at the elite level. This means that players of such ability can demand high salaries from their employers, safe in the knowledge that there are other clubs also willing to pay similarly high wages.

Players (and their agents) are also fully aware that clubs' incomes have risen significantly in recent years. Such awareness has resulted in higher wages. Sir Alan Sugar, the former chairman of Tottenham Hotspur, once said in relation to this: "The money coming into the game is incredible, but it is just the prune juice effect, it comes in and goes out straight away".

Figure 5.5 shows the growth in Arsenal's income and wage costs since the formation of the Premier League in 1992/3. Income has increased by 2,671 per cent since then, but wages have increased by 3,169 per cent during the same period. The relationship between income and wages has operated in a relatively narrow band of 45–55 per cent during that period, except for 2001/2, when it peaked at 68 per cent. Arsenal fans with very long

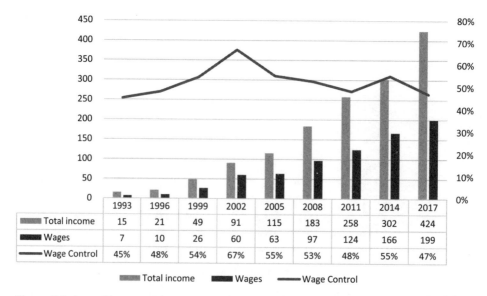

	1993	1996	1999	2002	2005	2008	2011	2014	2017
Total income	15	21	49	91	115	183	258	302	424
Wages	7	10	26	60	63	97	124	166	199
Wage Control	45%	48%	54%	67%	55%	53%	48%	55%	47%

Total income   Wages   Wage Control

Figure 5.5 Arsenal income and wage movement, 1993–2017

memories will no doubt point out that the increased commitment to paying wages in 2001/2 was a major contributory factor in winning the Premier League and FA Cup that season. This may be the case, although it could be that winning the Premier League itself triggered bonus payments that increased the wage cost significantly.

Player transfer fees and wages are an emotive and often misunderstood topic. The methods used to account for players make this even more confusing due to the seemingly inconsistent methods used to account for player purchases, sales, increases and decreases in value, and time taken to pay the fees. It takes time to familiarize with the industry practices for players but once the rules are understood then anyone reviewing the figures should have a greater understanding of some of the strange numbers that litter the accounts.

Agents

Five hundred pounds and answering some questions from an online drop-down menu is the cost of being registered as an agent (nowadays called an intermediary) in England. All you have to do is go to the FA website and complete a form, which includes questions that seek to establish an applicant's good character and reputation. Provided the applicant does not want to work with people under the age of 18 no further checks are required.

From 1 February 2018 to 31 January 2019 Premier League clubs paid agents £260 million, an increase of £49 million compared to the previous year and this has prompted much criticism from fans and commentators. When Manchester United signed Paul Pogba in 2016 the then record fee was shown in the – always excellent – Juventus financial statements as being €105 million. A few pages later the Italian club disclosed the amounts paid to agents and third parties in respect of player transfers and for the Pogba sale it was over €26 million. It is not known how much, if anything, was paid in addition by Manchester United to the agent in respect of this transfer. Clearly, Pogba's agent Mino Raiola was a major beneficiary from this transaction, but if the buying and selling clubs, along with his client, signed off on the deal one can ask has anyone lost out as a result of his involvement?

Speaking to people who have experience of the industry (and their names have been anonymised at their request) suggests that the sullied reputation of agents has some justification, but that as in all occupations there are both good and bad exemplars. According to a former member of a Championship club's management team some agents will "seek any entrance point" to a club in trying to gain a starting point for a deal in respect of their client. If rejected by one senior person at the club, they will then often seek others until someone starts being sympathetic to their proposals.

There are some clubs who are "agent led" and partnered with a specific agency where a club manager or other senior staff member's representative then becomes the preferred person for negotiating deals. Agent led means that the club's transfer policy is to an extent determined by the agent rather than the scouting team. This can result in some players being sold if they refuse to be represented by the preferred agent. Some clubs will have no scouting system and will rely on agents to find them a player for a particular position. This can lead to a conflict of interest as the agent will be looking for the best commission and doesn't necessarily have a knowledge of the player's abilities and how he would complement the playing and coaching of a team.

What is unusual in terms of football agents is the degree of nepotism in the sport. Many football managers or club owners have siblings or offspring who become agents regardless of their background or experience. This can result in players being recruited at a club because of the closeness of the relationship between agent and manager/owner rather than on the player's ability or the need from the club. The legacy of bad buys which are lucrative for the agent may be borne by subsequent managers who inherit these players.

Quite often a player may have more than one person who claims to be their representative and this causes problems when a club is trying to buy or sell the player. A chief executive of a Premier League club explained that when he attempted to sign a player from South America there were no less than ten people claiming to be the player's representative, all wanting a commission. It was only by taking a firm stance and stating that he was only willing to work with one representative that negotiations eventually proceeded, but if the club is desperate to buy the player then it may acquiesce and agree to work with multiple parties.

An agent can be beneficial to a club if they work in conjunction with all parties and take a long-term view of the relationship. If the agent is proactive and keeps in regular contact with the club in terms of what competitors are willing to offer in terms of wages, then everyone can be a winner. The player gets a regular pay rise in terms of a contract extension on improved terms, the club gets to keep a valued player for a longer period of time and the agent gets a commission from the improved contract. If eventually another club comes in with an offer that is significantly better both financially and potentially at a higher level, then the selling club will normally part on good terms.

There are many critics of FIFA in terms of its failure to have a global set of rules in relation to agents. In defence of the governing body it is almost impossible to police the activities of what happens in over 200 countries, especially as there may be conflicts with local cultural norms and laws. Whilst an unpopular view with fans, the consensus from those working in the game is that the agent/intermediary industry is effectively beyond regulation, and they are seen as a tolerable evil within football.

6

TICKET PRICES

In August 2018 the BBC published research showing that 11 clubs in the Premier League could have made a profit without charging fans for tickets, so why is it that ticket prices are so high?

1966 and all that

When England hosted the FIFA World Cup in 1966, it was possible to see seven games (three group games, a quarter final, a semi-final, the third/fourth place playoff and the final) for a total sum of £2.62. This was to watch the game standing on the terraces, which many fans find more enjoyable. If you wanted to sit in the best seats, the same package would have cost £15.10. Taking into consideration inflation between 1966 and 2017 in the UK, these two packages would cost £46.64 to watch standing on the terraces and £268.78 for the most expensive seats. Yet, for the 2018 FIFA World Cup in Russia, it would have cost you £985 for the cheapest route to the final, and £2,282 for the most expensive. Admittedly in 2018, you would have seen one extra game, as the number of teams participating in the competition has increased from 16 to 32 and so an additional knock out round is required. You are also allocated a seat at the match, compared to standing on a terrace.

Prices have therefore outstripped inflation (in sterling terms) by over 2,000 per cent for the cheapest tickets, and a mere 750 per cent for the most expensive. It is the same for domestic matches. Immediately after the 1966 World Cup it was possible to watch Manchester United, featuring superstar players George Best, Bobby Charlton and Dennis Law, for between 20–63 pence. To watch a match at Old Trafford in 2019/20 costs between £36–58, and Manchester United are one of the cheaper teams to watch in the Premier League.

So why have ticket prices risen so rapidly? Once again, we return to supply and demand. In theory prices are determined where supply (clubs selling tickets) meets demand (fans wanting to buy tickets). If you increase prices then demand falls, and if prices are cut then demand increases. This approach applies to football ticket prices too. So have ticket prices risen in recent years because demand has outstripped supply? However, it could also be argued that the nature of the relationship between clubs and fans is more complex than it is for other products and there are, in fact, many contributory reasons why ticket prices have risen faster than those of general prices.

Rising living standards

Whilst football ticket prices have risen far in excess of inflation over the last 50 years, living standards have increased faster over the same period. Consequently, households have far more of what economists call discretionary spending. We all have to pay for essentials such as housing, food, transport, clothing and similar goods and services, but compared to 1966 households today have far more money left over having paid for these essentials, which they can choose to spend on wants rather than needs and this is where football comes in. In 2016, according to the UK Office for National Statistics, households spent 13.5 per cent of their income on recreation and culture, including attending football matches. In 1966 this was less than 7 per cent. Football clubs are aware that individuals have more money in their pocket, and so have raised their prices accordingly. Clubs are also aware that football appeals to a wider audience than 50 years ago. Football is no longer the preserve of the working class and fans today cross all income levels, genders and age groups. If there are more fans and a limited number of matchday tickets, then prices are likely to rise.

Football is an addiction

When looking at prices for goods and services, economists use a term called price elasticity of demand to explain the behaviour of consumers (or in the case of football, fans). Price elasticity of demand measures the sensitivity of buyers to a change in price in terms of the quantity of goods they buy. It is calculated using the formula:

$$\frac{\text{Percentage change in demand for a good/service}}{\text{Percentage change in price for the good/service}}$$

Economists typically ignore the negative sign when talking about price elasticity of demand. Some goods are very sensitive to price movements. If price elasticity of demand is greater than 1 at a particular price level, it is referred to as elastic, and if less than 1, inelastic.

 If price elasticity of demand is elastic at the present price level, then the seller will find that revenue decreases by increasing prices at the present price level, as the fall in demand outstrips the increase in volume of sales. If price elasticity of demand is inelastic at the present price being charged, then the seller will increase revenue at the present price level by raising prices.

For example, a retailer called Jones sells on average 200 Liverpool football shirts a week at a price of £50 each. He then decides to increase the price to £60. None of the other retailers nearby increase their prices from the original £50. As a result, Jones' sales of Liverpool shirts fall to 80 per week. His price elasticity of demand is calculated as:

Percentage change in demand for Liverpool shirts = (80 − 200)/200 = −60%
Percentage change in price for Liverpool shirts = (60 − 50)/50 = 20%
Price elasticity is therefore 3 (60%/20%) (economists ignore the negative sign).

The reason why elasticity of demand is important to a seller is that if elasticity at the present price point is greater than 1, then an increase in price will lead to a decrease in total sales income. In the example of Jones above, the original income from the sale of Liverpool football shirts was £50 × 200 = £1,000 per week. After the price increase his income would be £60 × 80 = £480. The reason why his income has fallen is that most buyers want a Liverpool shirt, not a Liverpool shirt supplied by Jones. Many fans, assuming they know that other retailers are selling the shirt for £10 less, will take their custom elsewhere.

But when it comes to supporting their team the behaviour is different.

Imagine if both Liverpool Football Club and nearby Premier League clubs are selling season tickets at £500. Liverpool sell about 30,000 season tickets each year. Liverpool then decide to increase the price of season tickets to £600 a year and all the other clubs nearby keep theirs at the old price of £500. As a result of this price rise, sales of Liverpool season tickets fall to 29,700 (we will ignore that in reality Liverpool have a huge waiting list for season tickets). Price elasticity of demand for Liverpool season tickets at a price of £500 is calculated as:

Percentage change in demand for Liverpool season tickets = (29,700 − 30,000)/ 30,000 = −1%
Percentage change in price of Liverpool season tickets = (600 − 500)/500 = 20%
Price elasticity of demand is therefore 0.05 (1%/20%).

The reason why price elasticity is less than 1 is that for the vast majority of football fans, there is no alternative to watching the club they support. A Liverpool fan would never transfer allegiance to Everton, Manchester United or Manchester City, even if the fan could still watch Premier League football for £100 less a season. The fan is likely to be unhappy, moan to their friends, complain on social media and so on, but ultimately, he or she will pay, albeit reluctantly, the higher prices being charged by the club they love.

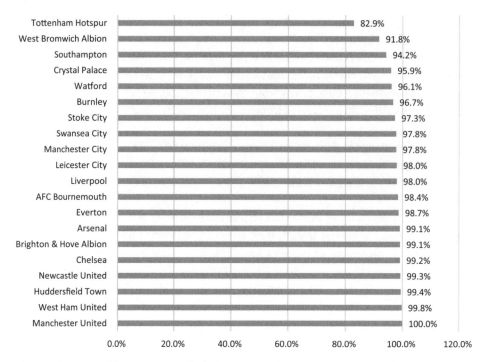

Figure 6.1 Seats sold as a percentage of capacity, 2017/18

Products that are addictive, or command significant brand loyalty, usually have inelastic price elasticity of demand at the present price level. Football match tickets have these characteristics, which is why so many fans travel the length and breadth of the country to watch their chosen team play home and away. From the club's perspective, selling something with inelastic demand has the additional benefit of higher income. In the case of Liverpool, original season ticket income was £500 × 30,000 = £15 million. After the price rise income would increase to £600 × 29,700 = £17.82 million.

Premier League clubs also have the benefit of being a popular product. As we can see from Figure 6.1 in 2017/18 Premier League clubs operated at, on average, 97.7 per cent capacity. This means that for every 1,000 seats on sale, clubs sold 977 of them. The only club to operate at less than 90 per cent capacity was Spurs, who have a valid reason in that their matches were being played at Wembley during the 2017/18 season during redevelopment. Because tickets for most matches are almost sold out every week, Premier League clubs (and their fans) know that there is a "use it or lose it" mentality, especially when it comes to renewing season tickets. If a fan fails to renew, such is the popularity of the game, then they may never again get the chance to see their team on a regular basis. Manchester United, for example, had 75,000 people on their waiting list for a season ticket in 2019 and Liverpool have had their waiting list closed for many years, as there is no realistic chance of ever getting a season ticket unless the stadium capacity is increased. Given this, does it mean that far from being too expensive, tickets for football matches, at the elite level at least, are in fact too low?

One way of reducing the waiting lists would be to increase prices, but clubs are reluctant to do so. Manchester United, for example, froze season ticket prices from 2011 to 2018/19. The club is aware that to try to use price rises to their advantage would result in a huge backlash from fans, who see their club earning huge amounts of money from commercial partners and broadcasting rights. Manchester United earned £437 from broadcasting and commercial partners for every £100 of matchday income in 2017/18, so to be seen "milking" the fans of additional cash might be deemed harmful to Manchester United's reputation and brand.

Some clubs, however, do try to increase income from fans by using what is called differential pricing. This can come in two forms. Some clubs vary ticket prices dependent on their matchday opponents. So a match against a local rival or a glamour team such as Manchester United or Liverpool would be more expensive than when the opposition is a smaller club such as Crystal Palace. The other way of maximizing income is to vary ticket prices depending on where people are located in the stadium. Fans are watching the same match regardless of where they sit, but proximity to the pitch, the half way line, elevation and so on can be exploited by the club if they know that these factors make an individual area of the stadium more or less desirable to fans. Spurs have taken this to the ultimate level by having 14 different price levels for adult season ticket holders in 2018/19, as the club planned to move to its new stadium. These prices varied from £795 to £2,200.

Whilst price inelasticity is true for clubs at the elite level of the major leagues, it does not necessarily apply further down the football pyramid. At a lower league level fans may be more sensitive to price increases. These clubs are less likely to have a sold-out stadium every week and therefore the club has to be very careful with its pricing structure. This is because a supporter of a team such as Rochdale or Morecambe knows that if they give up their season ticket there is a good chance that they can still easily watch their team play on a match by match basis simply by turning up at the ground at 2:55pm on a Saturday afternoon. This does not mean that an individual fan of Rochdale or Morecambe is any less "loyal" than a fan of a Premier League club. It's only that there are fewer of them and a club such as Rochdale does not have an army of people who will snap up any season or matchday tickets the minute they become available.

The rise of the football tourist

The Premier League is the most popular domestic sport contest in the world in terms of television audiences. The combination of a degree of unpredictability of match results, improved ground safety, all seater stadia, declining hooliganism and English being the most common second language in the world have created a new type of fan, the football tourist.

Many teams in the Premier League have official supporters' clubs based not only in other towns and cities in the UK, but overseas too. These fans may not get a chance to see their favourite club for every home match, but they do watch as many matches as their budgets and ticket availability allows. This type of fan is popular with clubs because they are more inclined to spend large sums of money on both tickets and club merchandise. There are benefits for the local economy too. Try finding a hotel at the weekend in Merseyside or Manchester when Liverpool or United are playing at home, such is the popularity of these clubs with fans from outside of the local area. Restaurants, bars, taxis and other employers linked to football tourism all benefit from financial boosts when their local elite teams are playing at home

Clubs who have a significant football tourist fan base can monetize this popularity in a variety of ways. Pre-season international tours where clubs are usually paid significant appearance fees, can be very lucrative. For example, Real Madrid generated €97 million in 2017/18 from international and friendly matches, which was 13 per cent of the club's total revenue. Some clubs deliberately restrict season ticket sales in order to maximize income from football tourists, who pay more for tickets for individual matches and are more likely to spend money on merchandise in the club megastore. Liverpool's Anfield stadium has a capacity of 54,000 but only sells 26,000 season tickets. This contrasts with West Ham United who had a capacity of 57,000 in 2017/18 but sell 52,000 season tickets. Liverpool generated an average of £1,526 per fan in 2017/18 compared to just £431 at West Ham for the reasons discussed.

All seater stadia

Following the Hillsborough disaster in 1989, where 96 Liverpool fans were unlawfully killed in a crush due to negligent policing and poor stewarding, the UK government authorized a public inquiry into the tragic loss of life. The findings of the subsequent Taylor Report, published in 1990, combined with the creation of the Premier League in 1992, led to English football grounds becoming all seater. This reduced the capacity at many grounds. For example, at Old Trafford capacity decreased from 56,000 to 44,000 in 1992, although this has gradually risen to over 75,000 due to a series of construction projects. Historically ticket prices for seated areas of grounds have been higher than on the terraces, where fans stand to watch the game. Clubs used the construction costs of converting terraces to seats as a reason to accelerate the price increases for tickets.

A decline in football hooliganism at grounds, partially attributed to all seater stadia, but also due to better policing methods and technological advancements such as enhanced

CCTV monitoring, has also helped to increase the number of people wanting to attend games. This has meant that football has attracted a broader demographic, more middle class, older (the average age of someone attending a Premier League match is 41), with more women attending and overall more people willing to pay the higher prices being charged by clubs.

Player costs

As we discussed in Chapter 5, the largest outlay for a club each season is typically wages. In nearly all instances, the key stakeholders in the club – fans and owners – want football success. For this to be achievable the club needs to invest in players and pay them a competitive salary. Players (and their agents) are aware of this desire for success, and therefore negotiate, at the elite level at least, high wages. Fans will often complain when their club is performing poorly that they pay the players' wages, but is this true?

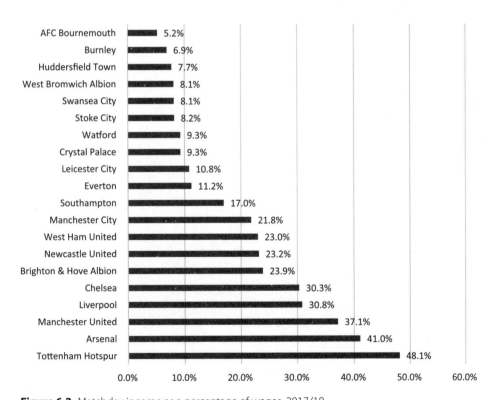

Figure 6.2 Matchday income as a percentage of wages, 2017/18

Figure 6.2 shows the relationship between the amount of income a club generates from matchday income, and the total wage bill. On average in the Premier League in 2017/18 matchday income accounts for only £23.88 of each £100 of wages, which is a decrease from £24.23 the previous season. Bournemouth and Burnley, both having grounds with small capacities, are unsurprisingly at the bottom of the scale. In the past football clubs would regularly use the promise of signing better players as a means to justify increased ticket prices, although in today's Premier League this is not so credible due to the greater significance of broadcast and commercial income for clubs. As a result, many clubs are freezing their ticket prices or only making small increases from season to season. Today elite clubs are far more likely to seek to extract better deals from kit and commercial sponsors, than hike up ticket prices.

The rise in ticket prices over the last couple of generations and the, for the most part, meek acceptance by fans is a sign of the rise in popularity of the game. Its gentrification, the growth of subscription broadcast models and big commercial deals have marginalized the traditional fans' financial contribution and as a result they are pushed farther down the order of importance when it comes to decisions made by footballing authorities. The only realistic sanction that fans could apply, that of boycotting matches and refusing to pay the ticket prices charged, is unpalatable given the emotional bond they have with the shirt of the team they support.

7

BROADCASTING AND SPONSORSHIP INCOME

Football loves television, and television loves football. The English Premier League deal with domestic broadcasters Sky and BT Sport is worth £5.1 billion, and the overseas rights a further £3.2 billion, for the seasons 2016–19. The Bundesliga comes second to the Premier League in terms of domestic rights, but still trails a long way behind (see Figure 7.1). It was not always the case. Prior to the creation of the Premier League there was a feeling amongst club owners and directors that television was the enemy, not the friend, of football. The common view was that live broadcasts would have a negative impact on people attending matches as people would prefer to watch the game on television from the warmth and security of their homes. Remember that matchday income, prior to the creation of bodies such as the Premier League, was the main source of income for clubs.

Table 7.1 shows how Manchester United have grown since the creation of the Premier League. Whilst all elements of the club's income have been significant, broadcast income has shown the fastest rate of growth, albeit coming from a low base prior to the formation of the Premier League.

Why do broadcasters like football so much?

Football, as a live product and a global one, is the most popular team sport in the world in terms of television viewers. In the United States the NFL (American football) had 20 of the 30 highest ratings for any television programme in 2018. People like live television, especially if it relates to a communal experience that can be watched at home or with others in a social environment, such as bars and restaurants. The English Premier League negotiators were quick to realize this and have marketed the game extremely well to broadcasters, both domestic and international. Clubs have worked hand in hand with the Premier League by arranging pre-season tours overseas to increase the interest in both the clubs and the overall EPL product.

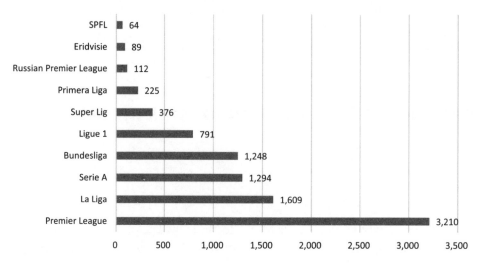

Figure 7.1 Annual income from broadcasting rights 1992–2022 (£ millions)
Source: Deloitte

Table 7.1 Manchester United income 1992 and 2019

Manchester United	1992 £'m	2019 £'m	Increase
Matchday	11.1	110.8	898%
Broadcast	1.8	241.2	13,300%
Commercial	7.2	275.1	3,721%
Total Income	**20.1**	**590.0**	**2,835%**

Source: Manchester United plc Annual Report

The rise of subscription services such as Sky and BT Sport in the UK has helped broadcasters to pay for football as a live spectacle. Broadcasters have found, both in the UK and overseas, that football, more than anything else, generates subscriber loyalty. The biggest fear for a broadcaster is that viewers will baulk at paying the sums being charged every month and cancel their subscriptions.

Football has a long season (August to May, if you exclude international competitions such as the FIFA World Cup, and pre-season friendlies) and is popular amongst a demographic that does not necessarily watch a lot of television (especially males aged 15–34). This also makes football attractive to advertisers who want to target such an audience, many of whom have disposable income. This provides a secondary income stream for the broadcasters on top of subscription fees.

One of the Premier League's best early business decisions was made by then chief executive Rick Parry to accept any short-term losses on international broadcasting deals,

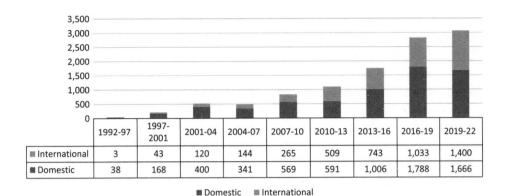

	1992-97	1997-2001	2001-04	2004-07	2007-10	2010-13	2013-16	2016-19	2019-22
◾ International	3	43	120	144	265	509	743	1,033	1,400
◾ Domestic	38	168	400	341	569	591	1,006	1,788	1,666

◾ Domestic ◾ International

Figure 7.2 Premier League television rights, 1992–2022 (£ millions)

in the hope that it would gain an advantage over competitors such as the Bundesliga and La Liga. This gamble has paid off, as the Premier League at last count sells its matches to more than 100 countries around the world. By being first to these markets, the Premier League has been able to build up interest and gain an advantage over the other major European leagues. English as the world's most common second language has meant that there are fewer barriers for local broadcasters to interview players. The Premier League is especially popular in Asia and the United States, and this is reflected in the price being paid by broadcasters in that region.

Broadcasting rights have traditionally been sold to cover more than one season. The first ever sale of television rights by the Premier League covered five seasons, although since 2001 this has been reduced to three. Figure 7.2 illustrates the willingness of overseas broadcasters to pay for Premier League rights. The increased disposable income of emerging markets, overseas pre-season tours by clubs, and reduced government regulation regarding football broadcasts have all contributed to the increase in bids for these rights. With the sale of domestic rights estimated to fall by 10 per cent in the 2019–22 sale cycle then overseas broadcasters could soon be responsible for over half of the money generated from broadcast rights for the Premier League and this could bring further issues in terms of changes to kick-off times that infuriate some fans.

Why does the football industry like live broadcasting so much?

Clubs generate not only income from television directly through the sale of broadcasting rights, but indirectly too. When a match is being broadcast live, it allows the club to charge more for perimeter advertising around the ground. Live broadcasts also help to develop an international fanbase for clubs, which in turn increases the value of deals with overseas commercial partners. The partners benefit from having the status of the official brand supplier for a club in products and services in everything ranging from motor cycles to snack foods. Having its affiliated football club on local television allows the partner to advertise and be associated with the success of the club. These partners can be extremely diverse. At Everton, a Premier League perennial but not a "Big Six" club, they have commercial partners as varied as gaming giant Angry Birds, Kenyan internet gambling company SportPesa and leading deodorant brand Sure.

Broadcasters also effectively provide free advertising and marketing for clubs, which would otherwise be costly. Dedicated television and radio channels keep the game in the public eye on a non-stop basis. This in turn helps to fuel demand for the broadcaster's product, as many fans feel the need to have seen the goals, saves, tackles and red cards either at the match, or more likely on screen, so that they can discuss them with friends and colleagues.

How is the money shared?

The distribution of broadcast income varies from country to country. In Spain, for example, historically clubs have sold their own broadcast rights, and this has given top clubs Real Madrid and Barcelona a substantial financial advantage over their competitors. In 2015/16 both these clubs earned €140 million each from domestic broadcasting, compared to €18 million for clubs such as Almeria and Granada at the bottom of La Liga. This practice was deemed illegal by the Spanish government in 2015. La Liga was then given a mandate to sell the rights for all the clubs in the division. Real Madrid and Barcelona are protected to a degree from the new ruling, which, fortunately for them, also states that no club can be worse off than before the changes were introduced.

In the English Premier League, there has recently been discord between clubs. At present the total sum earned from broadcasting is divided into a number of pots. The money from domestic broadcasters is split three ways. Half is distributed evenly between clubs regardless of size or success in the season. A quarter is based on "merit" and is linked to each club's final position in the league table. And a quarter is called a "facility fee" and is based on the number of times a club appears live on television.

Table 7.2 shows the total distribution from the Premier League to all 20 clubs in the division. For 2018/19 this meant that Manchester City, who won the Premier League, earned £151 million, but this was less than Liverpool, who appeared live on television more often and therefore generated slightly more money. This is because the financial benefits of two more matches being shown live on television exceeds the additional prize money for finishing one place higher in the table. In contrast, Huddersfield Town, who

Table 7.2 Distribution of broadcasting rights income to Premier League clubs, 2018/19 season

	UK Live	Equal Share	Facility Fees	Merit Payment	International TV	Central Commercial	Total Payment
Manchester City	26	£34,361,519	£30,104,476	£38,370,360	£43,184,608	£4,965,392	£150,986,355
Liverpool	29	£34,361,519	£33,461,785	£36,451,842	£43,184,608	£4,965,392	£152,425,146
Chelsea	25	£34,361,519	£28,985,373	£34,533,324	£43,184,608	£4,965,392	£146,030,216
Tottenham Hotspur	26	£34,361,519	£30,104,476	£32,614,806	£43,184,608	£4,965,392	£145,230,801
Arsenal	25	£34,361,519	£28,985,373	£30,696,288	£43,184,608	£4,965,392	£142,193,180
Manchester United	27	£34,361,519	£31,223,579	£28,777,770	£43,184,608	£4,965,392	£142,512,868
Wolverhampton Wanderers	15	£34,361,519	£17,794,343	£26,859,252	£43,184,608	£4,965,392	£127,165,114
Everton	18	£34,361,519	£21,151,652	£24,940,734	£43,184,608	£4,965,392	£128,603,905
Leicester City	15	£34,361,519	£17,794,343	£23,022,216	£43,184,608	£4,965,392	£123,328,078
West Ham United	16	£34,361,519	£18,913,446	£21,103,698	£43,184,608	£4,965,392	£122,528,663
Watford	10	£34,361,519	£12,198,828	£19,185,180	£43,184,608	£4,965,392	£113,895,527
Crystal Palace	12	£34,361,519	£14,437,034	£17,266,662	£43,184,608	£4,965,392	£114,215,215
Newcastle United	19	£34,361,519	£22,270,755	£15,348,144	£43,184,608	£4,965,392	£120,130,418
AFC Bournemouth	10	£34,361,519	£12,198,828	£13,429,626	£43,184,608	£4,965,392	£108,139,973
Burnley	11	£34,361,519	£13,317,931	£11,511,108	£43,184,608	£4,965,392	£107,340,558
Southampton	10	£34,361,519	£12,198,828	£9,592,590	£43,184,608	£4,965,392	£104,302,937
Brighton & Hove Albion	13	£34,361,519	£15,556,137	£7,674,072	£43,184,608	£4,965,392	£105,741,728
Cardiff City	12	£34,361,519	£14,437,034	£5,755,554	£43,184,608	£4,965,392	£102,704,107
Fulham	13	£34,361,519	£15,556,137	£3,837,036	£43,184,608	£4,965,392	£101,904,692
Huddersfield Town	10	£34,361,51	£12,198,828	£1,918,518	£43,184,608	£4,965,392	£96,628,865
		£687,230,38	£402,889,186	£402,888,780	£863,692,160	£99,307,840	£2,456,008,346

Source: EPL

finished bottom of the Premier League, earned £96.6 million, which was more than Bayern Munich earned in broadcasting rights from winning the Bundesliga the same season. Liverpool generated £1.56 for every £1 earned by Huddersfield from Premier League broadcast rights. This ratio is much lower than the split between top and bottom teams in other major European leagues. Supporters of the present agreement argue that this relatively equitable method of distribution increases the unpredictability of the Premier League in terms of match results and in doing so contributes towards its popularity.

The reason why there has been a fallout between clubs in the Premier League is in respect of overseas broadcast rights. When the Premier League first started in 1992/93, the value of overseas rights was so insignificant that the owners at the time agreed to split the revenue evenly between all 20 clubs. Fast forward 25 years and the value of the rights has increased significantly. Overseas broadcasters have seen that Premier League rights are a great way to generate, and maintain, subscriptions for their pay-to-view operations, as well as being popular with advertisers. Therefore, Manchester City and Huddersfield Town both earned £43.2 million from Premier League broadcasting rights sold overseas. In addition, the EPL has sponsorship deals with corporations who want to be associated with it, and the income from these deals is also split evenly between the clubs.

The "Big Six" clubs (a name given to Manchester United, Manchester City, Liverpool, Chelsea, Arsenal and Spurs by the media, despite Spurs not winning a league title since 1961) take the view that overseas fans only really want to see their clubs play and should be rewarded accordingly. They have therefore lobbied the Premier League to change the method of distributing the overseas rights, to something more in line with domestic television revenues. Whilst no one disputes that the Big Six are a more enticing draw for a global television audience, these clubs already have a significant advantage over their smaller competitors. For example, Manchester United generated £14.72 from matchday income and £40.72 from commercial income in 2017 for every £1 made by Watford.

Having a more egalitarian split of Premier League broadcast money (and remember, the Big Six almost have a monopoly on UEFA broadcasting income, as these clubs dominate the Champions League and Europa League places) is a way of giving the smaller clubs the resources that can give them a chance, albeit a slight one, of beating the larger clubs in a match. For example, in the 2017/18 season Huddersfield, Brighton and Newcastle, all newly promoted to the Premier League, defeated the Big Six's Manchester United, whilst Swansea beat Liverpool and Crystal Palace beat Chelsea. Part of the reason why these smaller clubs can achieve such results is that the present distribution of Premier League money allows them to compete successfully when recruiting players from elsewhere in the world against all apart from the elite. Whilst the likes of Watford, Sheffield United, Bournemouth and so on cannot compete with clubs of the stature of Real Madrid, PSG and Bayern Munich, they do have funds, on the back of their broadcast revenues, that make them able to outbid many other European clubs and so the overall standard of players in the Premier League is higher than elsewhere. The highly respected Deloitte Money League, published annually, had 13 Premier League entrants in the 30 biggest revenue generating clubs worldwide when it was published in January 2019.

This gives the Big Six a problem in that there are relatively few games in the Premier League that are easy. This increases fatigue in their squads and makes it more difficult to compete successfully in European competitions against other elite teams. Add to this Leicester City's amazing achievement in winning the Premier League in 2015/16, and the Big Six's iron grip on European qualification each season begins to look far more assailable. Changing the distribution rules so that the Big Six take a larger share of international broadcasting revenues would reduce (the already remote) probability of the likes of Leicester winning the Premier League again. However, it could be argued that by making it more difficult for smaller clubs to recruit high quality players, more guaranteed victories for the Big Six would follow and this would allow managers from top clubs to rest their players before crucial Champions League matches.

Premier League rules can only be changed if there is a two-thirds majority of clubs voting for any proposals and so any proposals would need to be supported by 14 Premier League clubs. The Big Six were initially rebuffed in their aims to grab a bigger share of the broadcast revenues as other Premier League clubs were, unsurprisingly, unhappy about giving up some of their income to those who were already far wealthier. In a fit of pique, the Big Six started making threats of leaving the Premier League set up to sell their own rights, or even as part of a European Super League. A vote on a change to the international distribution split was supposed to take place in October 2017 but deferred when it was clear that the Greed is Good brigade were not going to be successful.

John Henry, one of Liverpool's owners via the investment vehicle Fenway Sports Group, was quoted as saying in an interview in June 2018 "it's much more difficult to ask independent clubs to subsidise their competitors beyond a certain point".[1] It's perhaps understandable that an American billionaire might query why a club as internationally famous as Liverpool should be giving money to the likes of Accrington Stanley, Lincoln and Scunthorpe in the lower divisions as well as the minor clubs in the Premier League. However, Henry's comments also show a lack of familiarity with the pyramid system of football in England and Liverpool's historic success recruiting players from lower league clubs such as Scunthorpe (Kevin Keegan), Lincoln (Phil Neal) and Chester City (Ian Rush).

In June 2018 the Premier League announced that Amazon Prime had been awarded the broadcast rights to a small package of matches (20 games), although the price mysteriously has not yet been disclosed. This prompted much discussion in the media, which saw this as a potential move away from traditional broadcasters. In a classic case of a good

1. See https://www.espn.co.uk/football/story/3517872/liverpool-owner-john-henry-irritated-by-foreign-television-rights-split-among-premier-league-clubs.

day to bury bad news (for clubs in the EFL at least) there was also an announcement at the same time of a change in the distribution method. It is a work of genius in that it appeases the Big Six, in giving them in all probability more money, while ensuring that nearly all the other Premier League teams will be no worse off. The rules are fiendishly complicated, so skip the next part unless you like juggling numbers.

The rule change guarantees clubs their former shares of broadcasting revenues but any *increase* in international rights will be split half evenly between all 20 Premier League clubs, and half on the final league position in a similar manner to domestic payouts. There is a further caveat in that the club finishing top of the Premier League cannot earn more than £180 from the deal for every £100 given to the bottom team.

There has to be a party that bears the cost of this change financially and that loser is clubs in the English Football League. Under the terms of an agreement previously signed between the Premier League and the EFL, an agreed percentage of the monies split evenly between Premier League clubs was given to the EFL as "parachute payments" to clubs relegated from the Premier League and "solidarity payments" for the other EFL members. (Solidarity payments are an agreed payment from the Premier League to EFL clubs which are given in return for the EFL agreeing to certain rights over youth player transfers and other issues.) By allocating less money to the evenly split pot there is less money going into parachute and solidarity payments than would originally have been the case and so there is more money to divide between the Premier League clubs themselves. Historically, for each £100 million of additional overseas broadcast income generated by the Premier League, a non-parachute payment Championship club would receive £197,000, those in League One £47,000 and League Two £32,000. These clubs in the lower league will not be in receipt of such monies from 2019 onwards.

Whether the changes to the Premier League distribution model will keep the Big Six happy for long is debatable and there are already rumblings that the rich clubs still see themselves as victims in the deal and want to further change the terms in their favour in due course.

What of the future for broadcast rights?

Football is one of the few "crown jewels" still held by traditional television broadcasters and they are certainly not going to give up their prize assets without a fight. Sky TV, which is now owned by American giant Comcast following a recent takeover bid, has a business model that is dependent upon sports fans (mainly football) renewing their subscriptions annually. There are, however, suggestions that competition in the future will come from streaming media services that offer content directly to viewers via the internet bypassing traditional broadcast platforms (OTT providers), such as Amazon Prime, Facebook and Netflix. Amazon, as already noted, have won a small package of Premier League rights for

2019–22 in the UK for fixtures, mostly immediately after Christmas Day, where Amazon will use football as a way of driving more traffic towards its Amazon Prime service, which has proven to be very lucrative for the company.

Whilst OTT content providers are always looking to increase their consumer base, football rights, especially for domestic Premier League football, are a very expensive way of achieving increased market share and penetration. It is therefore more likely that OTT media services might apply for overseas rights especially when targeting new and/ or large markets, such as India, Brazil, Malaysia, etc., where for a relatively low price (compared to the UK) they can buy the rights and enhance demand for their other content and services.

In future negotiations the value of domestic rights for the Premier League will likely show a lower rate of growth. The decrease in the value of the most recent sale of domestic rights for the 2019–22 seasons has come about after Sky Sports and BT Sport, the existing rights holders, decided to stop fighting each other for individual packages of matches. This has resulted in the price paid by Sky Sports falling from £11 million to £9.3 million per match. This is because subscriber levels have limited growth potential and existing broadcasters may struggle to recoup the cost of paying more for Premier League rights by charging higher prices to subscribers.

Sport is the perfect product from a broadcaster's perspective: live, communal, unpredictable and emotional. Whilst these characteristics remain then subscribers will likely renew their packages and media companies will continue to pay top prices for exclusivity in broadcasting games. The greed of some clubs at the elite end of the game in wanting a greater share of the pie may end up reducing competitiveness and this could lead to a reduction in the value of the rights, but this is unlikely to have a serious fall in the prices paid. Sponsors want to be associated with success and have access to millions of consumers domestically and globally and they too will be prepared to pay high sums for clubs who represent their values and are watched by their target audience. The football income bubble for these sources has not burst yet and shows no sign of doing so in the future, albeit growth is unlikely to match the rates of the past decade.

8
FINANCIAL FAIR PLAY

Financial Fair Play (FFP) was a phrase initially associated with former UEFA president Michel Platini. Its stated aim was to prevent clubs from spending more than they earned in the pursuit of success and in doing so getting into financial problems. A more cynical view might be that the established European superclubs were concerned about the rise of newly monied rivals, in the form of Manchester City and PSG, creating a threat to the effective cartel in terms of how football riches and trophies were spread amongst the elite. Distributions from UEFA for the European Champions League at the final stages had traditionally been shared between a small number of clubs, giving the recipients a further financial advantage over their less wealthy competitors. This effectively acted as a glass ceiling, which prevented smaller clubs from challenging the elite unless they had owners who were prepared to underwrite large losses in recruiting and paying for some of the best players.

FFP is an umbrella term which covers a variety of ways of gauging the finances of football clubs. The rules are set by UEFA for those clubs that qualify for European competitions and by individual football authorities for their domestic competitions. FFP rules are split into two broad camps, one of which is profit related, and puts a limit on the maximum losses that a club can make, and the other is linked to wage control, usually set as a percentage of income. Both controls have some merits, but these approaches ignore a fundamental commercial rule. Businesses suffer financial difficulties because of an inability to pay their debts as they fall due, which is a cash flow issue and is not always connected to profit, which is an abstract accounting concept that can be manipulated.

In earlier chapters we established that profit and cash are not the same and so it seems baffling to have profit control methods if the sole aim is to minimize the chances of clubs entering formal insolvency/bankruptcy arrangements. The nature of these controls reinforces the view that some of them exist for reasons other than simply preventing clubs from going out of business.

UEFA rules

UEFA is honest in admitting that the purpose of FFP is not to create a level playing field between clubs, but instead they state,

> The aim of financial fair play is not to make all clubs equal in size and wealth, but to encourage clubs to build for success rather than continually seeking a "quick fix". Football clubs need an improved environment where investing in the future is better rewarded so that more clubs can be credible long-term investment prospects [...] By favouring investments in youth and stadium infrastructure and by setting the acceptable deficits in absolute million € terms and not relative percentage terms, the break-even assessment has been structured to be less restrictive to smaller and medium-sized clubs. In time, more [of the] smaller and medium-sized clubs will have potential to grow.

UEFA's statement appears on the face of things impressive and noble, but the reality is different. In introducing such rules UEFA has effectively stated that it wants to maintain the status quo in terms of clubs who qualify for the Champions League and in doing so has reinforced the financial advantage for qualifiers. Behind this is UEFA's fear that unless the existing elite clubs are given some form of advantage they will break away and form a European "superleague". FFP is a way of offering an olive branch to these clubs, as the breakeven model limits the amount a club can lose, and so restricts a nouveau riche club from spending large sums on wages to make itself more competitive with the existing successful clubs. The rules mean that clubs with new wealthy owners will find FFP a major obstacle in progressing the club to the next level of competing with the existing elite.

Figure 8.1 shows the distribution of broadcasting revenue by UEFA to teams in its competitions from 2013/14 to 2017/18 for the highest recipients. A financial advantage of up to €80 million per year for a team such as Juventus compared to clubs that do not qualify regularly for the Champions League, and so receive nothing, is nearly impossible to bridge under FFP when it comes to funding player transfers and wages whilst satisfying the FFP loss limits. The numbers in the table may appear confusing in some respects given that over the five-year period Real Madrid won the competition three times but received less income than Juventus, whose greatest achievement was to make the final twice. This is because the formula used to determine revenue distribution takes into consideration:

- The position in the league of the club when qualifying (Juventus won Serie A five times compared to Real only winning La Liga once);
- The relative amount of money paid by the domestic broadcaster for UEFA competition television rights;

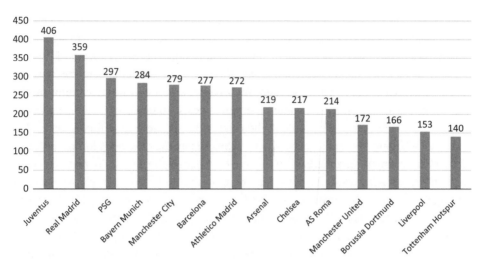

Figure 8.1 Distribution of broadcasting revenue by UEFA, 2014–18 (£ millions)

- The number of wins and draws in the group stages;
- The relative success of other teams in the competition from the same country. For example, Real Madrid "suffered" in 2016/17 as Atletico Madrid were in the semi-final of the competition, Barcelona the quarter finals, and Sevilla the round of 16. Real were fortunate that a further Spanish club, Villarreal were knocked out in the qualifying stages.

The rules for distributing money have been further tweaked from 2018/19 to consider a club's legacy achievements in European competition over the past ten years. This is to ensure that if a club such as Real Madrid or Juventus was eliminated at an early stage from the Champions League, because they have performed well in the competition in the previous decade, they would receive more prize money than a club who had qualified for the first time. Again, the motive for this adjustment seems to be UEFA's fear that the established elite may set up their own competition if they don't continue to take a large share of the cash generated by the competition.

UEFA FFP rules are such that clubs should operate on a breakeven model, ideally making no losses. Clubs are allowed to make an "acceptable deviation", which is a loss of €5 million over a three-year period. This can be increased to a €30 million loss if the owner injects equity (share capital) into the club. When calculating the profit/loss for FFP purposes some costs are excluded. This is to encourage clubs to invest in what UEFA considers to be sustainable growth and broadening the appeal and uptake of football. The costs that clubs can incur without contributing towards FFP include: stadium and infrastructure costs; training facilities; youth development; and women's football. As such costs can be significant it would be possible for a club to make large losses according to the profit or loss account and still satisfy FFP rules provided the club had significant expenditure in the areas that are deemed to be "good" and thus exempt from FFP.

The downside of such an approach is that there is scope to manipulate the figures if the club hierarchy is unscrupulous. There are broadly two approaches to circumvent the rules: either artificially inflate income or suppress costs. In terms of income a possible strategy for a club that wishes to bend the rules is to arrange commercial/sponsorship deals with a "friendly" related party who is willing to pay over the odds for a sponsor or partner arrangement. The increase in income then allows the club to increase its costs, inevitably player related and still fall within the allowable limits. For example, Manchester City signed a ten-year sponsorship and stadium naming rights deal with Etihad Airways in 2011. Etihad Airways is the state airline of the United Arab Emirates (UAE) and City are owned by Sheik Mansour of UAE. The agreement came into play in the 2011/12 season. As a result, City's commercial income almost doubled in 2012, increasing from £64.7 million to £121.1 million. Arsene Wenger, the Arsenal manager at the time, constantly sniped at City's close links to sponsors connected directly or indirectly to the owner, referring to the relationship as "financial doping". Similar allegations have been levelled at PSG, with their Qatari owners, from executives of rival European clubs.

UEFA do, however, have the right to review and consider whether or not such arrangements are at market value. UEFA have a "Club Financial Control Body" and a team of investigators to determine whether deals have been signed purely to circumvent FFP. The investigators are allowed to decide on what is a fair value of a commercial deal rather than the actual sum paid and use this instead when assessing FFP compliance. This is good news for the legal and accounting professions as clubs who are accused of artificially inflating income due to commercial deals with "related parties" inevitably argue that they have done nothing wrong and will use their professional advisors to defend their positions.

If a club is part of a multi football club ownership model, this too can provide opportunities to address FFP compliance as it allows costs to be "parked" in clubs that are not subject to UEFA scrutiny. This would allow the club that is subject to UEFA rules to reduce its own costs, which are nominally borne by a sister club in, for example, Australia or the United States, and therefore satisfy the FFP limits. For example, Manchester City Limited, announced a profit after tax of just over £1 million in the year to 30 June 2017. Yet during the same period the City Football Group Limited, which owns Manchester City, New York City, Melbourne City and Club Atletico Torque in Uruguay showed a loss of over £71 million.

The sanctions available to UEFA ranges from warning letters to exclusion from UEFA competitions. The legality of UEFA's sanctions has yet to be tested in a court of law, although UEFA is confident that it has taken appropriate steps to ensure the rules would be upheld. Since the rules were introduced, UEFA has found many clubs guilty of breaking the FFP rules. Manchester City was fined £49 million in 2014, part of which was refunded at a later date, and also had wage restrictions and reduced squad sizes enforced on them when playing in UEFA competitions until the club exited the sanctions in 2017. PSG have had similar sanctions and FC Porto have also been subject to squad size sanctions and were fined in summer 2017.

Clubs have been accused of going to significant lengths to avoid sanctions. Allegations of clubs using private detectives to check up on the UEFA Club Financial Control Body investigators are common, as are those of criticizing the recruitment by clubs of FFP experts who have the greatest knowledge of the loopholes. Manchester City's finance director is Martyn Hawkins, who previously was on secondment at UEFA from the prestigious Deloitte sports business group, which helped to draft FFP legislation. In any other business this would be seen as a smart move by Manchester City to recruit someone with insight and expertise in the legislative changes affecting the industry, but given the tribal nature of football fans such an appointment encouraged many conspiracy theorists claiming that Hawkins's recruitment gave the club an unfair advantage as he would be familiar with where the weaknesses within FFP exist.

Premier League rules

The Premier League Handbook, which runs to 608 pages, has two sets of rules in relation to financial controls. The most restrictive are in relation to wages. Prior to the broadcast deal that commenced in 2016/17, Alan Sugar's "prune juice" comments had some merit in that extra income appeared to be immediately matched by player wage rises that consumed the additional monies received by clubs. Indeed, Premier League clubs made a collective operating loss of nearly £87 million in 2015/16, but this changed to a £228 million profit the following season following the commencement of a new domestic broadcast deal. This was subsequently reversed in 2017/18 (see Figure 8.2) as revenues were relatively flat due to being in the middle of the three-year broadcasting deal whereas wages increased by over 10 per cent.

Short-term cost controls

The rules in relation to wages are called Short-Term Cost Control (STCC). Put simply, clubs can only increase their player wage bills by £7 million a season, plus adding in any increase in matchday and commercial income, and the average of profits for player disposals in the last three years. For clubs promoted from the Championship to the Premier League, or any club below a certain threshold, the club is allowed a player wage figure of a fixed amount, which is set at £74 million for 2017/18 and £81 million for 2018/19.

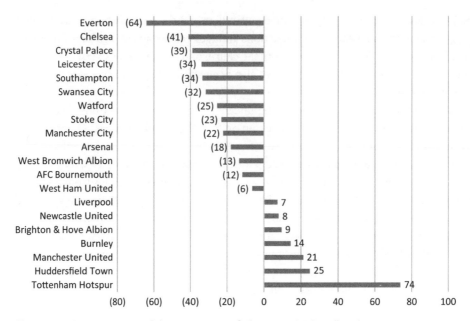

Figure 8.2 Premier League clubs operating profit/loss 2017/18 (£ millions)

If we look, for example, at Arsenal, the club had a wage bill of £195.4 million in 2015/16. If, for the sake of making life easier for ourselves, we assume this is all in relation to players, then for 2016/17 the STCC maximum allowable wage would be:

	£'m
2015/16 wage cost	195.4
Increase in commercial income in 2016/17	12.3
Increase in matchday income in 2016/17	0.1
Average of profit on player disposals for three seasons	12.6
Allowed annual wage increase	7.0
STCC wage limit for 2016/1	227.4
Actual wage bill for 2016/17	199.4
Amount within the limit	28.0

The above calculation perhaps shows that Arsenal were well within the limits for 2016/17 although failure to qualify for the Champions League would probably have had a detrimental impact on wages and bonuses in the season. The calculation also perhaps suggests why Premier League club owners are so willing to prostitute the history and heritage of the club through tie-ups with a myriad of commercial sponsors and overseas tours as these deals contribute to an income stream that allows them to subsequently pay higher wages.

With so many clubs either applying ticket price freezes or very modest increases due to resistance from fans the only way to increase matchday income is by increasing stadium capacity. This is perhaps why we are seeing the likes of Chelsea, Spurs, Manchester City and Liverpool making significant changes to the capacity of their stadia through ground expansion. Other clubs such as Everton and West Ham have either moved grounds or are planning to do so in order to boost attendances and matchday revenues. Additional income from extra stadium capacity is a contributory factor when calculating STCC compliance.

Strangely, just as it appeared that STCC rules had some bite and were going to impact upon many clubs in the Premier League, they were voted out by club owners and scrapped for the 2019/20 season.

Profitability and sustainability rules

The Premier League's profitability and sustainability (P&S) rules are similar to UEFA's FFP breakeven rules, although the limits are less onerous. Premier League clubs are allowed to lose up to £15 million over three years. These losses are extended to £105 million if the owner makes up the difference by injecting equity into the club. The Premier League made a collective EBIT (recurring profits) loss of £205 million in 2017/18 (see Figure 8.2) which suggests it is far less lucrative than many fans believe it to be. The same caveats that apply to UEFA rules in terms of "good" expenses that are exempt for P&S purposes also apply in the Premier League. Given the very generous level of losses allowed, especially if equity contributions are considered, it is highly unlikely that the rules will provide a significant deterrent to investors.

English Football League (EFL) rules

In the EFL, the rules vary depending on the division in which the team plays.

Championship

The Championship is presently the most concerning division in Europe financially. Clubs are unlikely to play in European competitions and so they are not subject to UEFA breakeven tests. A few years ago, Championship club owners did commit to a gradual aim to reduce FFP losses to £3 million per season, or £8 million if the owner made an equity injection. These rules were relaxed in 2015/16, allowing the losses to increase to £13 million for that season. Since 2016/17 the controls have been aligned with UEFA and Premier League rules. Under these rules clubs can lose up to £39 million over a rolling three-year period before sanctions are applied. Remember FFP losses exclude stadium and training facilities expenditure, youth, community and women's football expenses and so realistically a club could generate accounting losses of £60 million or more over three years and would still potentially be within the allowed limits.

The rules have been relaxed due to increased parachute payments earned by clubs relegated from the Premier League. Parachute payments are sums given by the Premier League to clubs relegated to the EFL in order to give those clubs time to acclimatize to receiving far less money from broadcasting. The parachute payments taper over a three-year period (two years for clubs that have been promoted to the Premier League and relegated in their first season there). Clubs not in receipt of parachute payments felt that the gap in income between themselves and those recently relegated was so large that the only way for them to have a realistic chance of competing for promotion was to allow their club owners to invest larger sums and so they voted for a larger FFP loss figure.

Figure 8.3 shows the parachute payments for clubs relegated from the Premier League for 2017/18. Clubs not in receipt of parachute payments in the Championship received approximately £7 million in EFL broadcast revenues and solidarity payments. Established Championship clubs therefore had an income deficit of up to £34 million at the start of the season compared to parachute payment recipients from broadcasting. Given that the average total income in 2017 for a non-parachute payment recipient club was £19.3 million, this is a substantial difference which makes competing for players and wages difficult.

The lure of Premier League riches is very attractive to club owners in the Championship and therefore the incentive to overstretch the club financially is significant. Total operating losses in the Championship in 2017/18, which exclude non-recurring transactions

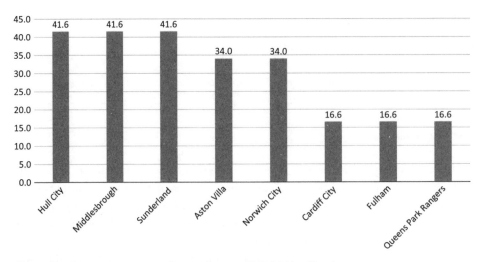

Figure 8.3 Premier League parachute payments, 2017/18 (£ millions)
Source: Premier League

such as profits on asset sales and legal settlement costs, were £580 million. By increasing the maximum losses available to Championship clubs, this increases the opportunities for non-parachute payment recipients to compete in terms of wages and player signings with clubs recently relegated from the Premier League. In recent years Middlesbrough, Brighton, Huddersfield and Sheffield United, none of whom were in receipt of parachute payments, were all promoted to the Premier League.

In 2017/18 Wolverhampton Wanderers, supported by new Chinese owners who invested heavily in the club, won the Championship. The increase in allowed losses under the new relaxed rules suggests the Championship is very competitive under the present arrangements, if eye-watering in terms of the financial losses that are being generated. From an owner's point of view, their club starts the season with a one in eight (3 in 24) chance of hitting a jackpot of £100–160 million a year in broadcasting income if the club is promoted to the Premier League, plus parachute payments should the club be relegated. Given these odds it is understandable how many owners are prepared to make financial gambles in the Championship and incur substantial losses.

Clubs that breach EFL rules now face an unlimited range of sanctions. They can be cautioned, given transfer embargoes, fined or even suffer a points deduction during the season. Money from FFP fines in the Championship was originally intended to be shared between the remaining clubs in the Championship, but the legality of this was queried and instead it was decided to distribute the fines to charitable causes instead.

The problem with FFP in the Championship is that if clubs do ignore the rules, gamble and succeed on promotion to the Premier League, they are then outside the jurisdiction of the English Football League. Queens Park Rangers (QPR) effectively took such an approach in 2013/14. The club had been relegated from the Premier League the previous season. Instead of taking the normal approach of relegated clubs in selling some of their best players (and reducing the wage bill at the same time) to match income and costs to Championship standards, QPR maintained much of their squad. The club spent £75.3 million on wages (the median that season in the Championship was £16.9 million) as well as £9 million signing players such as Charlie Austin, Matt Phillips and Karl Henry, along with five loan signings from the Premier League. The club was promoted back to the Premier League via the playoffs in May 2014. QPR's profit or loss account for 2013/14 showed an operating loss of £65.3 million, far in excess of the allowed FFP limit at the time, which would have triggered an estimated fine of up to £58 million. QPR's operating loss after taking into consideration parachute payments from the Premier League was about £28 million. By the time QPR announced their financial results, the club was in the Premier League and outside the jurisdiction of the EFL.

QPR could therefore ignore sanctions from the EFL whilst they were a member of the Premier League as the two bodies are independent of one another and not bound by each other's rules. The problem for QPR arose when they were relegated after one season in the Premier League and found themselves once again subject to EFL governance and rules. QPR's profit or loss account for the year ended 31 May 2014 showed an unusual income figure of £60 million below the operating loss of £65.3 million. Reviewing the footnotes revealed this sum to be the QPR owners writing off loans due from the club of £60 million and treating this as a negative expense in the profit or loss account.

The club defended this transaction by claiming: (1) The losses were within the FFP limits as a result of this transaction and therefore no fines were due, and also (2) FFP was illegal under Competition Law and therefore if the £60 million loan write off was ignored no fines were payable anyway. This case dragged on, earning little benefit except to the lawyers and accountants for both QPR and the EFL. An arbitration panel was commissioned and its verdict in October 2017 was in favour of the EFL. QPR decided to "consider their options", which resulted in yet another appeal or further prevarication before potentially paying any fine. The case was eventually finalized in the summer of 2018, and the punishment from the EFL, although expressed in the press release as a £42 million settlement, was considerably diluted.

QPR's owners agreed to convert £22 million of debt into shares. This was a sleight of hand action as the club would never have been in a position to repay the debt, so all that happened was one valueless piece of paper (loans that QPR realistically could not hope to repay) was exchanged for another (equity shares). QPR's owners had written off far larger sums than this in the past so for the EFL to claim this was a punishment is at best disingenuous. A £17 million fine was imposed, but this was spread over ten years from the settlement date, so in reality, given the offence took place in 2014, it meant that the club was paying the fine over 14 years. Plugging the numbers into a finance calculator and using the interest rate charged by banks to small businesses such as QPR, meant that the £17 million spread over 14 years was the equivalent of a £9.4 million fine being paid in 2014.

The QPR case, interesting as it is, does highlight further a problem faced by football authorities, namely that if clubs decide to use lawyers and accountants to delay FFP sanctions being applied it can take a very long time for any resolution to take place.

Leicester City also challenged the legality of the Football League's FFP regulations relating to when they too were promoted in 2013/14. Leicester had spent extensively under their owners King Power, the kings of duty-free shopping from Thailand. Wages rose that season by nearly £10 million, although some of this may have been due to promotion bonuses. What was unusual, however, was Leicester's income in the profit or loss account. Sponsorship and advertising income more than tripled from £5.2 million to £16.1 million. An investigation by *The Guardian's* David Conn in 2016 revealed that a company called Trestellar Limited acquired the rights to market the club in Asia and appeared to be very successful in selling naming rights and sponsorship agreements, despite appearing to have neither a website nor a registered telephone number. Trestellar's accounts for the year ended 31 May 2017 reveal the company had over £3 million in the bank at that date. This is a remarkable performance for a company with just two employees, run by the son of former Premier League chairman Sir Dave Richards, also, confusingly, called Dave Richards. Trestellar Ltd shares its premises with a glue making business, also run by Dave Richards Jr.

From the outside it does look very strange that a club such as Leicester, which had been in the Championship since 2004 with relatively constant levels of income suddenly found a lucrative revenue source thanks to the unusual involvement of newly formed Trestellar. It is this relationship that has led to the accusation of financial doping and artificially inflating income to avoid paying any FFP fines. Leicester did eventually settle with the EFL in 2017, paying a fine of £3.1 million, in the same year the club announced pre-tax profits of over £92 million and had participated in the Champions League.

In 2016 the EFL changed the rules in relation to stadium sales. Prior to then profits from fixed asset sales (including stadia) were specifically excluded from FFP calculations. The rationale here as per UEFA's Club Licencing and Financial Fair Play Regulations is "The profit on disposal … of tangible fixed assets in a reporting period is excluded from the calculation of the break-even result because the aim is to encourage the investment and expenditure on facilities and activities for the long-term benefit of the club".

Why the EFL changed the rules has never been made clear but some clubs have taken advantage of the relaxation of the rule and have sold their stadia to companies controlled by the club owners. In May 2019 the EFL play-off final, the winners of which would be promoted to the Premier League, took place between Aston Villa and Derby County. Both clubs had recently sold their stadia to other companies controlled by their club owners, generating profits of up to £40 million from these transactions which helped them comply with FFP.

Clubs taking advantage of the rule relaxation have been criticised by other owners, but can claim legitimately they are in compliance with the regulations. There have been further criticisms in relation to the sums for which the stadia have been sold in relation to whether these are at a fair market price or not. It does seem strange that Derby County's Pride Park, located on a retail park in the East Midlands city, where according to property website Zoopla the average house price is £207,000, was sold for £80 million whereas West Ham sold their stadium in East London, where the average house price is £429,000, for just £40 million a couple of years earlier. Similarly Sheffield Wednesday sold Hillsborough in 2018 for £60 million to a company controlled by the owner. The EFL have therefore decided to investigate further whether or not the sale prices at Derby and other clubs who have sold such assets to related parties are at true market values.

The EFL has also changed its rules so that clubs must now produce interim accounts and budgets covering the present season which estimate their profits. This would, in theory, allow the League to impose sanctions during the season in which the rules have been breached. In practice it seems reasonable to anticipate that if the EFL tried to impose points deductions for exceeding FFP limits during a season the case would be contested, and it could end up with promotion and relegation being decided in a court of law instead of on a field of play. This would be a very unsatisfactory outcome for players, fans, owners and everyone associated with individual clubs, bar, of course, those trusty lawyers and accountants.

The first points deduction for breach of profitability and sustainability limits arose in 2018/19 when Birmingham City were subject to a nine-point penalty. The decision was not finalized until March 2019 despite the EFL commencing proceedings against the club in August of the previous year. The deduction did shine some light on the process used to determine how points deductions are calculated but also highlighted "aggravating and mitigating" factors which could be used to increase or decrease the penalty. A deduction that is a combination of objective and subjective elements creates uncertainty for all parties involved, including other clubs in the same division whose promotion and relegation may be determined by whatever the adjudicating committee considers to be an aggravating or mitigating issue and who then turn that into a number of points to be added or subtracted.

Fans are desperate to know if their club is going to be subject to FFP sanctions and therefore campaign for greater information and transparency. The EFL is however duty bound to follow due process and procedure, which means keeping investigations and negotiations private until a final decision is made.

Leagues One and Two

In League Divisions One and Two the FFP focus is on wage control via Salary Cost Management Protocol (SCMP). Under these rules a club in League One can only spend 60 per cent of its regular turnover (effectively matchday, commercial and broadcasting income) plus 100 per cent of any "Football Fortune" income, which includes donations, prize money, net transfer income, parachute payments, and owner equity injections on "player related expenditure" (wages and benefits paid to players and their agents). The small print is, as always in these things, detailed and covers many issues, for example, if a club tries to evade the rules by promoting a particular player to a coaching or managerial role, 50 per cent of his wages and benefits are deemed to be for the playing part of his contract. It's a messy calculation, but clubs at least know where they stand at the start of each season.

In League Two the salary cap was 55 per cent of regular turnover and this was reduced to 50 per cent from 2018/19 onwards. Whilst lower league football does not generate many column inches in the national press, SCMP has been relatively successful in reducing the number of clubs who enter corporate bankruptcy in the form of administration or liquidation. That has not however stopped some clubs from trying to bend the rules. Chesterfield Football Club were fined £12,500 in July 2018 after it was discovered the wages of two players were paid by a private football academy owned by the club's former CEO. It is this type of cat and mouse that takes up time and money better spent elsewhere for the good of the game.

FFP in its various forms is here to stay and does have some merits, especially at a lower league level, in reducing the probability of club bankruptcies. The biggest criticisms of FFP come in relation to the rationale behind the rules at the elite level. The word "fair" is a complete misnomer if the intention of those who make the rules is to keep competition for major European trophies between the very few and prevent newly monied clubs from rising to challenge the existing cartel. There were fears that players would migrate away from countries which are bound by UEFA's relatively stringent rules, as wages outside of Europe, unregulated by FFP caps, might prove attractive to players. However, these fears now appear to be without foundation. The rise of the Chinese Super League (CSL), when President Xi Jinping was encouraging growth in football a few years ago, did appear to offer a potential talent drain away from Europe as CSL clubs were not subject to FFP. Initially the movement of players to the CSL, such as Jackson Martinez, Ramirez, Oscar and Hulk suggested there could be a major threat to clubs in Europe. But recent regulations in China, introduced in June 2017, has meant that there is now a 100 per cent tax on any player who is signed for more than £5.2 million. The CSL, which outspent the Premier League in the January 2017 transfer window, instead concentrated on much lower-cost transfers of domestic players in the summer 2017 window and this trend is likely to continue under present rules.

PART III
FOOTBALL CLUB FINANCIAL ANALYSIS

9

HOW TO ANALYSE CLUB ACCOUNTS 1: TREND ANALYSIS

Why would anyone choose to analyse a football club's finances? There must surely be more important and interesting things in life that warrant consideration, and this is the approach taken by most football fans. However, some fans want to know as much as possible about all aspects of the team they support. Alternatively, you may be a supplier to a club and are wondering whether to extend its credit terms. You may even be involved in the world of corporate finance and are seeking a "bargain basement" club for a client to invest in, or indeed many other reasons.

If you do want to analyse results, then you don't need to be mathematically gifted, most calculations are built around no more than adding, subtracting and calculating percentages. When looking at a football club, the first challenge can often be identifying exactly which company to investigate. This is because there can be a Russian doll-style group set up with a holding company perhaps owning another club (referred to as a subsidiary), which owns the football part of the business. The parent company may also own another company that owns the stadium and training grounds, yet another running the commercial arm. Ideally you should look at the company within the group that ultimately controls all elements of the club, which is usually the holding company.

Table 9.1 lists the various companies controlled by Manchester United Plc, whose shares are traded in New York on the Nasdaq stock exchange. It would seem logical for a fan to look at the accounts of Manchester United Football Club Limited in order to investigate the Red Devils, but doing that would exclude most of the commercial dealings of the club. Manchester United Football Club Limited made an operating loss of over £117 million in 2016/17, whereas Manchester United Limited, which is the commercial arm of the Glazer empire, made an operating profit of £183 million. Manchester United Plc combines all of the above companies and in their accounts they add together all the income from the different subsidiary companies. This would be the company that makes most sense to analyse, as it acts as the umbrella for all United's activities. Anyone thinking of buying the club would almost certainly be wanting to buy everything to do with United, so this is an additional reason for reviewing the parent company.

Once you've decided on the right company, you can then start on the analytics.

Table 9.1 Manchester United Plc subsidiaries, 2017

The following companies are the subsidiary undertakings of the Company as of 30 June 2017:

Subsidiaries	Principal activity	Description of share classes owned
Red Football Finance Limited	Finance company	100% Ordinary
Red Football Holdings Limited	Holding company	100% Ordinary
Red Football Shareholder Limited	Holding company	100% Ordinary
Red Football Joint Venture Limited	Holding company	100% Ordinary
Red Football Limited	Holding company	100% Ordinary
Red Football Junior Limited	Holding company	100% Ordinary
Manchester United Limited	Commercial company	100% Ordinary
Alderley Urban Investments Limited	Property investment	100% Ordinary
Manchester United Commercial Enterprises (Ireland) Limited	Dormant company	100% Ordinary
Manchester United Football Club Limited	Professional football club	100% Ordinary
Manchester United Interactive Limited	Dormant company	100% Ordinary
MU 099 Limited	Dormant company	100% Ordinary
MU Commercial Holdings Limited	Holding company	100% Ordinary
MU Commercial Holdings Junior Limited	Holding company	100% Ordinary
MU Finance pic	Debt-holding company	100% Ordinary
MU RAML Limited	Retail and licensing company	100% Ordinary
MUTV Limited	Subscription TV channel	100% Ordinary

Source: Manchester United Plc

Case study: Manchester United Plc year ended 30 June 2018

We've chosen Manchester United as our case study because their finances have a bit of everything: runners-up in the Premier League, FA Cup finalists, Champions League participation, commercial deals, substantial loans and activity in the transfer market. The principles involved however in the analysis of United are identical to those you would use if reviewing a company operating in a different industry, although there are some football specific financial metrics, and these are split into two broad areas, trend analysis and ratio analysis. In this chapter we shall consider trend analysis and in Chapter 10 ratio analysis.

Trend analysis is about looking at movements in key figures in the financials and obtaining an explanation for those movements, which can be caused by good and bad events and transactions. The logical starting point is the profit or loss account and the top line of revenue (Table 9.2). This is the figure used in the Deloitte Annual Money League tables, which showed Manchester United as the club that generated the third most income globally in 2017/18.

Of course, a figure in isolation is meaningless. If someone tells you that Manchester United had revenue of £590 million in 2017/18, is this good, bad or indifferent? You need to know what came before and how it compares with others to make sense of it all.

Table 9.2 Consolidated income statement, Manchester United

	Note	Year ended 30 June		
		2018 *£'000*	*2017* *£'000*	*2016* *£'000*
Revenue	4	590,022	581,204	515,345

Source: Manchester United

Historic comparisons

Figures must be put into some form of context, so it makes sense to first compare the club against itself on an historic basis. This is something we do in our personal lives regularly. It's no different to comparing your weight, your earnings, your half marathon personal best times and so on against your previous figures.

Manchester United's total revenue increased by £8.8 million in 2017/18. This looks modest compared to the previous year when it increased by £65.7 million (and in 2015/16 by £120.2 million). The revenue growth can also be expressed in percentage terms, at 1.5% for 2018, 12.8% in 2017 and 30.4% in 2016. These figures are a quick look at the "what" factor in relation to United's finances, but a good analyst will focus on the "why" – to identify the reasons behind the change in numbers. United's revenue must have increased for one or more reasons. Some of the explanations may be due to internal issues, related to management decisions made by Ed Woodward, the United executive vice-chairman and his fellow directors. Some of the revenue change may be due to external factors, over which the club has limited or no control. Here an analyst will use the management commentary from the board of directors, press releases, media commentaries and so on to identify what has caused the changes.

If it is possible to break the figures down, then this will help to identify the key drivers of revenue growth for the club. Under Premier League rules clubs are encouraged to split revenue into at least three categories (some clubs voluntarily show more) and these are: commercial, broadcasting and matchday. We can therefore calculate the growth rate in the individual income streams, as shown in Table 9.3. Let's take each in turn.

Matchday income

Matchday income is a function of the number of tickets sold multiplied by the price of tickets and the number of matches taking place at the stadium. Manchester United had frozen season ticket prices in the six years up to 2017/18 and every match was a sell-out. Matchday revenue increased in both 2015/16 and 2016/17 but fell in 2017/18 so the logical explanation must be related to the number of fixtures played. In 2015/16 United had the benefit of Champions League and Europa League fixtures, as well as winning

Table 9.3 Manchester United growth in revenue by category, 2015–18

Manchester United plc	2015 £'m	2016 £'m	Growth	2017 £'m	Growth	2018 £'m	Growth
Matchday	91	107	17.7%	112	4.7%	110	(1.6%)
Broadcast	108	140	30.4%	194	38.2%	204	5.2%
Commercial	197	268	36.2%	275	2.7%	276	0.2%
Income	395	515	30.4%	581	12.8%	590	1.5%

Source: Manchester United

the FA Cup. In 2016/17 winning the Europa League and the League Cup increased the number of matches too. Matchday revenue fell slightly in 2018 because Manchester United only progressed to the last 16 of the Champions League and therefore had fewer matches at Old Trafford.

What options do Manchester United have to increase matchday income significantly in the years to come? They are presented with three potential choices: either increase matchday prices and with that risk the wrath of their fans, expand the capacity of Old Trafford beyond the present 76,000 seats, or increase the number of events, such as music concerts or other sporting activities such as NFL matches, that take place at the stadium.

Broadcast income

Broadcast income grew in 2015/16 by 30 per cent. We can see that this increase was driven mainly by United's participation in the Champions League, as the Premier League television deal was in its final year of a three-year cycle at fixed prices. UEFA publish their distribution of broadcasting income each season, which is great from an analyst's perspective. United earned €41.9 million in 2016 from UEFA, split between €38.1 million from the Champions League, where United were eliminated at the group stage, and a further €3.8 million from the Europa League in which they then briefly participated. In addition all British clubs competing in Europe benefitted in 2015/16 from BT Sport doubling the price paid for Champions League and Europa Cup rights.

In 2016/17 broadcasting income increased mainly because of the new Premier League television deals that commenced that season and increased the sum paid by 70 per cent. Fortunately for analysts, the Premier League are very transparent and publish details of how money is allocated between teams. As a result, we know that Manchester United earned £141.1 million of broadcasting income for finishing sixth in the Premier League, compared to the previous season where they earned £96.5 million for finishing seventh. United won the Europa Cup in 2016/17, which earned them €44.5 million in broadcast distributions from UEFA. This was a marginal increase compared to the previous season. The 5.2 per cent increase in broadcast income in 2017/18 was partly due to Manchester United finishing second in the Premier League as this increased the club's merit award, worth an extra £1.9 million per place. UEFA allocate just under 77 per cent of their prize money to teams in the Champions League, so despite a relatively early exit from the competition in 2017/18 Manchester United still earned over €40 million.

Commercial income

For United, the increase in commercial income in 2016 was partially due to a change in kit manufacturer. Adidas had signed a ten-year £750 million agreement with the club that commenced in July 2015, which was significantly higher than the previous kit deal with Nike, who had been paying the club an estimated £30 million a year. The Adidas deal was announced in July 2014, which discouraged many fans from buying Nike manufactured merchandise in 2014/15. Further inspection of the United accounts reveals that of the £71.4 million increase in commercial income in 2016, £65.7 million of this was on the back of retail and licencing deals, the main one of course being Adidas.

United had some penalty clauses activated by sponsors in 2014/15 for failure to qualify for any UEFA European competitions, which reduced payments from this source. United signed relatively few new commercial deals in 2016/17, which restricted growth and they also only qualified for (and won) the Europa Cup, less lucrative than the Champions League. Had United failed to win the Europa Cup in 2016/17 and therefore not qualified for the Champions League for the third year out of four the following season, they would have suffered significant penalties from commercial partners, especially Adidas. It is therefore reasonable to expect that United's commercial income would rise slightly in 2017/18, as the club found themselves in the Champions League, with greater exposure for the club, which makes it more attractive to sponsors. Looking forwards this income stream should rise again in 2018/19 due to the club signing a sleeve sponsor deal with Kohler.

Competitor comparisons

Looking at the trends of a single club is fine as far as it goes, but if United are growing their revenue at 1.5 per cent in 2017/18, this can only be considered good if other clubs are growing their revenue at a lower rate (or even a fall) in the same financial year. We therefore need a peer group with which to compare performance. How you choose the teams in the peer group is a matter of personal preference, but an analyst would in practice use a series of filters, implicitly and explicitly, to determine who United's peer group should be. For United, there's a case for looking at the other members of the Big Six who are regularly competing for Champions League places in the Premier League. Alternatively, United could be compared to other clubs who are close to them in the Deloitte Money League, such as Barcelona, Real Madrid and Bayern Munich. Different analysts use different sets of rules and so may reach different conclusions. For this analysis Manchester United will be compared to the other members of the Big Six domestically.

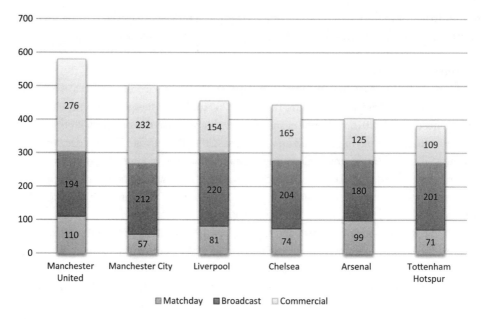

Figure 9.1 Premier League Big Six revenue, 2017/18 (£ millions)

Figure 9.1 shows that Manchester United have a substantial advantage over their peer group in terms of revenue generation, but this is not borne out over every income stream. Old Trafford has the highest capacity of any English football club stadium, which explains why matchday income is greater than that of its rivals. What is initially surprising is that for 2016/17 United's matchday income was 115 per cent higher than that of Manchester City, but Old Trafford's capacity is only 37 per cent larger than that of the Etihad Stadium on the other side of Manchester.

The analyst therefore needs to delve deeper. Further research reveals that United have 55,000 season ticket holders, compared to City's 40,000. This means that, after deducting 3,000 tickets for away fans for each home match, Manchester United can sell nearly 18,000 tickets to each match. These tickets are sold to corporate clients, who pay much higher prices for hospitality packages than regular fans, and day trippers and football tourists, who are more likely to spend money on merchandise in the mega-store than a diehard local fan who has had a season ticket for decades. These transient fans, although sneered at by the hard-core United fans for their half and half commemorative scarves, bulging carrier bags and selfie sticks, generate extra money for the club compared to those who attend matches at the Etihad and this is why there is such a difference between the two clubs. Despite having a huge television following globally, this is not converted into increased broadcast income as United are bound by collective agreements that determine how the Premier League and UEFA distribute broadcast income.

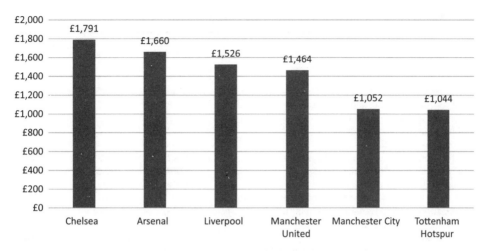

Figure 9.2 Big Six matchday revenue per fan, 2017/18

Figure 9.2 shows that it is Manchester City and Spurs, rather than United, who are the more unusual teams in the Big Six as they generated far less per fan during the 2017/18 season. Manchester City have a different demographic amongst those who attend matches compared to their peers. Spurs were playing at Wembley stadium in 2017/18 which inconvenienced many fans and so prices were kept competitive. The arrival of Spurs' new stadium is likely to see them increase revenue per fan substantially. Chelsea and Arsenal both have the advantage of being based in London, with Chelsea's Stamford Bridge stadium having a lower capacity (41,000) than that of its rivals it charges higher average ticket prices. Liverpool's strategy of selling relatively few season tickets bears fruit as they have a higher proportion of matchday tickets for sale and they can charge higher prices for them. Manchester United have slipped slightly behind these clubs due to their long-standing season ticket price freeze, although they still have a sizeable hospitality ticket operation. This isn't a good thing or a bad thing, it's just a thing. Fans from opposing clubs will seize upon the data to reinforce whatever prejudices they have for or against United (and City). An analyst will set the tribalism and emotion of football to one side and concentrate on looking for the on- and off-field drivers of change for the key numbers.

Costs

When looking at trends in costs, it makes sense to focus on the key ones for any business. For football clubs this is going to be football player costs, in the form of wages, amortisation of transfer fees, and gains on player sales. Let's take each in turn.

Table 9.4 Footnotes to financial statements, Manchester United

	2018 £'000	2017 £'000	2016 £'000
Employee benefit expense (note 7)	**(295,935)**	(263,464)	(232,242)
Operating lease costs	**(1,785)**	(2,316)	(2,392)
Auditors' remuneration: audit of parent company and consolidated financial statements	**(28)**	(27)	(26)
Auditors' remuneration: audit of the Company's subsidiaries	**(472)**	(476)	(436)
Auditors' remuneration: tax compliance services	**(212)**	(392)	(690)
Auditors' remuneration: other services	**(184)**	(456)	(143)
Foreign exchange (losses)/gains	**(994)**	(2,646)	7,760
Gain/(loss) on disposal of property, plant and equipment	**81**	(43)	(126)
Depreciation—property, plant and equipment (note 13)	**(10,625)**	(10,106)	(9,967)
Depredation—investment property (note 14)	**(130)**	(122)	(112)
Amortization (note 15)	**(138,380)**	(124,434)	(88,009)
Sponsorship, other commercial and broadcasting costs	**(25,907)**	(28,491)	(21,043)
External matchday costs	**(24,193)**	(26,892)	(22,244)
Property costs	**(21,620)**	(19,329)	(19,180)
Other operating expenses (individually less than £10,000,000)	**(41,705)**	(36,874)	(32,724)
Exceptional items (note 6)	**(1,917)**	4,753	(15,135)
	(564,006)	(511,315)	(436,709)

Source: Manchester United

Wages

Manchester United's wages appear in the footnotes to their accounts (see Table 9.4). This shows that wages ("employee benefit expense") increased by £31.2 million (13.4%) in 2017 and £32.4 million (12.3%) in 2018. These figures are significant changes so warrant further investigation. Wages can increase by increasing the number of staff and/or increasing the average wage.

A look elsewhere in the footnotes (see Table 9.5) reveals that employee numbers did increase substantially each year albeit by less than the increase in the wages, but in the case of a football club staff costs are skewed towards the first team players and management. In the summer of 2016 United replaced manager Louis van Gaal with Jose Mourinho, a decision that increased management and coaching costs. The club also signed Paul Pogba for a world record fee at the time, as well as Zlatan Ibrahimovic from PSG on a Bosman free transfer at the end of his contract. A player signing on a Bosman at the elite level is able to negotiate enhanced pay terms from the buying club, as the buyer has saved the cost of paying for the player's registration. Add in bonuses for winning the FA Cup, the Europa League and qualifying through the back door for the Champions League in 2017/18 and it is no surprise that the wage bill increased significantly. Similarly,

Table 9.5 Footnotes to financial statements, Manchester United

	2018 Number	2017 Number	2016 Number
By activity:			
Football—players	**81**	74	74
Football—technical and coaching	**165**	136	94
Commercial	**121**	120	111
Media	**87**	90	94
Administration and other	**468**	445	426
Average number of employees	**922**	865	799

The Group also employs approximately 3,858 temporary staff on match days (2017: 2,053; 2016: 2,124), the costs of which are included in the employee benefit expense above.

Source: Manchester United

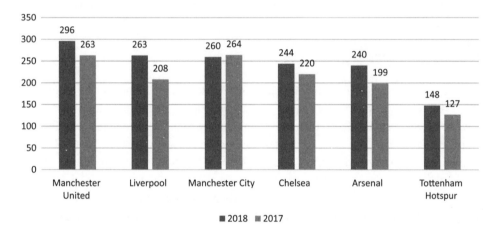

Figure 9.3 Premier League Big Six wage totals, 2017/18 (£ millions)

in 2017/18 the club recruited Lukaku, Matic, Lindelof and Sanchez for £243 million and spending money of this magnitude on players will drive up the wage cost further.

Part of the reason why the wage bill had to rise by double digit percentages each year could have been that United's rivals were also paying more. It therefore makes sense to compare against the chosen peer group.

Figure 9.3 shows that Manchester United to a certain extent have to keep paying higher wages to be competitive with their Premier League peer group. Liverpool's wage bill increased by over a quarter and in 2017/18 Arsenal, despite having a reputation for not trying too hard to compete at the top table, had a 20 per cent rise as the club signed Aubameyang, Lacazette and Mkhitaryan in a most un-Arsenal like spending spree of £166 million on new players. When Manchester United signed Alexis Sanchez in

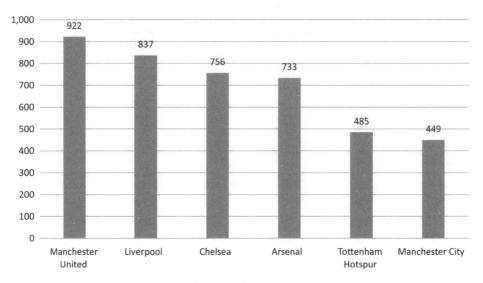

Figure 9.4 Premier League Big Six employee totals 2017/18

January 2018 he had the choice of going to the Etihad but the higher wages on offer at Old Trafford was a contributory factor to him making his decision. Manchester City's wage total decreased in 2017/18 which seems inconsistent with the club winning the Premier League that season. One reason for the decrease was that in 2016/17 City's income statement covered a period of 13 months as the club changed its reporting date. If City's total wage bill for 2016/17 is pro-rated down to cover 12 months the total would be about £244 million, giving a 6.5 per cent increase in 2017/18. Manchester City employs far fewer staff than its rivals (see Figure 9.4) which seems surprising given the club's ambitions, but this could be linked to being part of an organization that owns multiple clubs across the globe with some of the jobs being undertaken elsewhere or split between the different members of City Football Group Limited. Whilst Spurs also have fewer employees than most of its peer group, it also had a far lower wage expense, and both figures are likely to increase once the club is fully operational in its new stadium.

Player transfer amortisation

Figure 9.5 shows that Manchester United's amortisation expense was flat during the last five years of Sir Alex Ferguson's reign up to 2013. This was partly a consequence of him working to a tight budget as the club had huge finance costs resulting from the owners borrowing over £700 million to buy the club. Since Sir Alex retired the amortisation costs figures have risen, but effectively trail United's transfer activity. The amortisation

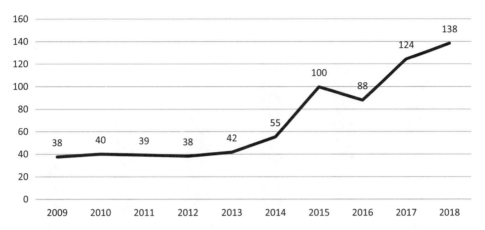

Figure 9.5 Manchester United player amortisation (£ millions)

expense decreased in 2016 compared to 2015 by almost £12 million. This is because United bought midfielder Angel Di Maria in 2015 for £60 million on a five-year contract, which works out as £12 million amortisation per year. He left the club a year later and so this expense was no longer being incurred. In 2017 amortisation increased from £88 million to £124 million as Jose Mourinho was able to spend on Paul Pogba, Henriukh Mkhitaryan and Eric Bailly for £205 million. Even on five-year contracts, this would increase the amortisation charge by over £40 million a season. A similar increase arose in 2017/18 on the back of the acquisition of Romelu Lukaku signing for £75 million on a five-year contract. This alone would have increased amortisation by about £15 million.

Manchester United do have amortisation costs in respect of some other intangible assets, but these are relatively insignificant compared to player registration amortisation and so for analysis purposes can be ignored.

Whilst Manchester United had the highest wage bill, they still trailed behind Manchester City and Chelsea in terms of amortisation (see Figure 9.6). This may be linked to Manchester United having more players coming through their academy into the first team, such as Marcus Rashford and Jesse Lingard who have not cost the club any money in terms of transfer fees, as well as other players who have been with the club for many years and so have a zero or very low amortisation charge such as David de Gea, Ashley Young, Phil Jones and Chris Smalling.

The figures for Arsenal and Liverpool show that over a medium-term period (3–5 years) their amortisation figures reflect that both clubs had fallen behind in player investment in terms of trophies won. Spurs amortisation figure stands out and shows the club's reputation for reluctance to engage in the transfer market is perhaps warranted. Further investigation shows that Spurs amortisation cost in 2017/18 was below three

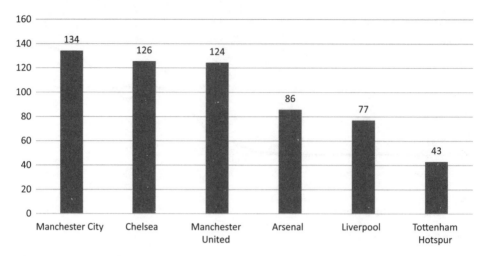

Figure 9.6 Premier League Big Six amortisation (£ millions)

other Premier League clubs in that season – Everton, Leicester and Crystal Palace – who are not part of the Big Six.

Gains on player disposals

This is always one of the most volatile figures in the profit or loss account for clubs who sign players for significant fees. Manchester United are no exception in this regard.

Table 9.6 shows an extract from United's accounts, which shows the club made profits on player sales in both 2018 and 2017, but that there was a significant loss in 2016. This is a result of the club signing players for large fees who did not then perform as expected. The main reason behind the loss made in 2016 is likely to have been the relative failure of Angel Di Maria and the fact that they were prepared to sell him at a loss. The advantage of doing so removed his considerable wages from the total staff cost expense. The profits in 2018 came from the sale of Mkhitaryan and Januzaj, with the former being in a swap

Table 9.6 Profits on player sales, 2016–18, Manchester United

	2018 £'000	2017 £'000	2016 £'000
Profit/(loss) on disposal of registrations	**14,709**	9,876	(9,786)
Player loan income	**3,410**	1,050	–
	18,119	10,926	(9,786)

Source: Manchester United

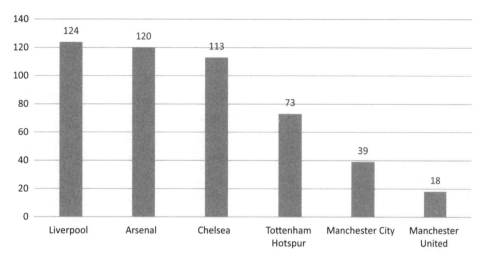

Figure 9.7 Premier League Big Six profit on player sales (£ million)

deal with Arsenal for Sanchez that may have been at prices that ensured that both clubs showed profits on the deals.

Manchester United are excellent in terms of their information disclosure in that they separate out loan income, unlike most other clubs. The £3.4 million of loan income on transfers for 2018 mainly relates to Pereira going to Valencia and some younger players joining Championship clubs to gain experience.

Compared to its peer group United show relatively low profits on player sales (Figure 9.7). This is partly due to the club generating so much money from other sources and so has less pressure to sell players to balance its books. Manchester United is also seen as a "buying club" rather than a "selling club" by players, many of whom only leave if they are not a success at Old Trafford and therefore tend to be sold for low rather than high fees. Figure 9.7 also highlights how a single transaction can distort profitability as highlighted by Philippe Coutinho's sale by Liverpool being responsible for nearly all their £124 million of player sale gains.

Profits: operating, EBIT and EBITDA

Manchester United have shown over a long period of time that they are a very successful operational business, and this is reflected in their profits. An initial look at United's operating profit figures of £68.9 million, £80.8 million and £44.1 million (see Table 9.7) and one might think that United's profits seemed erratic with 2018 being a particularly poor year. An analyst, however, would dig a bit deeper, identifying any non-recurring items and

Table 9.7 Consolidated income statement, Manchester United

	Note	Year ended 30 June		
		2018 £'000	2017 £'000	2016 £'000
Revenue	4	**590,022**	581,204	515,345
Operating expenses	5	**(564,006)**	(511,315)	(436,709)
Profit/(loss) on disposal of intangible assets	8	**18,119**	10,926	(9,786)
Operating profit		**44,135**	80,815	68,850
Finance costs		**(24,233)**	(25,013)	(20,459)
Finance income		**6,195**	736	442
Net finance costs	9	**(18,038)**	(24,277)	(20,017)
Profit on ordinary activities before tax		**26,097**	56,538	48,833
Tax expense	10	**(63,367)**	(17,361)	(12,462)
(Loss)/profit for the year		**(37,270)**	39,177	36,371

Source: Manchester United

examine earnings before interest and taxes (EBIT) and earnings before interest, taxes, depreciation and amortisation (EBITDA) profit measures.

Of course, different analysts have different approaches to calculating EBIT, but the approach used here (which is the same used by United in their press releases) is to eliminate player disposal gains and losses, because, while they arise every year, they are unpredictable. After that, it is a case of looking for any unusual forms of income or costs that are unlikely to be repeated. These items can be found in the footnotes or the face of the profit or loss account. Clubs might classify these as "exceptional items", or it may involve some judgement by the analyst.

Manchester United have, conveniently, labelled their exceptional items, although it is always worth checking the other footnotes to the profit or loss account to ensure nothing has slipped through the net which might be considered to be non-recurring in nature. In the case of Manchester United in 2016 these figures (Table 9.8) relate to the sacking of manager, Louis van Gaal and the impairment and then impairment reversal relating to Bastian Schweinsteiger (see Chapter 5).

When putting through adjustments it is important to correctly treat positive and negative figures when converting operating profits to EBIT. The key thing when converting profit from operating to EBIT is to reverse how the transaction has been reflected in the profit or loss account.

What is immediately striking from the figures in Table 9.9 is that recurring/underlying profits for Manchester United have fallen substantially in both 2017 and 2018. Intuitively one would have expected profits to be higher in 2017, as United won trophies and had the benefit of the new Premier League television deals. In 2018 the

Table 9.8 Exceptional items, Manchester United

	2018 £'000	2017 £'000	2016 £'000
Football League pension scheme deficit (note 30)	**(1,917)**	—	—
Impairment reversal/(charge)—registrations (note 15)	—	4,753	(6,693)
Compensation paid for loss of office	—	—	(8,442)
	(1,917)	4,753	(15,135)

Source: Manchester United

Table 9.9 Operating profit, Manchester United

	2018 £'m	2017 £'m	2016 £'m
Operating profit	44.1	80.8	68.9
Profit/(loss) on player sales	(18.1)	(10.9)	9.8
Impairment reversal/(charge)		(4.9)	6.7
Louis Van Gaal redundancy			8.4
Pension scheme deficit	1.9		
Earnings before income and tax (EBIT)	27.9	65.1	93.8

club had the benefit of Champions League participation so, again, first reaction would be to anticipate an increase. So why has EBIT fallen? A quick look at the figures already reviewed shows that revenue increased by £66 million in 2017, but this was all absorbed by wages increasing by £31 million and amortisation by £36 million. Increases in other matchday running costs, due to, for example, the club playing eight additional home games in 2016/17 following domestic and Europa Cup success, resulted in EBIT profits falling.

The 2018 revenue increase of £9 million was surpassed by a much higher increase in player costs in the form of wages (£32 million) and amortisation (£14 million), which led to the decrease in underlying profits. Here the analyst might start to think "so what" when reviewing the finances and consider the impact of changes in figures from the accounts on future decisions made by the club. This perhaps explains why United's board of directors were reluctant to allow Jose Mourinho to spend as much as he wished on player recruitment in the summer of 2018 having seen EBIT drop so rapidly in the first two years of his reign and with no wish to see the trend continue into 2018/19.

Manchester United typically quote EBITDA profits in their press releases. There are two reasons for doing so. Firstly, this financial metric will always be quite high as it eliminates player registration amortisation, which is a significant sum for clubs that are active in player recruitment and paying large transfer fees. In addition, EBITDA is used for valuation and assessment purposes by analysts as it is a proxy for a cash profit total. Remember to add back depreciation when calculating EBITDA, as it has already been

Table 9.10 Manchester United EBITDA

	2018 £'m	2017 £'m	2016 £'m
Earnings before income and tax (EBIT)	27.9	65.1	93.8
Depreciation	10.8	10.2	10.0
Amortisation	138.3	124.4	88.0
EBITDA	177.1	199.7	191.8

subtracted in arriving at operating profit. Depreciation and amortisation can be found in either the footnotes or the cash flow statement.

Table 9.10 shows that EBITDA increased by 4.1 per cent in 2017 but then decreased in 2018 to £177 million despite Champions League participation and United finishing in a higher league position than in 2017. This was due to the club once again increasing the wage cost disproportionately greater than income.

Analysing the balance sheet

The key balance sheet items analysed for a football club are likely to be intangibles, property, plant and equipment, trade debtors and creditors, and net debt. United's balance sheet (Table 9.11) shows assets totalling just over £1.5 billion. There has been little change in the property, plant and equipment total, which is to be expected as the club had no significant infrastructure projects in the year.

The intangibles note, however, is more revealing (Table 9.12). We can ignore goodwill; this is an accounting issue that has no impact on the club on a day-to-day basis. Player registrations increased from a balance sheet value of £241.7 million at 30 June 2016 to £369.5 million two years later, a 53 per cent increase. The analyst here would pick out the key reasons behind the movement.

In 2017/18 United bought players for £243.2 million, which is significantly higher than the £205.1 million they spent the previous season. This reflects market pressures as selling clubs, both domestic and overseas, attempt to exploit the enhanced Premier League broadcasting deal by demanding more money for their players. It is a commonly held view that there are two prices for football players in the present market, one of which is what sellers demand when a Premier League club is the potential buyer and a lower one for leagues in other countries where clubs have less wealth.

The "Mourinho effect" was also a major contributor to the increase in the squad net book value, as from the summer of 2016 the United board had acceded to the new manager's wishes to buy the players they hoped would help him return the Premier League trophy to Old Trafford. This is a common feature when there is managerial change as the new manager will often have a different playing style and strategy that needs a change of personnel.

Table 9.11 Consolidated balance sheet, Manchester United

	Notes	As of 30 June	
		2017 *£'000*	*2016* *£'000*
ASSETS			
Non-current assets			
Property, plant and equipment	13	**244,738**	245,714
Investment property	14	**13,966**	13,447
Intangible assets	15	**717,544**	665,634
Derivative financial instruments	18	**1,666**	3,760
Trade and other receivables	19	**15,399**	11,223
Deferred tax asset	25	**142,107**	145,460
		1,135,420	1,085,238
Current assets			
Inventories	16	**1,637**	926
Derivative financial instruments	18	**3,218**	7,888
Trade and other receivables	19	**103,732**	128,657
Cash and cash equivalents	20	**290,267**	229,194
		398,854	366,665
Total assets		**1,534,274**	1,451,903

Source: Manchester United

The natural view of a fan is to assume that the £243.2 million spent by Manchester United in the accounts relates to the summer 2017 and January 2018 transfer windows. But caution needs to be applied here; that total seems very high given the publicized signings and estimated transfer fees of Lukaku (£75m), Matic (£40m), Lindelof (£31m) and Sanchez (£40m) but these total £176 million, far less than the total given in the accounts.

A good analyst will then check dates in more detail to determine if something has been missed. Manchester United also signed Fred from Shakhtar Donetsk on 21 June 2018 for an estimated fee of £52 million. Because the club's year-end was 30 June 2018 he was therefore classified as a 2017/18 signing although he didn't make any appearances on the pitch that financial year. Adding this fee to those of the previous two transfer windows gives a total of £238 million, which is far closer to the figure quoted in the accounts. Had Manchester United had a 31 May financial year-end similar to Liverpool, Leicester and some other clubs in the Premier League then player additions would have been lower. Having Pep Guardiola arrive at Manchester City at the same time as Mourinho's appointment also helped fuel United's spending as the club did not want to be seen as the poor relation to their local rivals, who were busy recruiting expensive players of the same pedigree.

Although it is a figure that is not shown in the balance sheet, the gross cost of a playing squad is a figure worth monitoring. In the case of Manchester United this increased from

Table 9.12 Intangibles, Manchester United balance sheet

	Goodwill £'000	Registrations £'000	Other £'000	Total £'000
At 1 July 2016				
Cost	421,453	511,893	2,766	936,112
Accumulated amortization	—	(270,169)	(309)	(270,478)
Net book amount	421,453	241,724	2,457	665,634
Year ended 30 June 2017				
Opening net book amount	421,453	241,724	2,457	665,634
Additions	—	205,091	3,853	208,944
Disposals	—	(37,353)	—	(37,353)
Amortization charge	—	(123,695)	(739)	(124,434)
Reversal of impairment (note 6)	—	4,753	—	4,753
Closing book amount	421,453	290,520	5,571	717,544
At 30 June 2017				
Cost	421,453	645,433	6,619	1,073,505
Accumulated amortization	—	(354,913)	(1,048)	(355,961)
Net book amount	421,453	290,520	5,571	717,544
Year ended 30 June 2018				
Opening net book amount	421,453	290,520	5,571	717,544
Additions	—	243,182	4,495	247,677
Disposals	—	(27,201)	—	(27,201)
Amortization charge	—	(136,993)	(1,387)	(138,380)
Closing book amount	421,453	369,508	8,679	799,640
At **30 June 2018**				
Cost	421,453	785,594	10,379	1,217,426
Accumulated amortization	—	(416,086)	(1,700)	(417,786)
Net book amount	**421,453**	**369,508**	**8,679**	**799,640**

Source: Manchester United

£511.9 million at 1 July 2016 to £785.6 million at 30 June 2018. Managers sometimes complain about not being given support from the board in terms of player recruitment but in the case of Manchester United it wasn't the amount of money spent that was the problem, but the quality of the players signed, or perhaps the way they were coached, that contributed to a relatively lean period in the club's history, especially with Manchester City winning the Premier League in 2018.

To determine player sales income, it is necessary to take into consideration the accounting net book value of disposals, which United have shown as £27.2 million. Remember also that we then need to add to this figure the profit on player sales, which is found in the profit or loss account and totals £18.1 million. This gives a player disposal total of £45.3 million and shows therefore that United had a net spend (player purchases less player sales) for 2017/18 of £197.9 million. This was 26 per cent higher than the

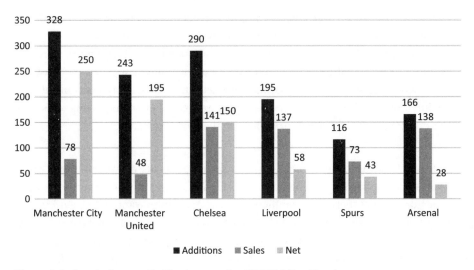

Figure 9.8 Premier League Big Six player trading 2017/18 (£ millions)

previous season and nearly double that of 2015/16 under Louis van Gaal. To give this some context it is useful to benchmark United's player trading spend against our chosen peer group as otherwise the figures are relatively meaningless (Figure 9.8).

What is noticeable from Figure 9.8 is that it is a very expensive business to compete at the elite end of the Premier League. The six clubs spent over £1.3 billion on new players. Manchester City were the highest as their relatively new manager Pep Guardiola identified areas of weakness from the squad he had inherited the previous year and recruited some high-cost replacements. Chelsea, who under Antonio Conte the previous season had managed to win the Premier League title with the benefit of not having UEFA competition distractions, spent nearly £300 million on a series of players that most fans would struggle to remember. Liverpool had a low net spend due to the sale of Coutinho and Arsenal were … Arsenal, frustrating their fans with a solid but unspectacular outlay as had been their habit in recent years. Spurs's focus on the new stadium meant that their net outlay was low, with the sale of Walker and Wimmer offsetting the investment in Sanchez, Moura, Aurier and Llorente.

Inspecting the footnotes can reveal further useful nuggets of information. On page 172 of the Manchester United annual report, buried in note 34, the following was disclosed:

34 Events after the balance sheet date

34.1 Registrations

The playing registrations of certain footballers have been disposed of, subsequent to 30 June 2018, net of associated costs, of £19,920,000. The associated net book value was £1,297,000. Also subsequent to 30 June 2018, Solidarity contributions, sell-on fees and contingent consideration totalling £3,557,000, became receivable in respect of previous playing registration disposals.

Subseqent to 30 June 2018 the playing registrations of certain players were acquired or extended for a total consideration, including associated costs, of £2,388,000. Also subsequent to 30 June 2018, sell-on fees and contingent consideration totalling £520,000, became payable in respect of previous playing registration acquisitions. Payments are due with the next 5 years.

This note highlights Manchester United's caution in the transfer market after their club's year end of 30 June 2018, spending only £2.4 million. During this time there was much press speculation that there were conflicts between Mourinho wanting to spend money to strengthen the defence and a board who were reluctant to sanction such spending. Whilst there is understandably much media interest in player transfer fees, the only definitive figures come from the accounts themselves. In the same summer 2018 transfer window after the business year-end the footnotes to the accounts of Manchester City show a net spend of £42 million but their accounts do not show a breakdown of the amounts spent and received. Similarly, Chelsea had a net spend of £125 million, Arsenal £61 million and Liverpool £181 million. Spurs made no player purchases in the two transfer windows of 2018/19 and so reported net income of £1 million as the club focused on the financing issues surrounding its new stadium.

Net debt

In the January 2019 UEFA Football Benchmarking Report Manchester United were revealed to have the highest net debt of any club in Europe, although they may be overtaken by Spurs in the next year or two as the costs of their new stadium escalate beyond the initial estimates. High debt levels may initially appear problematic, but United also had the third highest income of any club in Europe, and so have the resources to service that debt. Therefore, there is relatively little risk in relation to these loans.

When looking at debt it is a good idea, again, to check the footnotes to see if any loans are due for repayment in the near future. United's notes reveal that the club has two loans, one for $225 million due for repayment in 2025, and the other for $425 million due in 2027. The reason why the loans fluctuated in value in the balance sheet was due to movements in the exchange rate between sterling and the US dollar, rather than any repayments being made.

The low interest rates being charged on the loans (inter bank rates plus 1.25–1.75% on the $225 million loan, and 3.79% on the larger one), suggest that lenders have confidence in the club's ability to make repayments. As a rule, the riskier the loan, the higher the rate of interest charged. Manchester United are now perceived in the markets as being a major cash generating business with no possibility of relegation and this is reflected in the low rates demanded by lenders.

Receivables and payables

An analysis of receivables and payables often reveals the negotiating approach taken by clubs when signing and selling players. Manchester United have receivables of £29.2 million at 30 June 2018 (2017: £46.3 million) due from other clubs in respect of transfers. This suggests that players sold have been on credit terms, rather than for cash. The major sale made by the club in recent years was that of Angel Di Maria in August 2015 and the decrease in the receivables total suggests that the transaction was on an instalment basis with PSG making payments annually.

The same is true in respect of transfer payables but to a much greater extent. United owed other clubs £258.3 million in respect of transfer fees at 30 June 2018, up from £179.1 million the previous year. Of the £258.3 million, over £102 million was not due for at least a year. This would appear to indicate that major transfers, such as that of Paul Pogba and Romelu Lukaku were being paid in annual instalments.

Figure 9.9 shows Manchester United's recent history in respect of transfer payables, which indicates that the club has increasingly been using staged payments as a means of

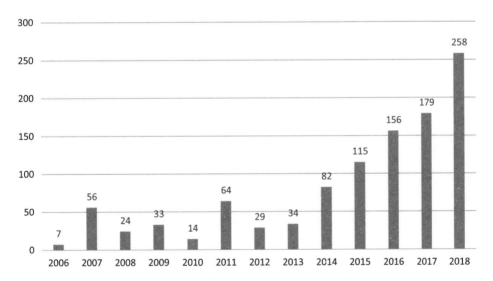

Figure 9.9 Manchester United transfer payables (£ millions)

recruiting players from other clubs. This is further evidence of the club owners supporting the managers of the post-Ferguson era in terms of player recruitment. Realistically this rapid escalation cannot continue indefinitely as the club would potentially be seen as having a credit risk if the total increased much further. The likely consequences of such a strategy is a tapering-off of player investment, as already seen in the summer 2018 and January 2019 transfer windows, or other clubs perhaps demanding larger initial payments when selling players to United if they are concerned about the credit risk.

10

HOW TO ANALYSE CLUB ACCOUNTS 2: RATIO ANALYSIS

Ratio analysis involves linking two or more figures from the accounts where they have a logical business relationship. The ratios are then used in comparative analysis on either an historic or peer group basis. When looking at ratios, one need not be concerned about the numbers themselves, they are merely tools and flags to help identify issues about the club's financial position. Instead, we need to ask:

- What does the ratio mean?
- What does a change in the ratio mean?
- What are the causes of the change in the ratio?
- And what are the consequences of the change in the ratio?

An analyst will focus on the "why" and the "so what" elements of a change in a ratio and identify the reasons behind the movement in the figures and their implications for the future, such as the ability to sign players, renew manager contracts, meet wage demands, and so on.

Performance ratios

Performance here means financial performance, not performance on the pitch, but some of the calculations can in fact be linked to on-field performance too. To measure how much profit is generated from each £1 of income we use the following:

Profit margin = Profit/Income × 100

There are other measures of profit too, all used by analysts to get an overall feel for the club's performance. We can have:

- Gross profit margin (not really appropriate for a football club, but if looking at a business linked to the club, such as a sportswear manufacturer, this would be valid);
- Operating profit margin;
- EBIT margin;
- EBITDA margin;
- Profit before tax margin;
- Net profit margin (and any other the analyst chooses to calculate).

When looking at profit margins it makes sense to distinguish between "dirty" margins such as operating and net profit ones, which include non-recurring items and "clean" margins such as EBIT and EBITDA where these are removed. Table 10.1 shows the data an analyst might extract from the accounts and put into a spreadsheet, which is typically how an analyst would crunch the numbers.

The EBITDA margin for 2018 is calculated as EBITDA profit (£177 million) divided by total income (£590 million) and multiplied by 100 to arrive at a figure of 30 per cent. What does this mean? It shows that, excluding player sales, one-off costs, depreciation and player amortisation, Manchester United generated 30 pence of profit for every £1 of income in 2017. Why has this fallen compared to the previous year? The main reason

Table 10.1 Manchester United key metrics

Manchester United plc	2015	2016	2017	2018
Income	**395**	**515**	**581**	**590**
Wages	203	232	263	296
Other costs	67	99	115	117
EBITDA	**125**	**184**	**202**	**177**
Amortisation	100	88	124	138
Depreciation	10	10	10	11
EBIT	**15**	**86**	**68**	**28**
Non-recurring income (costs)	(7)	(7)	2	(2)
Gain on player sales	24	(10)	11	18
Total Costs	**364**	**446**	**500**	**546**
Operating profit/(loss)	**32**	**69**	**81**	**44**
Net interest paid	35	20	24	18
Profit before tax	**(4)**	**49**	**57**	**26**
Tax	(3)	12	17	63
Profit after tax	**(1)**	**36**	**39**	**(37)**
Cleaned Net Profit	**(17)**	**54**	**26**	**(53)**
Effective tax rate	**75%**	**26%**	**31%**	**243%**
EBITDA Margin	31.7%	35.7%	34.8%	30.0%
EBIT Margin	3.9%	16.7%	11.7%	4.7%
Operating Margin	8.0%	13.4%	13.9%	7.5%
Profit before tax margin	(0.9%)	9.5%	9.7%	4.4%
Net Margin	(0.2%)	7.1%	6.7%	(6.3%)

is that United's wage bill and other costs rose faster than income. The EBIT margin fell faster than the EBITDA margin, mainly due to United's amortisation charge increasing by 11 per cent in the year, much faster than the increase in income. This increase in amortisation, driven by inflationary pressures in the transfer market, will be difficult to sustain in the long term if the club want to improve their profits, which is why it is beneficial that the club's academy continues to discover and develop player who can become part of the first team squad.

The operating and profit before tax margins decreased for the reasons given above despite United selling players at a greater profit in 2018 compared to the previous season. The operating profit is a "dirty" ratio, however, as it is impacted by volatile and non-recurring events, and so should be treated with caution. The net margin means that for every £1 of income for the club in 2018, it lost 6.3 pence for the Glazer family and other shareholders compared to a profit the previous season. However, the reason why this figure is negative is due to volatility caused by changes to the US tax system in the year in question.

Figure 10.1 compares Manchester United's profitability to some of its peer group and suggests that the different business models employed by some clubs aren't having an impact upon profitability.

Manchester United and Arsenal in theory both use the traditional profit maximizing objective of corporate entities. This is because both clubs have their shares traded on stock exchanges and as such are answerable to market forces (although Arsenal have subsequently been removed from the stock exchange after majority owner Stan Kroenke bought out the other main shareholders in 2018). Liverpool too, as part of the FSG group, would appear to be profit orientated. Spurs run a very lean business operation, and this is reflected in having high margins throughout.

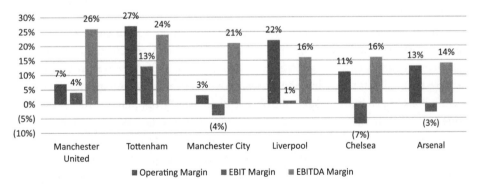

Figure 10.1 Premier League Big Six profit margins 2017/18

Table 10.2 Manchester United wages, 2013–18

Manchester United plc	2013 £'m	2014 £'m	2015 £'m	2016 £'m	2017 £'m	2018 £'m
Income	**363**	**433**	**395**	**515**	**581**	**590**
Wages	181	215	203	232	263	296
Wages/Income %	50%	50%	51%	45%	45%	50%

Both Chelsea and Manchester City should in theory be willing to accept lower profit margins because neither of their respective owners, Roman Abramovich and Sheik Mansour, bought the clubs as financial investments and so generating profits was not a priority. Both clubs had negative EBIT margins which perhaps shows that their owners were relaxed about profitability, but managed to convert this into a positive net margin due to profits on player sales. Manchester United, having the highest EBITDA margin of all the clubs, does show that excluding player signing costs it is the most profitable of the Big Six and why the club commands a premium value.

Cost control ratios

The following ratios focus on the main cost areas for clubs, which are wages and player trading.

Wage control = wages/income × 100
Operational player costs = (wages + amortisation)/income × 100
Total player costs = (wages + amortisation − gain on player sales)/income × 100

The wage control ratio looks at the cost of wages as a proportion of income. This is used in some variants of Financial Fair Play, such as those used in League One and League Two in the EFL.

Table 10.2 shows that Manchester United has shown fairly consistent wage control. Despite wages increasing by over £100 million in five years since 2012, the club's ability to generate income, especially the big commercial deals that came on stream in 2015/ 16, have ensured that wages have been easily covered by money coming into the club.

United also have better wage control than their peer group. Figure 10.2 shows that United are slightly more efficient at controlling relative wage costs than most of their competitors, with the exception of Spurs. This suggests that some of United's critics, who accuse United of fuelling an increase in unsustainable wage growth, are ignoring the key issue of staff costs, which is the ability to pay them from the income the club generates. UEFA recommend that clubs should aim to ensure that wage control ratios are kept below 70 per cent, however, some clubs in the Premier League exceed this regularly. The EFL Championship, which does not have the benefit of huge broadcasting income, had

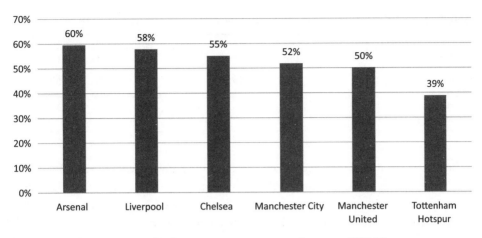

Figure 10.2 Premier League Big Six wages as a percentage of revenue, 2017/18

Table 10.3 Employment costs for Lakaku and Sanchez

	Romelu Lukaku	Alexis Sanchez
Contract remaining at previous club	2 years	6 months
Transfer Fee	£75 million	£30 million (estimated value of player swap with Henrikh Mkhitaryan)
Annual wage (estimated per press reports)	£13 million	£24 million
Four-year wage cost	£52 million	£96 million
Total cost over four years	£127 million	£126 million

an overall wage control of 107 per cent in 2017/18, which meant that the division as a whole paid out more money in wages than it generated in income, leaving nothing to pay the other running costs of clubs.

Just looking at wage control does not tell the whole story. In the present transfer market, elite players who are near the end of their contract can negotiate higher wages as the buying club can acquire them at a discounted price. When a club is acquiring a player, it takes into consideration the total cost over the life of the contract. The total cost includes both wages and amortisation. We can look at two deals at Manchester United in the 2017/18 season as an illustration.

Table 10.3 shows the total cost of employing Romelu Lukaku and Alexei Sanchez over a four-year period. Alexei Sanchez with two or more years remaining on his contract, would potentially have cost £100 million in the transfer market in 2017/18, but this figure declines as the contract expiry date approaches. Manchester City allegedly bid £55 million for him in August 2017 seeking to exploit the final year of his contract, but the deal was not finalized. Players are allowed to negotiate deals with suitor clubs when

Table 10.4 Manchester United wages and operational player cost control, 2013–18

Manchester United plc	2013 £'m	2014 £'m	2015 £'m	2016 £'m	2017 £'m	2018 £'m
Income	**363**	**433**	**395**	**515**	**581**	**590**
Wages	181	215	203	232	263	296
Amortisation	42	55	100	88	124	138
Operational Player Control %	61%	62%	76%	62%	67%	74%

in the last six months of their present contracts, in the knowledge that they will be able to leave on a Bosman deal and there will be no cost paid by the buying club to the seller. Sanchez's agent/advisors were (assuming the figures quoted in the media are correct) therefore able to negotiate higher wages for their client when he signed in a swap deal with Henrik Mkhitaryan.

From Manchester United's perspective they saved a considerable sum by signing Sanchez in the last six months of his contract and therefore were willing to pay a higher wage. Over the life of the contract, United are relatively indifferent as to whose bank account the money has been paid, be it Arsenal's or Sanchez's. The only danger of skewing the payments towards the player is that such an approach may cause other players in the Old Trafford dressing room to try to negotiate similar earnings and this creates wage inflation or player resentment if the club rejects the higher demands. Therefore, there is a case for combining wage and amortisation costs to see the total cost of players to a club as a proportion of income. This is called the operational player cost control (OPC) ratio.

Table 10.4 shows that whilst United have been able to limit wage rises in line with income, they have not been so successful in relation to transfer fees. Under Sir Alex Ferguson in 2013, United had a relatively restrained transfer budget. The reason for this was that the club had to ensure there were sufficient sums available to meet interest costs on the club's borrowings from banks. David Moyes continued this trend of frugal spending. The deemed failure of the Moyes regime (the club finished seventh that season and won no trophies) resulted in a change of policy in respect of player recruitment and a much larger investment in transfers for significant fees. This has resulted in the OPC ratio rising, as the club released the handbrake in terms of signing players under both Louis van Gaal and Jose Mourinho.

Figure 10.3 shows that Spurs have impressive player related cost control compared to the rest of the Big Six. How long this can continue without the risk of losing players to other clubs offering higher wages is debatable. Manchester United, even when taking into consideration the signings of the likes of Pogba and Lukaku in recent years have better cost control than the rest of the Big Six. This means there is less pressure on the manager to sell players to balance the books. The sharp rise in the Arsenal OPC figure is a result of the club spending money on new signings and income falling by 5 per cent due

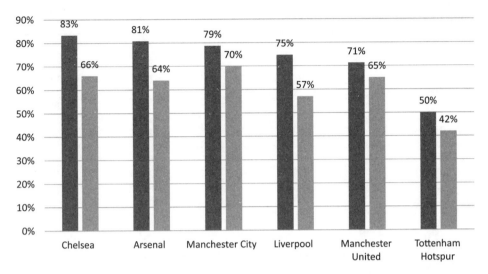

Figure 10.3 Premier League Big Six operational player cost 2017 (right) and 2018 (left)

to their failure to qualify for the Champions League in 2017/18. Manchester City have owners who have backed Pep Guardiola's endeavours to rebuild the squad he inherited when he became manager. City were also able to increase their player recruitment spend as a result of UEFA's punishment for breaches of FFP rules ending in 2016/17, which led to a surge in amortisation costs. Chelsea's OPC ratio is very high, which suggests that the club relies on selling players at a profit in order to cover all the other costs of running the business, so perhaps this needs further investigation. All six clubs had increases in this ratio in 2017/18, reflecting that wage and transfer fee inflation were far greater than revenue growth.

The final player cost ratio takes into consideration the gains made from selling players as well as wages and amortisation. This is the total player cost control (TPC) ratio. This reflects the overall impact of player trading on profitability and shows the different approaches taken at board level in terms of how the club operates in terms of buying and selling players. If a club can consistently develop players from their youth teams or unearth bargains to sell a couple of years later for much higher fees, then the TPC ratio will be much lower than OPC.

Table 10.5 suggests that Manchester United are not concerned with selling players to make ends meet as there is relatively little difference between their OPC and TPC ratios. In most years TPC is a couple of percentage points lower than OPC, except for 2016, when Angel Di Maria was sold at a loss to PSG.

If we look at United's peer group (Figure 10.4), the club most affected by the TPC ratio is Chelsea. Its TPC is significantly lower than its OPC and brings the club much closer in line with the other Big Six clubs. This is because Chelsea have a policy of selling their players,

Table 10.5 Manchester United operating expenses

Manchester United plc	2013 £'m	2014 £'m	2015 £'m	2016 £'m	2017 £'m	2018 £'m
Income	**363**	**433**	**395**	**515**	**581**	590
Operating expenses						
Wages	181	215	203	232	263	296
Gain on player sales	9	7	24	(10)	11	18
Wages/Income %	50%	50%	51%	45%	45%	50%
Operational Player Control %	61%	62%	76%	62%	67%	74%
Total player cost/income %	59%	61%	70%	64%	65%	71%

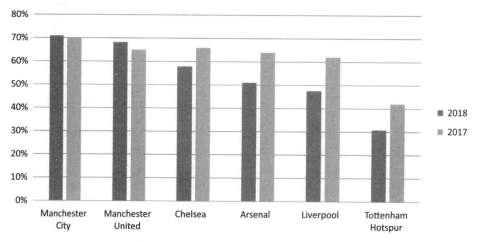

Figure 10.4 Premier League Big Six total player cost control percentages, 2017 and 2018

even to rivals such as Manchester United (Mata and Matic) if the price offered is acceptable. Chelsea generated gains on player sales of £272 million in the 2013–18 period, whereas Manchester United only made a profit of £43 million in the same period. Chelsea have been accused by critics of "player harvesting", the practice of recruiting large numbers of youth players, either from their own academy schemes or those of other clubs, then sending them out on loan to see which ones develop, with a view to selling them on at a profit. At the start of 2017/18 Chelsea had 40 players on loan at other clubs. Spurs's TPC total also stands out and shows that the club is competing with its wealthier rivals on a far lower budget.

Matchday income to wages

Even for a club like Manchester United, with the largest stadium capacity in the country, fans' contribution as a proportion of the wage bill has fallen noticeably in recent years.

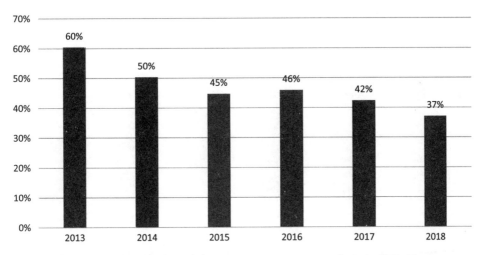

Figure 10.5 Manchester United matchday income as a percentage of wages, 2013–18

This is because clubs have been unable (or unwilling) to increase ticket prices, but wages have risen, especially in the first year of a new broadcasting deal. Instead clubs have relied upon improved broadcasting and commercial deals to bear an increasing element of wage costs. Figure 10.5 shows that Manchester United's matchday fans were paying 60 pence for every £1 paid out in wages in 2012/13, but this had fallen to 37 pence in the pound by 2017/18.

When we consider the peer group (see Figure 10.6), the clubs are significantly different. Arsenal and Spurs fans will not be surprised to know that they pay the greatest propor-tion of the wage bill because, whilst their matchday income is similar to that of United's, the wage bill is much lower. Chelsea are constrained by currently having a relatively low ground capacity compared to both United and Arsenal, which limits the club's ability to turn Stamford Bridge into a cash cow from matchday income. This follows a deci-sion by owner Roman Abramovich to halt a proposed move to a new 60,000 capacity stadium. Liverpool have had a policy of season ticket price freezes which has restricted income growth, although the recent expansion of Anfield has allowed the club to increase matchday income, albeit still £20–30 million below that of Manchester United and Arsenal. Manchester City's business strategy is to grow the supporter base by offering relatively cheap ticket prices. City also have fewer football tourist fans compared to the other clubs and so generate less money per fan, as regular fans, as we have seen, are less lucrative on a match by match basis than those that attend occasionally.

Overall in the Premier League matchday income accounts for less than a quarter of the wage bill with some clubs like Burnley and Bournemouth with small stadia having a figure as little as 7 per cent.

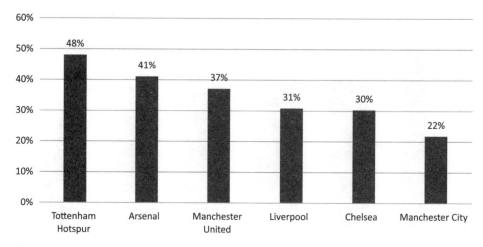

Figure 10.6 Premier League Big Six, matchday revenue as a percentage of wages, 2018

Income per fan

The success or otherwise of clubs extracting cash from fans can be measured by looking at the average income generated over the season from each fan: total matchday income/average attendance. Manchester United have generated about £1,400–£1,500 per fan per season in recent years with the exception of 2015.

Figure 10.7 shows the importance for clubs of qualifying for European competitions. Matchday income per fan is a combination of the average price paid to attend a match and the number of fixtures played in the season. In 2013/14 under David Moyes Manchester United failed to qualify for Europe. This contributed to a reduction in fixtures the following season (44 compared to 55) and so there was a significant reduction in matchday revenue. Clubs like Manchester United, with a global fanbase, are able to monetize this appeal through not only ticket prices, which are moderate by Premier League standards, but also through corporate hospitality and merchandise sales.

Figure 10.8 show that the Big Six extract about the same amount of cash per fan per match, with the exception of Manchester City and Spurs who generate about a third less than the other clubs. This is due to City needing to be more price conscious having to build a fanbase as success has been relatively recent, as well as the relative lack of lucrative football tourists amongst those that attend the Etihad. Spurs had the move from White Hart Lane to Wembley in 2017/18 which resulted in ground capacity doubling and so priced tickets to encourage new fans to attend, as well as to compensate existing regulars for the inconvenience of having to travel further to see their team.

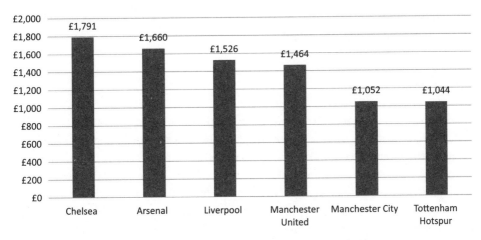

Figure 10.7 Big Six matchday income per fan, per season, average 2013–18

Figure 10.8 Premier League Big Six matchday revenue per fan, 2018

Other clubs might have a pricing strategy of expensive matchday and hospitality tickets as well as having a greater proportion of season tickets at premium prices. Clubs with large numbers of corporate hospitality seats can if they wish subsidize ticket prices for regular fans. Bayern Munich charge as little as €140 for a season ticket at the Allianz Arena as analysts estimate it generates as much matchday income from business seats and luxury boxes as it does from the rest of the stadium. The culture of football in Germany is different to that in England. Bundesliga fans tend to be more organized and militant in their opposition to club behaviour that they don't like and as a consequence ticket prices are priced to keep the fanbase happy.

Interest cover

Some clubs, such as Manchester United, have significant borrowings from banks and other financial institutions. It is imperative that all businesses, including football clubs, can meet their finance commitments, both capital and interest, to the bank. Failure to do so can result in the bank imposing sanctions ranging from fines and penalties to forcing the business to sell its assets (which for a club is likely to mean star players and even potentially the stadium). Interest cover shows how easily a football club can meet its interest costs from the current level of profitability. It is calculated by dividing profit before interest by interest payable and is normally expressed as a multiple. The lower the multiple, the riskier the investment.

Figure 10.9 calculates Manchester United's interest cover using operating profit as the profit element. It shows that those who lent to the Glazer family to finance their purchase of the club took on a lot of risk, especially in the early years of the takeover. With United's loans peaking in 2010 at £778 million and with interest cover often below 1.0, it could be argued the club was spending more time trying to manage its interest payments than investing in the playing squad. Some of the club's borrowing was in the form of "payment-in-kind" (PIK) loans, where the lender does not receive interest in the form of cash, but

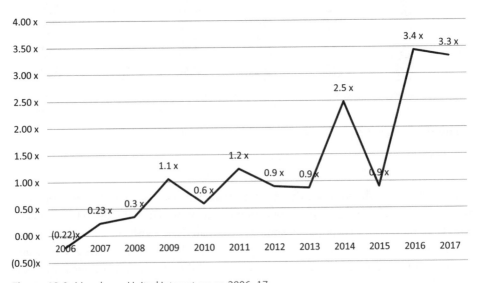

Figure 10.9 Mancheser United interest cover, 2006–17

instead the borrower can defer interest payments by issuing additional securities until the term of the loan is over when interest on the interest is charged. A PIK loan enables the debtor to borrow without having the burden of a cash repayment of interest until the loan term is ended. It's useful for a club with a liquidity problem but it is high-risk and expensive as the interest is charged on a compound basis. United's PIK loans were initially £138 million in 2006 and ended up at £235 million by 2010.

United used a share issue in late 2010 to repay some of its borrowings. The proceeds of the share issue, along with much higher broadcasting revenue from improved rights deals signed by the Premier League coming on stream in 2014 and 2017, helped the club to achieve interest cover ratios that were less worrying for lenders. Consequently, United were able to reschedule their loans at much lower interest rates to reflect the lower risk felt by lenders.

Effective tax rate

The effective tax rate is calculated as profit or loss account tax charge/profit before tax. Popular belief is that Premier League football clubs generate large sums of money, so it should logically follow that they pay large amounts of tax. This is not the case in reality. Whilst the tax authorities do benefit from employment taxes on players' wages and VAT on matchday ticket sales, clubs are taxed on their profits, rather than their income.

In theory a football club would pay corporation tax on their profits at the rate set by government (19% in the UK in 2019). However, under current rules, all businesses are assessed on their *taxable profits*, which are calculated using different rules from the accounting profit figures we see in the profit or loss account. The complexities of tax law are outside the remit of this book, but suffice to say, the rules are long-winded and involve many sections and subsections of tax code, and clubs employ expert and expensive advisors to ensure they pay the appropriate amount of tax on their profits.

Manchester United's tax expense (Table 10.6) can really only be described as bizarre. The club's decision to register in the Cayman Islands, a well-known tax haven, is no doubt a contributory factor. How the club managed to achieve a £155 million tax credit in 2013 in a season in which they made losses is surprising and evidence that tax affairs of clubs are perhaps best left to the professionals. The unpredictable nature of tax charges means that most analysts are cautious when assessing clubs on their post-tax profits.

Table 10.6 Manchester United tax expense, 2013–18

Manchester United plc	2013	2014	2015	2016	2017	2018
Profit before tax	(9)	41	(4)	49	57	26
Tax	(155)	17	(3)	12	17	63
Effective tax rate	1765%	41%	75%	26%	31%	243%

Balance sheet ratios

Player based ratios

Analysing ratios based on player trading has to be dealt with carefully, as the figures are distorted through swap transactions, Bosman signings and first-team players coming from the youth development programme. The amount of money spent by clubs on players is certainly one that gets fans excited and often irate (especially if they support Newcastle United, whose owner Mike Ashley has been subject to regular criticism in respect of the net sums spent on players since he purchased the club in 2007).

Player signings to income
Player additions/income × 100 provides the player signings to income ratio. This measures how much the club spends on player transfers for each £1 of income generated. At many transfer windows there are media reports of record amounts being spent by clubs and discussions as to whether this is a bubble that will burst. This ratio gives an indication as to whether the amount of money spent by clubs is sustainable, by comparing it to previous years.

Figure 10.10 shows United's transfer activity to income since the Glazer family acquired the club in 2005. In the early years of ownership, when the club's focus was on debt management, Sir Alex Ferguson had to be cautious in terms of player recruitment. In 2005/06 the club only spent 14 pence for each £1 of income, and whilst there were some fluctuations, this figure continued to be low until 2014. The managers since Ferguson's retirement have all had a much freer rein in terms of spending. This is because the share

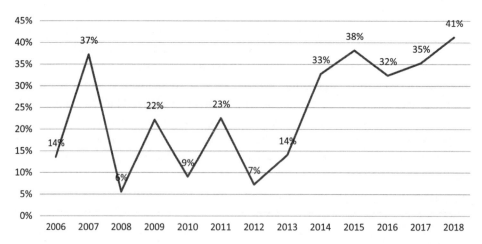

Figure 10.10 Manchester United player additions as percentage of income, 2006–18

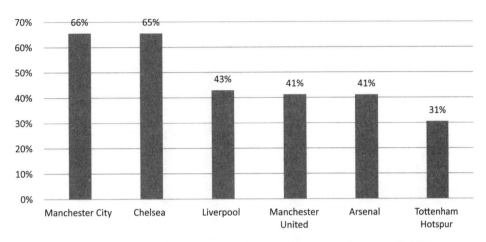

Figure 10.11 Premier League Big Six player purchases as percentage of revenue, 2017/18

issue proceeds in 2010 were used to pay off the PIK loans, reducing the interest charge and freeing up funds to invest in the playing squad. Whilst fans may have little interest in off-field topics as dry as debt and equity funding of the club they support, these issues can impact upon what happens on the pitch in terms of player signings.

Figure 10.11 shows that despite Manchester United spending a record £243 million on new players in 2017/18 the club was relatively restrained in the transfer market compared to the two non-profit seeking clubs, Manchester City and Chelsea. City's high figure is mainly due to the purchase of expensive players identified by Pep Guardiola to improve the squad after his first season in charge. The recruitment policy appears to have been successful given that Manchester City broke so many records in winning the league that season. Chelsea's budget may have been high because the club was competing in the Champions League unlike in the previous season. Arsenal's relatively low figure is consistent with the view of many of their fans that the board are reluctant to invest in new players to the same extent as other leading clubs. It could be argued, as some fans do, that this was a contributory factor to Arsenal failing to achieve Champions League qualification for the first time in more than 20 years. Liverpool had a relatively quiet year in terms of recruitment, but still managed to qualify for the Champions League and reach the final in 2018. Spurs' often cited reluctance to invest large sums in players is confirmed by trailing far behind in the table which is a contributory factor toward the lack of trophies won by the club in recent years.

Player reinvestment rate
The player reinvestment rate is calculated as player additions/player amortisation × 100. This measures how much is being invested in new players compared to the proportion of

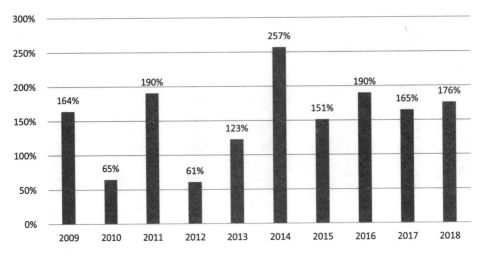

Figure 10.12 Manchester United player reinvestment percentage

contracts being consumed through amortisation. Intuitively you would expect this figure to be greater than 100 per cent as the current market price of players is constantly rising, whereas the amortisation figure is in relation to players acquired in previous years when player prices were lower. If the figure falls below 100 per cent consistently it suggests that the club either has financial pressures that are restricting player signings, as has been levelled at Spurs since they committed to move to the new stadium, or they have a very productive youth academy that brings through new players making signing from elsewhere unnecessary.

Figure 10.12 shows once again that Sir Alex Ferguson worked with a relatively restricted budget and was unable to spend significant sums to replace players. He was in charge for the first six seasons shown in the graph when United won the Premier League and finished runner-up twice. Since then, under David Moyes, Louis van Gaal, Jose Mourinho and Ole Gunnar Solskjaer, the club has finished seventh, fourth, fifth, second and sixth respectively. This is despite reinvesting more in the squad each year on new players than the cost of amortising existing players.

Many United fans have accused their noisy neighbours at the Etihad stadium of "buying" success by spending large sums on players and Figure 10.13 suggests this has some merit in 2017/18, with City spending £244 on new players for every £100 of amortisation costs, far more so than runner-up United, but even so City's reinvestment in the squad was little different to that of Liverpool, who finished fourth. The table does suggest that transfer fee inflation in the Premier League is rampant and that clubs are having to pay substantially higher sums to replace players as their contracts expire or leave for another club. That Spurs are top of the table might feel intuitively wrong, but

Figure 10.13 Premier League Big Six player signings/amortisation 2017/18

this indicates that the club has historically invested little in buying new players and so the amount spent in 2017/18 was relatively high compared to the club's purchases in previous seasons, which may surprise some fans.

Squad ageing

Squad ageing ratio is calculated as accumulated amortisation/player registration cost × 100. This measures how much time is left on players' contracts. At lower league level such a ratio is largely irrelevant because most players are on one or two-year contracts. At the elite level it is much more of an issue. Clubs do not want to risk their star players coming to the end of contracts and leaving for a reduced fee or on a Bosman transfer, as happened with Arsenal who lost Aaron Ramsey in 2019 to Juventus when he was just 28 years old and in the prime of his career. Most players who sign on multi-million-pound deals do so on four/five-year contracts, so if the squad ageing ratio is above 60 per cent it usually means that the squad on average has less than two years remaining on their contracts. After this date player values start to fall as buyers may be prepared to delay making a purchase allowing the player to run down the contract and then buy the player at a reduced price or on a Bosman deal. The length of individual contracts is widely known in the football industry, but if the squad ageing figure does rise significantly it can indicate that the club (a) may be struggling to negotiate new deals with players, or (b) wants to get rid of unwanted players coming towards the end of their contracts.

Figure 10.14 shows that Manchester United had quite a few players at the end of the Ferguson era who were nudging towards the end of their contracts. Under the managers who succeeded Sir Alex, United have signed players on longer contracts, often five years where previously they may have been for four years and had contract extensions for existing squad members.

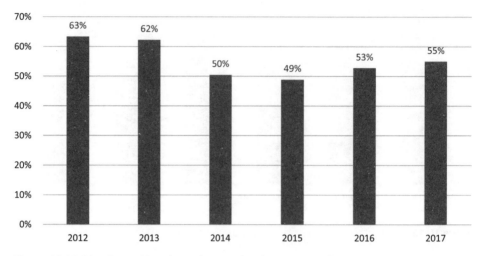

Figure 10.14 Manchester United squad ageing (% of contract term)

Transfers owing percentage

Transfers due to other clubs/revenue measures the proportion of the club's revenue that is owed to other clubs for transfer payments. The number itself is relatively unimportant, but the trend compared to previous years can be significant as it can signal a club's ability to buy in future transfer markets.

Figure 10.15 shows that under Ferguson Manchester United owed relatively little to other clubs for transfer fees. After his departure in 2013, not only did United spend more money on transfers, but many of these were based on credit deals rather than for cash, with instalments spread over years rather than months. Even though United's income rose spectacularly during the period, it could not keep up with the rise in transfer fees owing.

Financial gearing (leverage)

The gearing ratio – debt or net debt/equity – measures the proportion of the club's finances that come from borrowing. The higher the ratio, the greater the risk of non-payment of loan instalments and the more difficult it is for the club to borrow additional funds. Net debt is borrowings less cash balances. Borrowings can be overdrafts, loans and documents promising to pay lenders issued by the club, usually referred to as bonds or loan notes. The equity figure is the total invested by shareholders in terms of the cash generated from shares issued as well as profits, should they be made, being reinvested in the club.

Football is unusual in that some clubs have negative net debt, which arises when cash exceeds borrowings, especially if they have wealthy benevolent owners who prefer to invest in the form of shares rather than through loans and who may be reluctant to borrow money from traditional banks for either cost saving or cultural reasons.

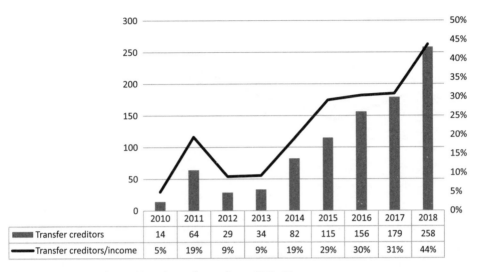

	2010	2011	2012	2013	2014	2015	2016	2017	2018
▬▬ Transfer creditors	14	64	29	34	82	115	156	179	258
▬▬ Transfer creditors/income	5%	19%	9%	9%	19%	29%	30%	31%	44%

Figure 10.15 Manchester United transfer creditors, 2010–18

Manchester United is an example of a leveraged buy-out (LBO) acquisition by the Glazer family. An LBO arises where an acquirer buys a business by borrowing to fund the purchase price. They then use the cash generated by the business to pay the interest payments on the loans. It is a risky approach, which, if successful, can make a huge return for the investor. The initial years of an LBO tend to be the riskiest as failure to meet loan payments can lead to sanctions from lenders and there is then the potential for the business to become insolvent.

Manchester United's gearing, shown in Figure 10.16, as measured by debt to equity, was zero in 2005 because the club was so wealthy that they received over £2 million in interest from £65 million in the bank, with no overdrafts or loans. By the time the club had produced its next set of accounts in 2006 there were £364 of borrowings from lenders for every £100 of equity invested by shareholders. By 2017 this had fallen to £117 of borrowings for every £100 of equity investment, although this has been creeping upwards over the past five years.

Trying to work out Manchester United's true level of gearing is a challenge. The transfer of ownership and debt from company to company controlled by the Glazer family is at times bewildering. Whether it is correct to use Red Football Limited, Manchester United Limited, Red Football Shareholder Limited, or Manchester United Plc as a means of calculating gearing is somewhat of a lottery, so different analysts will arrive at different ratios when assessing the club. The reason why lenders were charging high interest rates was due to the gearing levels of the club in the early years of the takeover. Gearing peaked in 2010 as Manchester United Limited paid a dividend of £266 million to its shareholders,

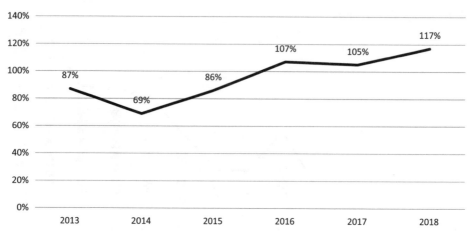

Figure 10.16 Manchester United gearing percentage

reducing the equity base of the club. Gearing has fallen significantly since 2010 initially due to the club's share offer listed on the New York NASDAQ stock exchange, which raised cash used to pay down some of the outstanding borrowings. This repayment also allowed the club to terminate some loans at high interest rates and replace them with ones that had more advantageous terms. The original lenders charged the club £22 million in 2013 to replace loans upon which interest was being charged at 8.375 per cent with ones with much lower borrowing costs.

Critics of the United owners will point out that gearing calculated on a net basis is far lower. At 30 June 2018, for example, the club had £242 million of cash in the balance sheet and if gearing was calculated using net debt, by subtracting this cash sum from borrowings, the figure would fall from 117 to 60 per cent. Some might take the view that the huge cash balance that United have would be better spent on paying down the loans rather than earning a paltry rate of interest from investing the cash in a bank account. They point out that executive vice-chairman Ed Woodward is a former investment banker and may have divided loyalties between the club and his former profession which makes money out of lending and earning money from the resultant interest charges. There's little evidence to support this view, as the loans taken out by United have large repayment penalties for early settlement and so it is questionable if there would be any net financial savings.

Gearing, like nearly all figures from the financials, is a meaningless number unless it can be given context from the club's activities. From Figure 10.17 we can see that Spurs had the highest gearing of the Big Six, with net borrowings representing £107 for every £100 of equity investment due to the costs of the new stadium being far

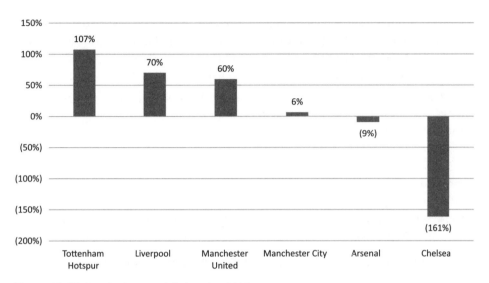

Figure 10.17 Premier League clubs' gearing 2018

higher than expected. This ratio is likely to increase substantially by the end of 2018/ 19 with Spurs having to borrow further sums, eating up a large proportion of the cash balance of £101 million they had at 30 June 2018. Provided the stadium redevelopment generates more revenue than the interest costs on the loans, the club should be better off overall financially.

In 2018 Liverpool had the second highest gearing of 70 per cent mainly due to the club borrowing a large sum to fund the expansion of the main stand to increase capacity at Anfield to 54,000. The Glazer purchase of Manchester United in 2005 was clearly a gamble given the borrowing required to buy the club, but from a financial perspective it has proven to be successful. Arsenal have had a historically high gearing that reflects the costs of moving from Highbury to the Emirates stadium in 2006 and the relatively (compared to Manchester United's) cautious approach to player spending taken by the main shareholder "Silent" Stan Kroenke. Gearing had however been reduced to zero by 2018 and Arsenal's matchday income has been first or second highest in the Premier League since the move. Both Chelsea and Manchester City have benevolent owners who have underwritten the cost of being an elite club in the Premier League. City have not only trophies, but also a new stadium which can potentially be used to increase income. Chelsea have trophies but risk being left behind by the Manchester clubs due to Stamford Bridge having a lower capacity. Chelsea's gearing figure is relatively meaningless due to the club having negative equity from substantial losses as well as over £1 billion of borrowings from Abramovich's own company Fordstam Limited.

Gearing is often used in conjunction with interest cover, reviewed earlier, to determine the level of financial risk of the business. Manchester United still had half a billion pounds of debt at 30 June 2018, but such is the success of the business that this amount is now relatively easy to service. Whilst gearing has edged up slightly since 2015, part of the reason is that United's loans were taken out in US dollars and sterling has fallen in value against the dollar. It could be that in future years the debt levels decrease if this fall in the value of sterling reverses.

Conclusion

An analyst will typically summarize the work undertaken and make various observations. In respect of Manchester United's finances this could be on the following lines:

- The Glazer takeover was a huge financial risk, which has proved to be successful for the new owners.
- Manchester United's commercial department is in a league of its own when it comes to striking deals with partners.
- Sir Alex Ferguson worked wonders with a relatively restricted budget during the early years of the takeover, as money generated by the club was used to meet financing obligations. Those who followed in his footsteps have not been so successful.
- Had United not had the huge levels of debt taken on by the Glazer family, the club's managers would have had far more leeway in terms of signing players and offering more competitive wages. Arguably, for a club the size of United, to have won the Champions League only once since 1999 is a relatively poor return for an institution that markets itself as the world's "greatest football club".
- At present the only club in a position to challenge Manchester United financially, domestically, is Manchester City, due to their different financial structure and ability to utilize the owner's status with commercial partners in the Middle East. Liverpool is a potential threat to United's leading financial position only if the club can deliver trophies and use that to leverage on its global fanbase and this seems feasible following the success in winning the Champions League in 2019.

Analysing financial statements isn't a straightforward task, but a forensic approach and a desire to determine the causal reasons behind movements in key indicators, and the consequences of such changes, is of value to anyone interested in the club financially. The easiest trap to fall into is to focus only on calculating numbers, ratios and trends without backing them up with comparative analysis and plausible, business derived explanations.

11

VALUING A FOOTBALL CLUB

This chapter examines the different approaches – part art, part science – used to value a club when it is sold. There's no "correct" price for a football club, just as there is no "correct" price for a football player, a house or a piece of art. This is due to the nature of what is being traded. There are some guidelines that help to narrow down prices to a realistic range and then it comes down to the negotiating skills of both parties, the extent of the need to sell and the ability of the buyer to finance the deal. Often buyers and sellers will use professional advisors to estimate a price for the club. Whilst a lot of time and effort can go into determining these values, they are potentially flawed for many clubs because of the elephant in the room that is the impact of relegation or promotion on a club's finances, especially in relation to the Premier League. Cynics might also suggest that some of the methods used by "professional" advisors are there to justify their exorbitant advisory fees, rather than to give an accurate measure of the true worth of a club.

Our case study will be Newcastle United, which, according to media reports, is up for sale, with its owner Mike Ashley allegedly looking for a price of £300–350 million.

Balance sheet value

The simplest way to value a club is to look at the net assets total in the balance sheet and use this as the figure. Newcastle's accounts at 30 June 2018 (see Table 11.1) show the club had net assets (assets less liabilities) of just over £8 million. The footnotes to the accounts also show that the club owed their owner Mike Ashley £111 million in loans on top of this sum, so a buyer would presumably have to repay him these loans too, which would take the net total to £119 million.

A balance sheet valuation method is a poor one to use. We've already established that the balance sheet tends to vastly undervalue players. This is because some players are not shown as assets in the accounts due to being recruited via the club academy system at a zero cost, or Bosman transfers with no purchase fee but a potential sale value if the

Table 11.1 Consolidated statement of financial position, year ended 30 June 2018, Newcastle United

	Note	2018 £000	2018 £000	2017 £000	2017 £000
Fixed assets					
Intangible assets	12		**93,965**		93,500
Tangible assets	13		**62,206**		62,406
			156,171		155,906
Current assets					
Stocks	15	21		16	
Debtors: amounts failing due within one year	16	46,122		42,570	
Debtors: amounts failing due after one year	16	23,973		40,932	
Cash at bank and in hind	17	33,831		–	
		103,947		83,518	
Creditors: amounts falling due within one year	18	**(101,066)**		(86,315)	
Net current assets/(Liabilities)			**2,881**		(2,797)
Total assets less current liabilities			**159,052**		153,109
Creditors: amounts falling due after more than one year	19		**(117,216)**		(118,412)
Provisions for liabilities	23		**(12,244)**		(21,997)
Deferred income	25		**(21,334)**		(23,041)
Net assets/(liabilities)			**8,258**		(10,341)
Capital and reserves					
Called up share capital	26		**6,655**		6,655
Share premium account	27		**68,944**		68,944
Capital redemption reserve	27		**831**		831
Retained earnings	27		**(68,172)**		(86,771)
			8,258		(10,341)

Source: Newcastle United Ltd

player has joined and signed a long-term contract, or increasing in value due to market inflation. Assets such as the stadium tend to be undervalued too, as the accountants measure them at the original cost figure, which may be decades old, less depreciation, rather than the current market price. Other assets, such as the loyalty of fans in renewing season tickets, the brand value of the club and its database of customers/fans and their buying habits in relation to football are also ignored in the balance sheet. In addition, the balance sheet only shows the assets and liabilities of a club on a particular date, so if the valuation is months later the balance sheet will be out of date and not reflect subsequent changes in the club finances.

Stock market values

The value of a company on the stock market at any one time is the value of a single share multiplied by the number of shares. Therefore, for Manchester United in October 2019 the club had 164 million shares with a price of $16.03 each, giving a total market value of $2.63 billion. This calculation is fine for someone looking to make a small investment by buying a few shares, but someone wanting to control the club would need to acquire at least half of the voting shares and it could be that some existing owners are reluctant to relinquish their shares. The only way to persuade them to sell would be to offer them extra money over and above the current share price. Therefore, the current market price of the club tends to undervalue the value for a takeover scenario.

There is an additional issue for the football industry in that relatively few clubs have shares that are bought and sold on the stock market. Apart from Manchester United, it is only Arsenal amongst Premier League clubs whose shares have recently been on a stock exchange. Arsenal's shares however ceased to be traded when their majority shareholder Stan Kroenke increased his investment beyond 90 per cent in the summer of 2018, which allowed him under UK rules to remove the club from the stock exchange. Most football clubs who have had their shares traded on a listed stock exchange have subsequently departed because the compliance costs and demands of the market have typically exceeded the benefits of having access to fresh investment.

Comparative sales values

If you were about to buy a house one way of working out an appropriate price to pay for it is to look at the prices for similar sized properties. If the houses that are being compared are nearby then a buyer can start to get a feel for the right price to pay. The houses might be slightly different, in terms of the number of bedrooms, size of garden, date of most recent decorations and so on, but it's a starting point. If the houses are in different geographical areas, then it becomes more difficult. A 700 square metre apartment in Central London or New York will command a far higher price than a similar sized one in a less affluent location, such as Derby or the American Midwest.

Adopting a similar approach when valuing a football club has the same pros and cons. For example, a club that has been in the top six of the Premier League for a number of seasons will command a higher price than one that has just been promoted to that division for the first time. This is because the club that has just been promoted has a far higher chance of being relegated back to lower divisions, where broadcast and commercial income streams are far lower. Even if the clubs are in the same division and in close proximity, there still may be significantly different valuations. London-based Arsenal, with a relatively new 60,000 capacity stadium and regular qualification for European

Table 11.2 Prices paid for English football clubs, 2016–19

Club	Date	Price (£'m)	Amount bought	Division
Huddersfield	May 2019	38	75%	Championship
Arsenal	August 2018	1,833	100%*	Premier League
Barnsley	December 2017	20	80%	Championship
Southampton	August 2017	210	80%	Premier League
Everton	February 2016	87.5	49.9%	Premier League
West Bromwich Albion	August 2016	150	100%	Premier League
Aston Villa	June 2016	76	100%	Championship
Wolverhampton Wanderers	July 2016	45	100%	Championship

*Owner already owned 65% of the club.

competition, would command a much higher price than a small London club such as Crystal Palace, whose stadium at Selhurst Park only holds 25,000 fans, despite Palace having had some successful seasons in the Premier League.

The football club market is quite active, with many deals negotiated over the course of the past decade or so. Trying to find a definitive price for deals done can be challenging as the sums involved are not always publicized, but we can use values quoted in the media as a guideline.

Table 11.2 shows the prices paid in recent years for English football clubs. There is a wide range of prices and it doesn't provide much comfort for a prospective purchaser, but it is possible to perhaps choose a price of one or more clubs that are similar in size, stature and recent history to Newcastle. In the list perhaps Everton and Southampton are the best choices. Both are provincial clubs who have been in the Premier League for a few years (and of course in the case of Everton, never relegated). Neither are a perfect match, as Newcastle have a larger ground capacity, but with matchday income being the smallest element of total income for most clubs, it's a starting point.

Southampton's owners sold 80 per cent to a new investor, Chinese businessman Gao Jisheng, for £210 million, which gives the club an overall value of £262 million. Everton's new owner Farhad Moshiri paid £87.5 million for just under half the club, which gives a total value of £175 million. The latter value may appear low, but the transaction took place about 18 months before that of Southampton and football club inflation, just like football transfer fee and wage inflation, has seen recent sharp rises.

Comparative profit or loss account multiples

Football is an unusual industry in that some clubs are bought for vanity rather than profit-making purposes. Even so, regardless of the motives of prospective owners, they might be keen to buy a club based on its ability to generate income. Until a few years ago this

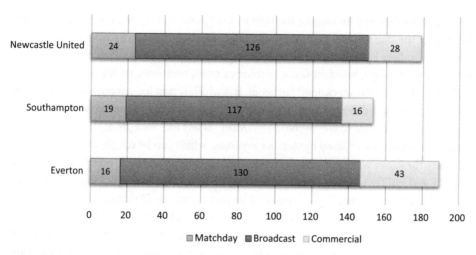

Figure 11.1 Everton, Southampton and Newcastle revenue 2017/18

would have been folly in the Premier League because so many clubs were losing money. The last couple of broadcasting deals, combined with the cost controls associated with various forms of Financial Fair Play, have made a comparative profit-based valuation approach more valid. If we drop down into the Championship then this approach would not work, because almost every club in that division loses money.

If we look at the revenue figures in Figure 11.1 for all three clubs for 2017/18 we can see that Newcastle had total income of £179 million, Southampton £153 million and Everton £189 million. One way to value a club is to consider the price paid for the club as a multiple of total income. For Everton this is × 0.92 (£175 million divided by £189 million) and for Southampton it is × 1.71 (£262 million divided by £153 million). The Deloitte Sports Business Group, who are probably the most experienced team in the football finance industry, reported in 2008 that deals had gone through at between 1.5 and 2 times revenue, so Southampton's figure is well within that range while the Everton one is perhaps a little low because the owner only bought half of the club. We can then use these multiples to value Newcastle. This gives us a price range of £165 million using the Everton multiple (£179 million × 0.92) and £306 million using the Southampton multiple (£179 million × 1.71).

This clearly is a wide range of figures and the calculations would have produced different numbers too if it had added deals involving the likes of West Bromwich Albion or Crystal Palace into the equation. The valuer would use their judgement, experience and industry knowledge to consider which of the above two values is most appropriate. Southampton is the more recent deal and also involves an acquisition of a larger proportion of shares, for which buyers usually pay a premium, so perhaps this is a figure with which there would be more confidence.

Valuing a club using an income multiple is one option, but an investor would be ideally looking for the club to generate profit so the ability of a club to control costs is an alternative. The problem here is deciding which profit measure to use? When looking previously at the profit or loss account, we identified a number of profit measures, such as operating profit, EBIT, EBITDA, net profit, cleaned net profit, but which is best for valuation purposes? One approach is to use a different profit measure to generate a range of valuations and then discard any which give unusual/extreme values. Most valuers will use a pre-tax profit multiple to remove the distortions caused by club tax expenses, which can be volatile from year to year. Similarly, the valuer will use their judgement when calculating "cleaned" profit measures such as EBIT and EBITDA. This is because they have to decide whether or not unusual expenses or income should be classified as recurring or non-recurring. Different valuers may reach different conclusions, and this is why there is no one agreed figure for a club value.

In Figure 11.2, profit is adjusted for non-recurring and irregular items such as gains on player sales, redundancy costs, the costs of settling legal disputes and similar transactions. At first glance the numbers give an indication as to why Southampton was sold at such a premium price compared to Everton, as the club is far more profitable on an operating profit basis. It is not possible to calculate profit multiples for negative figures, so some of the above numbers immediately become redundant when looking at Southampton and Everton. Southampton made an operating profit including gains on player sales of £35.3 million. This gives a profit multiple of 7.42 (£262 million divided by £35.3 million). It's not possible to use a similar approach for Everton as the club made an operating loss that year after player sales. Multiply Newcastle's profits (including player sales) by 7.42 gives a value of £157 million. This seems low but could be explained by looking further at Southampton's accounts which reveal gains on player sales of £69 million in 2017/18, compared to Newcastle's £3.6 million.

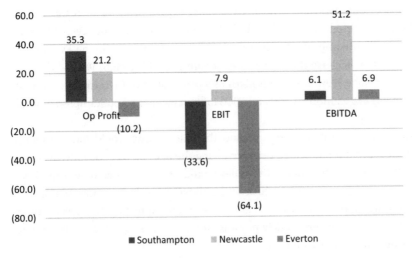

Figure 11.2 Everton, Southampton and Newcastle profit measures 2017/18

Southampton do have a reputation as a club that develops players and sells them at a profit, but it is unlikely they will be able to repeat such gains on player sales every year for the foreseeable future and maintain their Premier League status. Therefore, this valuation is perhaps best discarded. It is not possible to use an EBIT valuation multiple (which removes gains on player sales, and in the case of Everton, the cost of sacking manager Roberto Martinez) for either comparative club, as these figures are negative. A positive profit measure is required, which means using EBITDA multiples. These exclude not only the gain on player sales, but also the non-cash transfer fee amortisation cost from the profit or loss account.

Everton have an EBITDA multiple of 25.36 (£175 million divided by £6.9 million) and Southampton 42.95 (£262 million divided by £6.1 million). Applying these multiples to Newcastle's EBITDA profit of £51.2 million using Everton as a basis results in a value of £1,298 million (£51.2 million × 25.36) and Southampton £2,199 million (£51.2m × 42.95). These calculations are clearly nonsensical, but further investigation suggests some housekeeping is perhaps needed. What the calculations should do is make the valuer curious as to why the figures appear so high.

The financial factor that correlates best with final league position for a club in the Premier League is player costs. This makes sense as it is players who win and lose matches and better players command higher transfer fees and wages. Newcastle under Mike Ashley were relatively low wage payers in the Premier League.

Figures 11.3 and 11.4 show Premier League wages levels and the clubs' final league position in brackets after the team name. Whilst even at the lower end of the wage table players are still earning million pound plus salaries, on a relative basis, if you pay

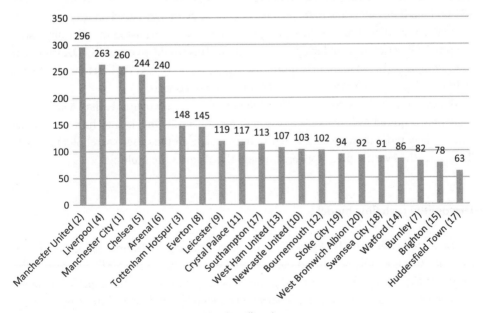

Figure 11.3 Premier League wages 2017/18 (£ millions)

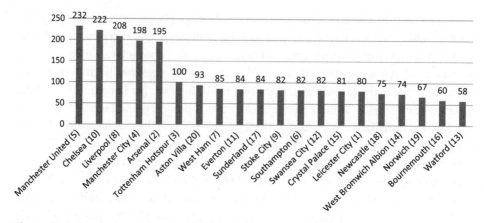

Figure 11.4 Premier League wages 2015/16 (£ millions)

low wages, you often end up in a relegation fight. The table for 2015/16 also highlights Leicester's amazing achievement in winning the Premier League that season. Newcastle's wage bill in 2017/18 was the seventh lowest in the Premier League and in 2015/16 it was the fifth lowest. If Newcastle could be certain of Premier League survival with such a wage policy, then the very high looking valuations using EBITDA multiples could be justified. Newcastle's wage bill was about £20 million lower than the median for the division in both seasons. If we therefore added £20 million to Newcastle's costs, reflecting the wage and amortisation cost that would give them a more competitive playing squad and a greater chance of being a long-term Premier League club, then EBITDA would fall to £31 million. If further adjustments were made for prize money based on league position relative to the other clubs and previous player write-downs whilst in the Championship the previous season it would drop to £11 million. This would give an EBITDA valuation of £472 million (based on Southampton) or £279 million (based on Everton). These put Ashley's alleged asking price of £300–350 million into context.

The Everton based value is also distorted because the new owner Farhad Moshiri initially only acquired 49.9 per cent of the club for £87.5 million. He may have had to pay substantially more than twice that figure to persuade all the other shareholders to sell. Therefore, the Everton price appears low and this distorts the multiple.

Discounted cash flow model

A discounted cash flow (DCF) model is based on valuing the future cash generated by the club. This is another valuation measure that was invalid for most EPL clubs until the Premier League only recently started generating large cash sums. The approach in practice can be very complex, but can be stripped down to the following four steps.

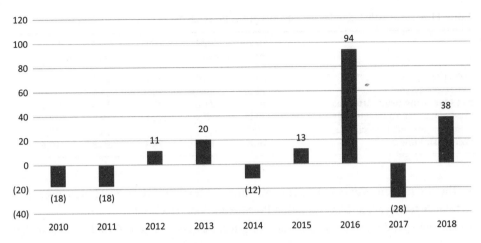

Figure 11.5 Newcastle United player trading, 2011–19 (£ millions)

Step 1: Calculate the free cash flow (FCF)

Free cash flow (FCF) represents the residual cash after paying the day-to-day running expenses of the club (except for finance costs) as well as the cash invested in player transfers and infrastructure spending. The cash that is left over belongs to debt and equity investors and is called FCF. These cash flows are estimated for about five to ten years into the future, using different growth rates and scenarios. Such an approach is fraught with difficulty, as the one thing that is certain about the future is that it is uncertain. This is especially true for a club such as Newcastle, where the relegation risk under Mike Ashley has been high and it cannot be certain in which division it will be playing in future years.

Looking at Newcastle's investment in player transfers under Mike Ashley since 2008 shows the erratic nature of spending on the club's key investment asset category. Between 2008–15 Ashley had a net annual spend on player signings of only £702,000 a year (see Figure 11.5). It was then a case of too little, too late in 2015/16 to rectify the situation as Newcastle were relegated despite spending over £100 million on player signings in the season. Once in the Championship in 2016/17 Newcastle reverted to their previous cautious net spending approach.

Nevertheless, an attempt can be made to estimate future cash flows based on the following working assumptions:

1. The club will finish each season in fourteenth position in the Premier League;
2. Recurring operating profits before player trading (EBIT) is £25 million for 2018/19 and will grow by 4 per cent a year;

Table 11.3 Newcastle United free cash flow projections, 2019–23

	2019 £'m	2020 £'m	2021 £'m	2022 £'m	2023 £'m
Recurring operating profits	25.0	26.0	27.0	28.1	29.2
Tax on profits	(4.3)	(4.4)	(4.6)	(4.8)	(5.0)
Net Operating profit after tax	**20.8**	**21.6**	**22.4**	**23.3**	**24.3**
Expenditure on players and PPE	(20.0)	(20.8)	(21.6)	(22.5)	(23.4)
Amortisation and depreciation	16.0	16.6	17.3	18.0	18.7
Free Cash Flow	**16.8**	**17.4**	**18.1**	**18.8**	**19.6**

3. The tax rate on profits is 18 per cent. After subtracting tax on EBIT this gives us a finance term called "Net Operating Profit After Tax" (NOPAT);
4. The net spend on players and other long-term assets will be £20 million in 2018/19 and will grow by 4 per cent a season;
5. Depreciation and amortisation will be 80 per cent of the net spend on players and other long-term assets each year. This figure is added back to profit because it is a non-cash item.
6. There will be no change in other operational assets and liabilities (inventories and other merchandise, receivables, payables, etc).

Sticking all of these assumptions (which are, of course, there to be questioned, especially by Newcastle fans familiar with Mike Ashley's parsimonious spending history) into a spreadsheet gives the free cash flow totals in Table 11.3.

Step 2: Calculate the weighted average cost of capital (WACC)

One problem with looking at future cash flow is that £1 earned in 2023 is worth less than £1 earned today. It is therefore necessary to adjust future cash flows considering that the further away the date is for the cash to be received, the lower the value today. Investors are either shareholders (equity) or lenders (debt). WACC is the minimum return that the combination of shareholders and lenders would expect for investing in the club.

Keeping things simple, lenders tend to be willing to accept a lower return on their investment than equity investors. This is because lenders take a lower risk as they usually have some form of security, in the form of a mortgage or similar, in respect of the sums advanced. The WACC takes into consideration the proportion of the investment that comes from each party. For the sake of simplicity, a WACC of 10 per cent has been chosen for assessing Newcastle. The rate would increase if the investment risk increases, such as might be the case if there was a high probability of relegation. Each year the value of the cash flows therefore decrease by a compound 10 per cent. We calculate the impact on the cash flows by multiplying by a "discount factor", calculated as $1/(1 + WACC)^n$ each

Table 11.4 Newcastle United present value of FCFs

	2019 £'m	2020 £'m	2021 £'m	2022 £'m	2023 £'m
Free Cash Flow	16.8	17.4	18.1	18.8	19.6
Discount factor	0.91	0.83	0.75	0.68	0.62
Present value of FCF's	15.2	14.4	13.6	12.9	12.2

year, where *n* is the number of years from the present date. This gives us what we call the present value of the FCFs (see Table 11.4). If all of the FCFs are added together the total cash flow sum is £68.3 million, which clearly is far too low for a value of Newcastle United, but a further calculation is required called the "terminal value".

Step 3: Calculate the terminal value (TV)

The club will generate free cash flows from 2024 onwards, but it's not feasible to create a spreadsheet that carries on for an infinite number of years. The terminal value is calculated as a profit multiple (usually of EBIT or EBITDA) in the final year of the analysis. The multiple is usually based on the sale prices for other clubs that have been sold in recent times. There is a lot of experience to be had from looking at similar deals and an equal amount of guesswork that goes into calculating a terminal value multiple. The terminal value total is then discounted to a present value using the discount factor in the final year of the analysis.

For Newcastle a terminal value of seven times EBITDA has been chosen. Seven was chosen as it ties in with the figure for similar deals for clubs in previous years. EBITDA in 2023 is £48 million (recurring (EBIT) profit of £29.2 million plus depreciation and amortisation of £18.7 million) and so the terminal value is £335.7 million (£48 million × 7). Then discount the terminal value using the discount rate of 0.62 in 2023 to arrive at a figure of £208.5 million.

Step 4: Calculate the total value

The total value of the club is the present value of the FCFs from Step 2 – £68.3 million – plus the present value of the terminal value in Step 3 – £208.5 million – which together come to a total figure of £276.7 million.

The above steps are very much an oversimplified summary of DCF valuation but are aimed at showing the process that the valuation team would take in arriving at a final figure. Depending on the assumptions used in the calculations then the value of the club would be higher or lower. In practice an analyst would run a series of calculations based on different assumptions to get a range of prices.

The Markham Multivariate Model

All of the valuation methods seen to date have used approaches taken in other industries and then applied them to football. The Markham Multivariate Model (MMM) is a specific valuation measure devised for football clubs by Tom Markham, on whose PhD thesis it is based. Dr Markham is presently the head of business development at Sports Interactive, the makers of the Football Manager videogame. However, prior to taking up this role he wanted to devise a specific formula for valuing Premier League football clubs. Aware of the limitations of traditional valuation methods, especially with so many clubs not generating positive profits or cash flows, he decided to use some specific football metrics instead. He looked at the quoted prices for a number of deals, identified the key differences in terms of the clubs being sold and the prices for the transactions, and arrived at the following valuation formula:

(Revenue + net assets) × (net profit + revenue)/revenue × (stadium capacity %)/ wage ratio %

The formula takes into consideration some of the key drivers of football club success. Although it appears complicated, it is relatively easy to calculate. It is worth breaking the formula down into its components to show the relative importance of each issue.

(Revenue + net assets)

A club needs revenue in order to pay its key costs, especially player wages, therefore revenue contributes to the ability of the club to be successful, as without it clubs would not be able to create a competitive advantage over their rivals. The net assets of the club (assets less liabilities) consist mainly of the stadium and the playing squad. These provide the infrastructure and the product that fans (and viewers) come to watch.

There is, however, a problem when it comes to owner loans. Should these be treated as liabilities or equity? Loans from banks are always treated as liabilities, but Newcastle owner Mike Ashley has lent the club £144 million *interest free*, so the loans are not impacting upon profitability as no finance costs are being incurred. As such it could be argued they are similar in nature to the owner buying shares in the club and the club not paying a dividend. Other clubs, such as West Ham, have owners who have lent money, but do charge interest. David Gold and David Sullivan, the West Ham owners lent the club £45 million in 2012 but have since charged over £14 million in interest on those loans. These loans would certainly be better treated as liabilities. Ultimately there is no correct treatment, it is a case of using experience and judgement, or calculating two values, one as a liability and one as equity and seeing the significance of the difference.

In the calculations below a cautious approach has been adopted and the loans have been treated as liabilities.

(Net profit + revenue)/revenue

This gives a multiplier effect to the (revenue plus net assets) figure above. If the club is making profits, then this figure will be greater than 1 and represents additional resources that can be invested into new players. There is a case for perhaps tweaking the net profit figure to take into consideration non-recurring events such as legal settlements with kit suppliers or redundancy payments to managers that have been sacked. Profit is also impacted by gains on player sales, which tend to be volatile, so here a three-year average of player sale profits is perhaps more appropriate as this also ties in with some of the Financial Fair Play rules. If the club is making a loss the figure will be less than 1. When this is multiplied by (revenue plus net assets) it will reduce the total club value, as this reflects the drain on resources caused by being a loss-making business.

Stadium capacity percentage

This figure shows how many tickets clubs sell as a proportion of the capacity of the stadium. This shows how efficiently the club is utilizing its asset that generates income. For most clubs in the Premier League nearly all tickets are sold, so this figure is close to 1 and has little impact on the value. For those clubs who have alienated their fans and so are not selling out their stadia the club value falls.

Wage ratio percentage

The wage ratio is the wage bill divided by income. The lower the figure, the greater the control over costs of the club. This can however be a double-edged sword. The Big Six clubs tend to have a relatively low wage control percentage figure. This is because they have the benefit of increased income from the UEFA Champions League and Europa Cup competitions. This also makes these clubs more attractive to commercial partners, as their products and services are likely to be seen by a wider audience when European matches are watched live and on television. This extra income allows these clubs to pay higher wages, but they can also retain some of the income for other purposes.

As previously discussed, by signing players for relatively low fees, Mike Ashley has also managed to reduce Newcastle's wage/income ratio from over 90 per cent to less than 60 per cent. Under normal business circumstances this would be applauded. In the world of Premier League football this is a dangerous ploy, as the players recruited, on wages that are not always as generous as those of other clubs, were not marquee signings. The recruitment of non-household names such as Remy Cabella (£9 million), Siem De Jong (£8 million) and Emmanuel Riviers (£5.5 million) failed to light up the Premier League, or, more importantly, failed to prevent Newcastle from dropping into the Championship in 2017. This strategy of keeping player-related costs relatively low impacted upon Newcastle's league position and was a contributory factor towards the club being relegated twice to date under Ashley's tenure.

The MMM calculation

The components of the MMM are therefore as follows:

Revenue + net assets (£178.7 million + £8.3 million) = £187 million, this includes a loan of £111 million from the owner within net assets.

(Adjusted net profit + revenue)/revenue = (£18.6 million + £178.7 million)/ £178.7 million = 1.10

Stadium capacity % = 51,992/52,354 = 99.3%

Wage ratio % = 57.8%

This gives a MMM total of 187 × 1.10 × 99.3% / 57.8% = £353 million.

If the Ashley loans are treated as equity, the model would produce a value of £464 million, which seems disproportionately high so is best ignored. Alternatively, an adjustment could be made to Newcastle's profitability to take into consideration that under Mike Ashley the club was paying wage levels that increased the likelihood of relegation and this would reduce the value.

The MMM has some merits, the key one being that it is relatively quick and simple to calculate and also often produces some very accurate figures. When Stan Kroenke bought out rival Alisher Usmanov's 30 per cent stake in Arsenal in summer 2018 for £550 million, it valued the club as a whole at £1.83 billion. Three months earlier the University of Liverpool Football Industry Group valued all the clubs in the Premier League using the MMM (see Figure 11.6) and estimated Arsenal's value at £1.82 billion. The MMM model can also be relatively easily tweaked. One concern with it, however, is the disproportionate impact that player sales in a single year have on profits, so by taking the average profit for a period of three to five years gives a more balanced total. If this is applied to Newcastle over three years, the value is estimated at £383 million.

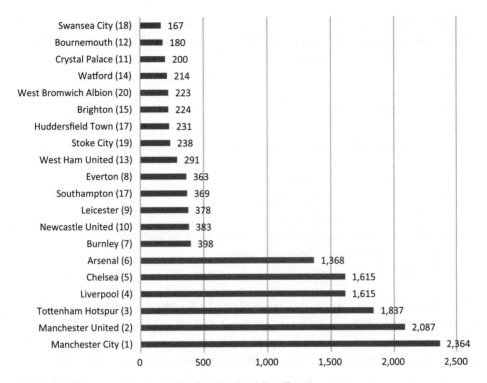

Figure 11.6 Premier League MMM values, 2017/18 (£ millions)

The MMM model highlights the struggles that ambitious clubs will have if they want to break into the Big Six given that these clubs appear to have such a large financial advantage over the rest of the division. The MMM approach does need to be treated with caution, as do all models, and some figures do appear anomalous, such as Manchester City being measured at a higher sum than Manchester United, and Burnley being valued as the highest of the non-Big Six clubs. What the values do highlight is the overall quality of management at the clubs involved and prompt questions as to why some clubs' values appear higher or lower than one would expect.

In the case of Manchester City, a combination of unusually lucrative commercial deals, low employee numbers and zero debt are all contributors to the value of £2.36 billion. The sale of 10 per cent of the City group in November 2019, which includes the other clubs in New York and elsewhere, for £370 million suggests that City's valuation is not as unreasonable as some critics have suggested. Manchester United are perhaps weighed down by having to pay out large sums in the form of finance costs and shareholder dividends, neither of which benefit the playing side of the club, as well as a recent history of poor investment decisions in terms of player recruitment that has left the club with expensive assets who contributed little to the playing success of the club. In respect of Burnley the value highlights that the club has been managed extremely efficiently, with the owners not needing to contribute financially, yet still achieved a Europa League place on the back of a successful season under Sean Dyche in 2017/18.

Summary of values

Listing the results of all the methods gives us the following valuations for Newcastle:

Balance sheet value: £119 million
Revenue multiples: £165–306 million
EBIT multiple: not possible
EBITDA multiple (adjusted for higher wages): £279–472 million
Discounted cash flow valuation: £277 million
MMM valuation: £353–383 million.

Clearly the methods produce a wide range of figures, but there is a broad consensus of values in the £275–300 million range (see Table 11.5). This is what is usually called a "quick and dirty" analysis but it gives a potential buyer an indication of price before they decide to take the issue further. Anyone who was serious about buying the club would normally request to see the club finances in far more detail than those figures available publicly. This would allow them to determine an offer with greater accuracy. And any interested parties would have to sign a non-disclosure agreement to keep the information private. According to media reports, the most recent offers for Newcastle have been in the £250–300 million range, with some sums conditional upon future performance and other issues, but these were rejected by Mike Ashley. As can be seen from all the models examined, the figures are mainly assumption based and so must be treated with a degree of caution.

In September 2019 a document from an American consortium, GACP Capital Sports, was leaked to a number of journalists (including myself). This valued the club at £300 million and the 46 page prospectus to potential investors was based on some of the methods detailed in this chapter.

Table 11.5 Summary of Newcastle values 2017/18 £'m

	Low	*High*
MMM	353	383
DCF	277	277
EBITDA	279	472
Operating profit	157	157
Revenue	165	306

12

OWNERSHIP MODELS: LOVE, VANITY AND INSANITY

Why buy a football club? Most businesses are there to make profits for their owners, but football is a unique industry because the investments made are frequently emotional or political instead of just financial. Ask a fan what is meant by success and their focus would be on trophies and on-field performances, not a financial return on investment. No two owners are exactly the same, but we can identify some broad ownership models that help us understand how clubs work, or not work, financially.

The local fan made good

Ask a football fan what would they do if they won a huge sum on the lottery and many would reply that they would buy the club they have supported all their life. And for some clubs this is effectively what's happened, but instead of a windfall the fan has been successful in business and so has been in a position to purchase the team they've always supported.

In 2017 Huddersfield Town and Brighton & Hove Albion were both promoted to the Premier League for the first time. This would not have been achieved except for the money and devotion of local fan-owners. At Huddersfield Dean Hoyle had followed the club since a boy. He ran a successful greetings card company and joined Huddersfield's board in April 2008, when the club finished tenth in League One, with matchday crowds averaging less than 10,000. Initially he bought 30 per cent of Huddersfield but Hoyle then took over as chairman at the start of 2009/10 and bought the remaining shares from the previous owner. Hoyle then sold his greetings card company to venture capitalists and used some of the proceeds to improve the club he loves. Since then Dean Hoyle has lent the club over £50 million, as well as effectively writing off £6.5 million of debt by converting loans into shares.

As can be seen from Figure 12.1 Hoyle's approach was incremental, investing a few million from year to year. Firstly, there was promotion to the Championship in 2012 and then a period of consolidation before his perseverance was rewarded in 2017 when Town

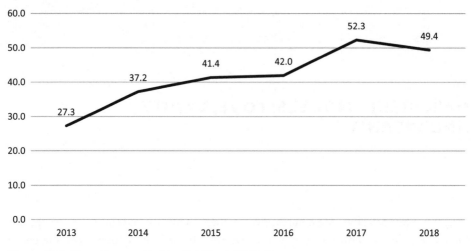

Figure 12.1 Owner loans to Huddersfield Town, 2013–18

were promoted on penalties at Wembley in the Championship play-off final. Hoyle was in tears as Town scored the final penalty to secure promotion, which is how, from a fan's perspective, it should be. He was then quoted as saying "Dreams really do come true … I never thought I would ever see Huddersfield Town as a Premiership club. I think there were many supporters who also felt the same, but believe you me we are". Huddersfield's first successful season in the Premier League allowed him to recover a small amount of his debt investment in the club, but without him they would never have hosted matches again against top flight opposition. After two seasons in the Premier League and with his own health concerns to deal with too, Dean Hoyle sold Huddersfield Town for an estimated £50 million following their relegation back to the Championship. Fans gave him a rousing reception at the final home match in the Premier League as appreciation for all that he had done for both them and the club.

Tony Bloom at Brighton took a similar path. His grandfather and uncle were both former board members at the club and after a successful career in the betting industry where he used his skills as a maths graduate, he took a controlling interest in the club in 2009. At that time the club's stadium was a converted athletics stadium with portacabins for changing rooms and more than half the seats uncovered, meaning that fans had to sit and deal with all weather conditions. The club had applied for a site for a new stadium, which had been rejected initially. And funding for the stadium was also a problem. Having also spent time as a professional poker player (nicknamed "The Lizard") Bloom, if he had assessed the probabilities at this stage, would no doubt not have involved himself with the club's development. Instead he thought as a fan, underwrote the losses of Brighton at their old ground and then financed the construction of the Amex Community Stadium

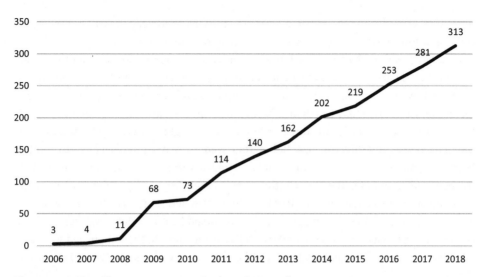

Figure 12.2 Tony Bloom investment in Brighton & Hove Albion, 2006–18

at an initial cost of over £90 million and then provided further funding for its expansion and a new training ground. By the time the club was promoted to the Premier League his total investment, in the form of both shares and loans, was £280 million and even the riches received therein weren't sufficient as Bloom put more money into the club to fund further infrastructure spending (see Figure 12.2).

The advantage of having a genuine fan as an owner is that if they do lend money to the club it is likely to be interest free. This can save the club millions of pounds in finance costs in future years. Both Dean Hoyle and Tony Bloom have never charged their local clubs any interest. Not all fan-owners are as benevolent and this is reflected in their popularity with those who watch their teams. Talk to a Brighton or Huddersfield fan and they will have nothing but praise for their owners.

The downside of having such a relationship is that the owner-fan may have a limited amount of money to invest. Whilst being a millionaire is beyond the wealth of most regular fans, the sums required in the top leagues to keep a club afloat are likely to challenge even these people. In addition, having a fan in charge can be counterproductive as decisions are sometimes made from the heart and not the head. When the owner's money runs out they may sell the club simply to get rid of it and not pay too much attention to whoever takes over. Bolton Wanderers were for many years owned by Eddie Davies, a lifelong Wanderers' fan who made his fortune from electrical devices. Under Davies Bolton thrived for many years in the Premier League and he underwrote losses every year as the club recruited players such as Nicolas Anelka, Jay-Jay Okocha, Ivan Campo and Youri Djorkaeff and finished in the top eight of the Premier League four seasons in a row. Bolton were then relegated to the Championship in 2012 but the financial losses continued despite being in receipt of parachute payments.

In failing health and with limited funds Davies put the club up for sale, but there were few interested parties in a club that had accumulated total losses of £189 million. In desperation Davies wrote off £175 million owed to him and sold the club in 2016 for £1 to former player Dean Holdsworth and Ken Anderson, the latter having been previously banned from being a company director in the UK for eight years, but who still satisfied the EFL's "owner and director" test. Bolton then went from one financial crisis to another, borrowing money at exorbitant rates, before Holdsworth left, and the club was solely in the hands of Anderson. The club continued to struggle financially under Anderson and went into administration early in 2019 with tales of unpaid staff having to use foodbanks and no hot water at the training ground due to unpaid heating bills. Anderson claimed, correctly, not to have been paid a salary whilst at the club, but still managed to charge Wanderers £525,000 for consultancy fees (the club also paid his son £125,000 for similar services).

Bolton were relegated in 2018/19 from the Championship and were unable to fulfil their fixtures that season as the players went on strike over unpaid wages. The club was then penalised ten points at the start of the following season for going into administration and initially had to play fixtures with youth players as they were unable to offer contracts for senior professionals whilst under the management of the administrators, who finally managed to sell Bolton to new owners in August 2019.

The butterflies

Some owners move from club to club. West Ham United are owned by David Sullivan and David Gold, who at times have had a toxic relationship with the club's fanbase. The pair bought West Ham in January 2010 after the previous Icelandic owners had problems due to the global recession and Iceland's collapsing banking industry. Gold and Sullivan had previously owned Birmingham City Football Club but sold it in 2009. Under FA rules a person cannot control two clubs in the same country, so this sale allowed them to acquire West Ham in due course.

Gold and Sullivan both lent money to West Ham, which in the end totalled £45 million. These loans came at an annual interest rate of 6 per cent, which was reduced to 4 per cent in 2017. The owners claimed that this was good value for the club as prior to their involvement the club was paying interest at 10 per cent. The interest was not paid on the loans until August 2017 when they received £10 million as a part settlement, but millions more were still outstanding. Gold and Sullivan claimed that they were significant losers in terms of the loan arrangements because they had to cash-in other investments that were earning a far higher return than the 6 per cent they charged to West Ham to find

Table 12.1 West Ham group turnover by revenue class, 2016/17

3 Group Turnover

An analysis of turnover by class of business is provided below. All turnover is derived in the United Kingdom.

	Group	
	2017 £000	2016 £000
Match receipts and related football activities	28,606	26,923
Broadcast and central sponsorship distributions	119,322	86,711
Commercial activities	25,828	19,035
Retail and merchandising	9,584	9,394
	183,340	142,063

Source: West Ham United Ltd

the £45 million to loan the club. This is one of the reasons why fans are unhappy. If, as claimed, the owners are lifelong fans themselves, it seems inconsistent for them to profit from their involvement through lending and charging interest on their loans. The move from the Boleyn Ground to the London Stadium has also caused resentment. The hopes of the West Ham fanbase when the club moved to the 2012 Olympic venue, the London Stadium, were dashed as the dream they were sold of the club being able to challenge the established Premier League elite failed to materialize.

As can be seen from Table 12.1, an extract from the accounts, the move from the 35,000 capacity Boleyn Ground to the supposed 66,000 capacity (disputes with the stadium's owners initially restricted this to 57,000) London Stadium should have resulted in a surge of matchday income, but instead it only increased by 6 per cent to £28.6 million, a fraction of other major clubs in London such as Arsenal (£100 million) Chelsea (£66 million) and Spurs (£45 million). Without substantial extra money coming from the move to the new stadium, the attitude of many fans is that they have sacrificed their beloved Boleyn Ground for a larger but soulless home which was never designed for football in the first place. It would appear that for all the comments from the two owners, they are keen to extract a return from their investment, which is an accusation that could not be levelled at the likes of Hoyle and Bloom. To add to the fans' sense of injustice, the profits on the sale of the Boleyn Ground have never been fully explained as the property appeared to pass through the books of more than one company before finally being acquired by the Barrett Group.

The accounts of West Ham's Holding Company, WH Holding Limited, showed a profit on the sale of the Boleyn Ground of £8.7 million. Elsewhere in the accounts (see Table 12.2) there is a disposal of freehold property at a net book value of £30 million (£39.1 million cost less £9.1 million depreciation). Putting these together gives sale proceeds for the stadium of £38.7 million.

Table 12.2 Notes to financial statements year ended 31 May 2017, WH Holding Ltd

12 Tangible Assets – Group

	Freehold land & buildings £000	Plant, fittings & equipment £000	Motor vehicles £000	Total £000
Cost or valuation				
1 June 2016	51,836	19,786	86	71,708
Additions	5,885	2,205	–	8,090
Disposal	(39,109)	(8,211)	–	(47,320)
31 May 2017	18,612	13,780	86	32,478
Accumulated depreciation				
1 June 2016	9,354	15,527	79	24,960
Charge for the year	723	735	5	1,463
Disposal	(9,112)	(8,211)	–	(17,323)
31 May 2017	965	8,051	84	9,100

Source: W H Holding Limted

The sale was made to a company called the Galliard group, who appeared to have excellent credentials. West Ham vice chair Karren Brady said in a press release at the time:

> We opted to reach an agreement with Galliard because they are a local London developer and employer with origins in East London [...] We know they are committed to working closely with the local community and Newham council on proposals to transform the site into a residential and retail village, which will benefit the local community and East London's regional economy ... The deal demonstrates that we have been true to our word by securing the regeneration of two areas of East London through our move to the Olympic Stadium in 2016 [...] In addition, and most importantly for us, we can see that Galliard are passionate about working with West Ham United to engage their supporters to help deliver a fitting legacy that will honour the tradition of the famous ground [...] We are confident that West Ham United fans will be excited about their vision and the way they plan to respect more than 100 years of West Ham history at Upton Park.[2]

At the time of the transaction this looked to be a good deal for the club and the community. Further investigation however shows that the Boleyn Ground appeared to be subsequently sold on to BDW Limited, part of Barratt Developments Plc, based in Leicester. The paper trail is difficult to follow, but a company called Boleyn Phoenix Limited, which

2. See https://www.theguardian.com/football/2014/feb/10/west-ham-sell-upton-park-olympic-stadium.

is part owned by Galliard produced a profit or loss account in which it had sales of £60 million on a property that cost close to £40 million. This appears to be the Boleyn Ground. Defenders of Gold and Sullivan would point out that they did their best to secure the best price via a sealed bid auction. Boleyn Phoenix Limited bid cleverly and West Ham were potentially £20 million worse off as a result. There is nothing to suggest any wrongdoing by the West Ham board, but it would appear the sale price for the Boleyn Ground could have been negotiated higher.

The trophy asset

You are extremely wealthy, have a huge yacht, mansions, private jet and all the trappings of such a lifestyle, so why not add a football club to your portfolio of trophy assets? Football clubs, especially those in the top divisions, add kudos, recognition and glamour to an individual's standing due to their scarcity value and constant media attention. Not only are you incredibly rich but you own an asset that is the focus of ceaseless news and social media coverage. The advantage of having such an owner is that they may be willing to provide the club with sufficient cash to elevate it to positions that were previously unachievable. The biggest downside is that if things don't go to plan, they may lose interest and stop backing the club.

In 2003 the then unknown 36-year-old Roman Abramovich bought Chelsea for £59.3 million as well as taking on an estimated £80 million of the club's debts. The club previously had only won the top division title once, in 1954/55. Jose Mourinho was recruited as manager in 2004 and given a transfer budget that was far greater than that of his predecessors.

Figure 12.3 shows that in the season before Abramovich's arrival Chelsea spent only £1.2 million on new players, but in the first three seasons after he acquired the club this

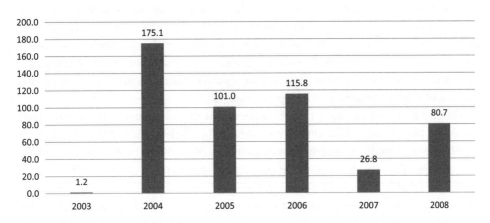

Figure 12.3 Chelsea player signings, 2003–08 (£ millions)

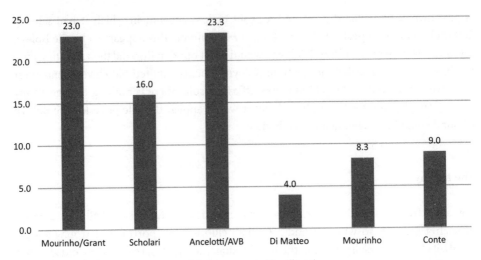

Figure 12.4 Chelsea recent managerial change costs (£ millions)

rocketed to £392 million, which brought with it two Premier League titles. The downside with a club being a rich person's plaything is that the owner is not answerable to anyone apart from themselves as they have total control of the club. This manifested itself in Abramovich's case by sacking the manager after a few bad results, albeit with the consolation for the manager of a large payoff.

Chelsea have had 13 managerial appointments since Abramovich bought the club and this has proved to be costly for the club and owner (see Figure 12.4). It is suspected that the figure for Carlo Ancelotti of £23.3 million may include the payoff that Chelsea made to Villas-Boas's former club, Porto, of £13.3 million to release him from his contract as manager in June 2011. Antonio Conte, who was successful in winning the Premier League in his first season in charge in 2016/17, was then sacked a year later at an estimated cost of £9 million. Since acquiring Chelsea Abramovich has invested over £1.1 billion in the club, mainly in the form of loans. His wealth has transformed the club from an occasional cup winner to a member of the Premier League elite. The money injected by Abramovich has been interest free which has allowed a succession of managers to invest in the playing squad and deliver domestic and European trophies.

Another downside of being a trophy asset is that the owner may want to have their say in the playing side of the club. Some signings by Chelsea under Abramovich, such as 29-year-old Ukrainian Andriy Shevchenko have appeared to be on the whim of the owner rather than the desire of the manager. Shevchenko was signed for a then record fee for an English club of £31 million in 2006, but never appeared to fit in and scored just nine goals before being allowed to depart to Dynamo Kiev on a free transfer three years later. Similarly, Abramovich has also seemed to change his mind quickly, which can be a problem for those working under him. After years of negotiation and planning, in January 2018 Chelsea were given the green light to build a new 60,000 capacity stadium to replace Stamford Bridge, only for plans to have been put on hold by the club because of a cited "unfavourable investment climate". Although Abramovich may never have committed himself to fully fund the stadium, he certainly had the resources to make a financial contribution and guarantee any commercial loans taken out by the club, which would have reduced the credit risk involved and allow Chelsea to borrow money at a lower interest rate.

The flipper

Nearly all football clubs, including those in the Premier League, were losing money until 2013. Since that date a combination of significant increases in broadcast income, along with wage control due to the Short Term Cost Control rules, have resulted in the Premier League being an industry where annual profits are now common. Whilst this has not resulted in owners necessarily paying themselves dividends (apart from those of Manchester United) as a means of withdrawing those profits, it has resulted in potential gains for the owners should they wish to sell the club to another party. This has meant that some clubs have been subject to a series of owners whose aim has been to buy the club, run it for a short time and then "flip" it for a profit. This is especially the case when a club is in financial distress and can be bought for a relatively small sum. Clubs such as Portsmouth and Leeds United have had a succession of owners who saw the potential of a large fanbase but were reluctant to invest in the playing side of the club because they wanted to make a profit on the deal. There is nothing presently in the rules set by governing authorities to prevent such behaviour and this allows some clubs and their fans' loyalties to be exploited by owners who know that regardless of their behaviour people will turn up and pay money to watch the team every match.

Fan owned/member clubs

In Spain in particular some clubs are owned by the fans instead of having shareholders. Clubs operate a membership scheme where for a fee fans can vote for and elect a president and board of directors. The advantage of such a model is that the board are accountable to the members and if they instigate policies that are unpopular can be voted out of office. The downside of this is that presidents spend a lot of time campaigning for re-election and making populist promises that are not always in the club's strategic long-term interests. In such scenarios, with the club having large income streams, it is able to borrow money from the capital markets to fund expansion, so they can be seen to operate in a similar manner to other non-football businesses.

In England there are some examples of fan ownership, in particular associated with "phoenix" clubs which were set up following ownership failures. Swansea City, Portsmouth, Wycombe Wanderers, AFC Wimbledon and Exeter City are just a few of the examples of clubs where there has been greater fan representation, although this does not guarantee sporting or financial success. The financing of such clubs is, however, more complex. Membership is usually on a one person/one vote basis and individual members have no obligation to fund any deficits beyond their membership fees. This can result in the club operating a more cautious financial strategy as fans often don't have the wealth to underwrite losses.

The history of such clubs is mixed. Swansea City Supporters' Trust was instrumental in helping rescue the club from oblivion in 2001 and bought a 21 per cent stake in the club in order to have some involvement in the decision-making process. When a majority stake in the club was bought by two American investors, Jason Levein and Steve Kaplan, the Trust claimed that it had been bypassed and that other investors made millions of pounds in the process. This highlights that even with significant shareholdings supporters' representatives can be eliminated from key events.

FC United of Manchester was set up as a fan-owned club in 2005 as a protest following the Glazer acquisition of Manchester United. It started off in the tenth tier of English football, but with attendances reaching over 6,000 in its first season was able to progress through the pyramid system and acquire its own stadium after initially ground sharing with Bury FC and some other clubs when there was a fixture clash. The club had a one person/one vote constitution regardless of the sums invested in the club. This has not prevented fallouts between the club board and the membership, which has resulted in conflict in terms of the future direction of the club.

This chapter has shown that there are many motivations for owning a football club, all of which have merits and demerits. The biggest investor in a club however is usually the fanbase, most of whom commit themselves emotionally to supporting the club for a life-time, whereas the owners, many of whom are well meaning, are more transient. Football is not the same as other industries as it provides people with an identity and can provide moments of collective joy and misery for towns and cities that no other business does, and for that reason clubs should be given greater protection from the few rogue owners that sometimes get involved with the game.

There are many examples of fine owners in all divisions, many of whom are unher-alded, such as Andy Holt at Accrington Stanley and Mark and Nicola Palios at Tranmere Rovers, who are dedicated to making the club the hub of the local community whilst also ensuring the club lives within its means financially.

13

RED FLAGS: THINGS THAT MAKE YOU GO "HMMM"

There are some common issues that fans should concern themselves with if ever they should choose to review the finances of their club. Whilst the majority of club owners and accounts have no issues surrounding them, there are some discrepencies and disclosures that anyone should look out for if they are concerned about the financial well-being of the club they support.

Better late than never

All UK limited companies must submit their accounts to Companies House, the government registrar of companies, within nine months of their financial year end. This is part of the price that limited companies pay for the benefits of being incorporated. The main advantage of being a "limited" business is that should the company enter into a corporate bankruptcy arrangement (which has been a common occurrence for football clubs in the past) then the maximum loss to the owners would be the value of the shares bought in the club. This could be a considerable amount of money, but creditors are unable to pursue the company owners on a personal level for monies owed, which would be the case if the club operated as a sole trader or partnership business. The downside to limited liability status is that companies are subject to greater regulation, such as submitting their accounts to a government agency where they are subject to public scrutiny.

Preparing a set of accounts is not something that can be done overnight for a football club with revenue of anywhere between £2 million and £600 million, but at the same time it should not take more than nine months. If clubs are late in submission it can only be if there is an item in the accounts that is being disputed at board level and the directors cannot agree, or the club doesn't want fans (and other interested parties) to see some of the figures, for whatever reason.

Crystal Palace have a financial year end of 30 June and have operated as CPFC 2010 Limited since their owners had bought the club from the administrators in 2010. At 31 March 2018 they had still not submitted figures for the year to 30 June 2017. At this stage there were two other stragglers from the Premier League in 2016/17, one of which was Sunderland, who at least had the equivalent of a note from their mum excusing them from attending PE lessons, in the form of two relegations and a takeover to deal with, as well as publish their financial results on time. Eventually Companies House had enough of Palace's owners' refusal to submit the figures and issued a notice of compulsory strike off on 5 June 2018. After some unflattering comments in the media, the club published a press release saying the delay was due to "technical reasons". This energized the club into action, firstly in appealing against the strike off notice, which if actioned, would have seen the assets of the company become those of the Crown.

Palace then published their accounts on 19 June, 11 weeks late. From reviewing these accounts it appeared that there were potentially some issues in terms of interest being paid on owners' loans. In the notes to the accounts there was an interest charge of £359,000 on these loans, but they then went on to say that the interest had been waived post-year end. If this was the case, why show the interest in the 2017 figures in the first place? Elsewhere in the accounts Palace's total wage bill had risen by 39 per cent, which for an established Premier League club seemed high. As a result, the club had the highest wages to income ratio in the division for that season (see Figure 13.1). Palace fans (and executives) may claim that delaying the submission of the figures until after the end of the following season gave them a competitive advantage over rivals when negotiating with

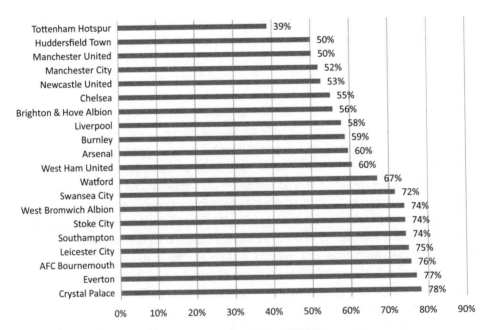

Figure 13.1 Premier League wage control percentages 2017/18

teams and players for transfers and wages, but this seems a high-risk strategy if it involves upsetting government agencies and being subject to a striking off notice.

Controlling the narrative

Many clubs are keen to promote a particular message in relation to their finances. They do this by initially publishing a press release which contains a select set of financial information, accompanied by carefully chosen words that promote a viewpoint, often in terms of the club owner's relationship to the club. On 18 May 2018 Newcastle United announced their results via a press release for the 2016/17 season, when the club were promoted as champions of the EFL Championship following relegation the previous season. The press release stated (amongst other things) that Newcastle had made an operating loss of £91 million, that the wage bill was £112 million and that "with the support and backing of the owner we took what was, in essence, a financial gamble on securing immediate promotion". Later on, the article read "Our ability to withstand the financial impact of relegation, and adopt the approach that we did, was therefore only made possible by the continued financial support of our owner, who injected a further £15m interest-free loan into the club in 2017".

The message being promoted by the club was clearly trumpeting the benevolence and altruism of Mike Ashley, the club's owner, who tends to split the Newcastle fanbase (they either hate him a little, or they hate him a lot). His unwillingness to invest in the playing squad since acquiring the club is legendary and many fans hold him responsible for the club being relegated twice during his ownership, despite selling out its 51,000-capacity stadium most weeks.

As previously discussed, under Mike Ashley Newcastle United has been cautious when investing in player recruitment, with the total net spend on players in the ten years of his ownership being less than £72 million, which is about the same as Chelsea spent on Real Madrid striker Alvaro Morata in 2017 in a single transaction. The announcement of the financial results could be seen as an attempt to redress the balance with the hope that the story might be picked up by local and national media who would act as an echo chamber for the club's message. Newcastle did not send their accounts to Companies House until 22 May 2018, by which time the media scrutiny had evaporated. A close look at the full accounts shows that whilst the club did make substantial losses in 2016/ 17, perhaps the Doomsday scenario implied by the announcement on the club website was overplaying the case.

In terms of the wage bill, the club paid £10 million for promotion bonuses and £22 million to players who did not play for the club in 2016/17, with Newcastle either paying up their contracts and/or sending them on loan and paying most of their wages. This brought the wage bill relating to those who were at the club down to about £80 million. If these figures are added back then the club made EBIT (recurring) losses of £59 million, still significant, but far less than the figure signalled by the club. And as for Ashley's loans, he had indeed lent the club £15 million during 2016/17. One could argue, however, that the major beneficiary of this was Mike Ashley. Having put the club onto the market to try and find a new owner in October 2017 with an asking price in the range of £300–350 million, compared to about £80–100 million as a Championship club, it was therefore in his interests to lend the club money whilst in the Championship so that he could potentially recover a larger sum should the club be sold in the Premier League. The gamble has paid off and Newcastle are an attractive proposition to a potential investor, with a price to match.

Loopholes

Companies that satisfy at least two of the following criteria: turnover of less than £10.2 million, total assets of less than £5.1 million, fewer than 50 employees, are classified as "small" and are allowed to submit a pared down set of accounts to Companies House. In particular, they do not have to make available for scrutiny their profit or loss account and the notes that relate to it. In addition, the balance sheet disclosures are significantly reduced. Who cares? Well, if your business is a small retailer, publisher, manufacturer, etc., then frankly no one tends to read your accounts, as the shareholders and directors tend to be the same individuals. But football clubs are different. Fans may not have legal possession of the shares of the club, but they are the emotional and spiritual owners. Football clubs are community assets, even if legally they are owned by private individuals. Fans are the people who travel the length and breadth of the country, in all types of weather, often with little chance of seeing a victory. Fans are the ones who commit every year to spend money for a season ticket months in advance of the first match taking place, not knowing which players they will be watching, or how much will be spent on recruitment and so on.

As such surely the least clubs could do is to allow their fans to be able to see, if they so desire, the key financial figures relating to their team, which would allow them a slightly more informed assessment of the decisions made by the club's directors. To be fair, some lower league clubs do show full sets of accounts even when there is no legal obligation to do so, but the commitment is not universal. The fan group, the Football Supporters Association, have lobbied the English Football League for a rule change to require full financial accounting disclosure but have had a negative response. This is because it is the club owners themselves who vote on the rules and there is insufficient enthusiasm for this to proceed. The Football Association could make it a rule that all professional clubs are obliged to publish full accounts if they want to participate in FA competitions but they have done nothing. The FA's indifference towards public scrutiny of stewardship of individual clubs by owners does not reflect well on an organization that is supposed to be the guardian of the game.

Consequently, clubs can end up showing accounts as brief as those, for example, from Bradford City, which effectively consist of three pages and very little detail. Fans are kept in the dark and the opportunities for financial abuses can potentially increase if there is limited content to scrutinize. Many small club owners are fantastic and work tirelessly for little reward or appreciation, but the scope for abuse increases if there is an information vacuum.

Without singling out Bradford City, such a short and thin set of accounts, with no profit or loss information and only an abbreviated balance sheet does means that Bradford City fans are unable to know how much revenue the club has generated. It should be noted that the club has a very progressive pricing policy that for many years has reduced season ticket prices should applications reach a particular threshold. This has created loyalty amongst its fans and the club had over 18,500 season ticket holders paying as little at £149 to see 23 games at Valley Parade in 2017/18. But do these season ticket sales cover the wage bill, the interest cost on any borrowings? How much money have the directors paid themselves during the year? And to what extent has money been invested in the playing squad? None of these questions are answered because the club publishes such little information. Many fans will shrug and couldn't care, for them football is 90 minutes of getting behind their team, a few drinks and a chat with their mates before and after the game. That's fine, so long as you always have a club to support. Bradford City were placed in administration in 2002 and 2004, which suggests that financial management skills and good corporate governance might have been lacking then, so can fans be assured that such abilities exist today? It also means that fans are putting their total faith in the board of directors, many of whom are, of course, as committed to the club as the fans themselves, but not all have such noble motives. In 2016/17 one club in the Championship (and we are looking at you here Barnsley), seven in League One and fourteen in League Two took such an approach and submitted a cut-down version of their accounts to the government registrar.

Corporate social responsibility is defined as a business approach that contributes to sustainable development by delivering economic, social and environmental benefits for all stakeholders. Given that fans are a key stakeholder group whose support is critical for the continued existence of the club they should be able to assess the financial consequences of decisions made by the directors.

Another legal loophole is to change the financial year end. Most football authorities insist that clubs have a financial year end between 31 May and 31 July of each year. Some clubs will change the figures to coincide with the end of a different calendar month (Liverpool in 2012 changed from 31 July to 31 May and Manchester City in 2017 changed from 31 May to 30 June). There are often logical business reasons for such a change, and whilst it means that comparisons with other clubs are slightly more difficult as an 11 or

13 month financial period has to be pro-rated to the 12 months of other clubs, it is little more than a tweaking of a spreadsheet for an experienced analyst.

If a company changes its year end by one day, then under UK legislation (section 442 of the 2006 Companies Act for those who like that type of thing) a company then has three months from that date to submit the accounts to Companies House. Bury Football Club Limited did this on 27 February 2018, a day before the deadline for its accounts for the previous financial year of 31 May 2017 were due. This meant that Bury had until 30 May 2018 to submit their accounts compared to the original submission. The club actually sent them in a month later, knowing full well that the registrar usually gives companies a month's grace before starting to instigate sanctions against the company involved.

Bury then forgot that they had changed their year-end and published accounts to 31 May 2017. To give Bury some credit, they did submit full accounts to the registrar when they could have submitted cut-down versions, but it would give some potentially unscrupulous owners the opportunity to keep fans and other interested parties further in the dark for a longer period of time.

Clubs may claim that they need the extra time in the case of a takeover and the new owners need to get to grips with the finances and the accounts. This may have some legitimacy in cases where the previous owners hadn't kept proper financial records, but is far more likely to be a red herring and simply a delaying tactic. Bury's accounts showed the club had been losing over £50,000 a week for some time, so perhaps it is understandable that the owner would want to delay such information being in the public domain. The then Bury owner, Stewart Day, was unable to continue to underwrite these losses and sold the club for £1 to a local businessman Steve Dale. Within a couple of months Steve Dale had stopped paying staff wages on time, as well as sums due to other creditors. He then failed to supply the EFL with evidence of proof of funding in relation to how he proposed to run the club and it was expelled from the EFL in August 2019 as relations between the two parties soured.

Perhaps the master of Section 442 year-end adjustments is Mike Ashley, the owner of Newcastle United via his personal company MASH Holdings, which lists 23 companies related to Newcastle football club. Whilst not wholly related to football clubs, his personal company, MASH Holdings Limited adjusted the financial reporting date of his company nine times in four years up to 2019 which has allowed the company to submit the financial statements approximately a year, instead of nine months, after the year-end. The financial activities are eventually produced, but as information decreases in value the longer it takes to produce from the event it relates to, Ashley's machinations reduces timely scrutiny of his companies' activities.

Complicated club structures

A football club company in theory should be a simple business to run, with a few income streams and easily identifiable costs. Therefore, for many clubs, especially those in the lower leagues, there is one company that deals with everything. This is not always the case. As we've just seen in the case of Newcastle United, there can be many companies involved, with Mike Ashley's Mash Holdings Limited owning 100 per cent of 23 companies with "Newcastle" or "NUFC" in their titles. What then arises is a set of Russian dolls in terms of the club structure, with one company owning another that owns a third company and so on. This has both positive and negative consequences for anyone wanting to analyse a club. Ultimately if you want to check the activities of a club the best thing to do is to review the consolidated accounts of the parent company (the one that directly or indirectly has over half the shares in other companies in the group). It is then possible to potentially see how well the activities of individual parts of the overall business are performing by drilling down to the accounts of individual subsidiaries, although the information shown here can be hit and miss.

There are some logical reasons for such company structures, which can involve elements of tax planning (more money for the club owners and the accountants who are responsible for these schemes, less for the tax authorities) and property ownership. In theory it would also allow a club owner to sell off elements of the club (such as the commercial or broadcasting elements) to another party without losing control of the football club itself. Complicated group structures do allow club owners to hide costs within the group.

Manchester City Limited is a 100 per cent owned subsidiary of City Football Group Limited, who own/control a number of other football clubs in the United States, Australia and Uruguay, as well as having minority stakes (i.e. less than 50%) in clubs in Japan and Spain. In Spain the City Group own 44 per cent of Girona, with the other main shareholder being Pere Guardiola, the brother of Manchester City manager Pep Guardiola. There is nothing wrong with such a setup, but critics of City and conspiracy theorists (who in football are never far away) claim that it gives the owners scope to allocate costs between the different football clubs in such a way as to ensure FFP compliance.

Table 13.1 shows the proportion of income and costs that are generated and borne by Manchester City Limited compared to the group as a whole for 2016/17. It's unsurprising

Table 13.1 Manchester City as a percentage of City Group income and costs, 2016/17

	Manchester City Limited	City Football Group Limited	MCFC as % of total
	£'m	£'m	
Income	473.4	515.4	91.9%
Wages	264.1	327.5	80.6%
Amortisation	121.7	121.8	99.9%
Other operating costs	120.2	177.0	67.9%
Loss before player sales	(30.2)	(105.1)	28.7%
Directors Pay (£'000)	Nil	4,252	0%

that Manchester City generate the vast majority of overall income given the club's participation in the Premier League and Champions League. Similarly, Manchester City being responsible for nearly all the transfer spending by the City Group, which is then reflected in the amortisation charge, is to be expected. What prompts critics to point their fingers at Manchester City is the treatment of wages and other costs. City Football Group Limited has many types of central costs such as HR, legal, marketing, IT, accounting and so on. These costs are then allocated to the individual football clubs within the group in a way determined by City Group Limited. Manchester City Limited being responsible for only just over two-thirds of "other costs" validates, in their own eyes at least, those who believe that the creation of City Group Limited is a means of giving Manchester City an unfair advantage over rival clubs. There is scope for a disproportionate amount of these central expenses to be allocated to the other football clubs within the City Football Group, allowing Manchester City to bear a lower proportion of the costs and so ensure compliance with FFP. Alternatively, these cost "savings", should they exist, could be used to spend more money on player signings and wages and improve Manchester City's playing competitiveness.

The devil is in the detail: footnote disclosures

Let's be honest, company accounts are dull (have you ever thought of downloading a copy of Vodafone's latest annual report to take on vacation for a bit of light reading?). The number of people likely to read them is relatively few to begin with and then they will usually concentrate on the headline figures. Owing to company legislation and accounting rules, there can, however, be interesting snippets of information in the back pages of the accounts. In addition, quite often the club chairperson will have a review of the club's activities which can illuminate some of the numbers.

These notes may reveal that the club owners are not quite as benevolent as they would have you believe. The following note to current liabilities in QPR's 2017 financial statements is a case in point:

> The revised convertible shareholder loans relate to the following amount which is interest bearing:
> £46,000,000 from Total Soccer Growth Sdn Bhd repayable on 31 May 2018. £30,000,000 has an interest rate of 1% per month, the remainder £16,000,000 has an interest rate of 2% per month. As at 31 May 2017 the total interest of £7,486,367 charged has been capitalised, further information in relation to this is shown under note 21.

The owners had lent the club money, which is perfectly legitimate and, in many ways it is great to see owners supporting the club financially. The note, however, reveals that interest is being charged at 1 per cent a month on part of the loans (works out at 12.7% a year) and 2 per cent a month on the remainder (26.8% a year).

For the year ended 30 June 2017 CPFC 2010 Limited, the company that rescued Crystal Palace from administration, paid one of their directors (almost certainly CEO Steve Parish) £2.15 million. Again, there is nothing illegal about such payments, companies are entitled to pay their staff whatever they choose and many of the first team squad would have been on more money that this anyway. Parish has worked tirelessly for the club and is entitled to financial rewards for his efforts.

On page 28 of the accounts, in note 23, there was a further revelation:

> During the year £234,000 (2016: £78,000) was charged to the Group by Smoke & Mirrors Group Limited, a company controlled by S Parish (a director), for rent payable under a tenancy agreement that can be terminated by giving six months' notice, with a further amount of £ nil being accrued at the year end (2016: £78,000).

Steve Parish was also renting out a property through a company called "Smoke & Mirrors Group Limited" to Palace for £234,000. Calling a company such a name does display a sense of humour, which is to be applauded. However, when Palace are also trying to justify to fans that they have limited sums to spend on players the following season, the joke backfires somewhat.

Case study: Derby County

Some of the above issues can combine to provide a layer of fog over the finances of a club. Let's consider Derby County. The Derby County Football Club Limited was incorporated in 1896. It has detailed the accounts of this fine club ever since. Anyone who has been to Derby for a match will tell you it has traditionally been a great day out for away fans, either at their former home, the Baseball Ground, or at Pride Park and locals call everyone "duck" which is endearing if a little odd. In September 2015 Derby County Football Club Limited were acquired by SevCo 5112 Limited, a company set up by local businessman Mel Morris when he bought the club from its previous owners. SevCo 5112 Ltd's accounts for the first year of trading were for the twelve months to 31 August 2016, which is perfectly acceptable. It did mean that including the results for Derby County Football Club Limited was a bit tricky, as Derby's accounts were to the year ended 30 June 2016.

Under the new regime Derby invested heavily in players in 2015/16, spending £26.6 million (see Figure 13.2). Manager Paul Clement was sacked by Morris in February

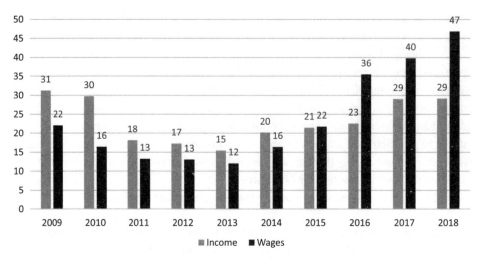

Figure 13.2 Derby County income and wages, 2009–18 (£ millions)

2016 for not playing football "the Derby way" and the club missed out on promotion to the Premier League after being eliminated in the play-offs by Hull City. On 28 March 2018 the club via the official website, published the following press release:

> Derby County have today announced their financial results for the 2016/17 season, reporting another record turnover and more strategic investment on the playing side, operational functions and infrastructure of the club [...] The financial year 1 July 2016 to 30 June 2017 saw a best ever Championship turnover (in non-parachute payment years) of £29m, up £6.4m on the previous year [...] The signing of players including Matej Vydra, David Nugent and Ikechi Anya were made during ... the year ... the sales of Jeff Hendrick, Lee Grant, Will Hughes and Tom Ince in this financial year contributed to a profit on player registrations of £16.2m [...] Total staff costs across the Club rose from £33.1m to £34.6m [...] The overall result was a loss of £7.9m in the financial year, compared to £14.7m in the previous year.

The website did not, unlike the approach taken by many other clubs, publish the accounts themselves. The local media summarized the press release in an article and as the results seemed an improvement on the previous year, there seemed little to get excited about so everyone lost interest quickly. On 6 April 2018 the accounts of Derby County Football Club Limited were submitted to Companies House. When compared to the press release, a detailed analysis of the accounts revealed, as C&C Music Factory used to sing, "Things to make you go hmmm...". The income total had indeed increased

Table 13.2 Derby County FC wages, 2017

Employees

Staff costs, including directors' remuneration, were as follows:

	As restated	
	2017	2016
	£	£
Wages and salaries	**29,971,254**	29,338,856
Social security costs	**4,568,443**	3,435,214
Other pension costs	**27,793**	153,112
	34,567,490	33,127,182

The average monthly number of employees, including the directors, during the year was as follows:

	2017	2016
	No.	No.
Players and apprentices	**25**	62
Management and coaching	**31**	60
Groundsmen, kitchen and cleaning	**11**	16
Administration and marketing	**85**	113
	152	251

In addition to the above the Company employs on average 252 [2016: 282] casual matchday staff at a total costs of £413,055 [2016: £455,935].

Source: Derby County Football Club Ltd

by £6.4 million (an impressive 29%) compared to the comparative figures for the previous year, and the wages figure by a far more moderate 4 per cent. On the face of things this looked as if the club had controlled costs well for the year.

The wages note (Table 13.2) also revealed that the average number of employees at the club had plummeted from 251 to 152 which seems strange given the club had not changed its activities in the year and so it seems difficult to justify a 40 per cent reduction in staffing levels. In the strategic report there was reference to companies called "Club DCFC Limited" and "Stadia DCFC Limited", but no reference to how many, if any, jobs were being transferred to these companies.

The profit or loss account (see Table 13.3) did show a loss of £7.9 million for 2017 as per the press release. The loss shown, however, was after player sales, which as has been discussed before, are volatile and unpredictable. The operating loss for Derby was over £23 million. The Derby press release referred to the sale of Tom Ince and Will Hughes as being included in the profit on the sale in the year ended 30 June 2017. The excellent Hughes was sold on 24 June 2017 for an estimated £8 million to Premier League Watford, a transaction perhaps accelerated to book a decent profit in the 2017 profit and

Table 13.3 Derby County FC proft and loss account, 2017

	Note	2017 £	2016 £
Revenue	4	29,029,577	22,558,821
Direct operating costs		(135,261,413)	(35,003,199)
Gross loss		(6,231,836)	(12,444,378)
Administrative expenses		(12,003,8881	(11,608,379)
Amortisation of players' registrations, levies and associated costs		(5,041,196)	(3,370,103)
Operating loss	6	(23,276,920)	(27,422,860)
Profit or disposal of players' registrations, levies and associated costs		16,154,429	199,661
Exceptional operating income	5	–	12,433,568
Loss on ordinary activities before interest		(7,122,491)	(14,789,631)
Interest receivable and similar income		–	64,278
Interest payable and expenses	10	(750,224)	–
Loss before tax		(7,872,715)	(14,725,353)
Tax on loss	11	–	–
Loss for the financial year		(7,872,715)	(14,725,353)

Source: Derby County Football Club Ltd

loss account. Ince, however, was not sold by Derby until 5 July 2017. Some would argue that the profit on the sale should therefore be delayed until the year ended 30 June 2018, although the accounting rules here are ambiguous.

Another figure that looked unusual was that of player amortisation, which if you recall is the price of a transfer fee spread over the contract life. Derby spent £51 million on players in 2016 and 2017 according to the accounts, yet the amortisation charge in 2017 was only £5.1 million. Until 2015, Derby's accounting policy in respect of transfers was identical to that of all other clubs:

> Amounts paid to third parties for players' registrations, Football League levies, agents' commissions and compensation for mangement and coaching staff are capitalised as intangible assets and amortised on a straight line basis over the period of the players' or other employees' contracts. Players' registrations are written down for impairment when the carrying amount exceeds the amount recoverable through use or sale. (Derby County FC)

But the club then changed its policy to the following:

> The costs associated with acquiring players' registrations, inclusive of EFL levies, or expanding their contracts, including agent fees, are capitalised and amortised over the period of the respective players' contracts after consideration of their residual values. (Derby County FC)

It may not look significantly different, but the key words are the final ones "amortised over the period of the respective players' contracts *after consideration of their residual values*". Under such a policy a club has the opportunity to be creative with the figures to reduce the annual amortisation charge and so perhaps comply with FFP rules.

Consider the following: Fulchester Rovers signs a player for £12 million on a four-year contract. Most clubs would therefore have an annual depreciation charge of £3 million a year. If the club however allocates a residual value of the player (residual value is the expected value of the player at the end of the contract) of say £8 million, then the annual amortisation charge falls to £1 million a year ((£12m − £8m)/4). This would boost profit or reduce losses by £2 million in a year.

Figure 13.3 shows the amortisation charge as a proportion of the average cost of players at the start and end of the year for 2016/17. A low figure means that amortisation is only

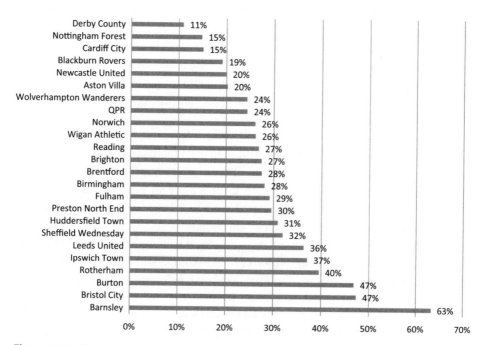

Figure 13.3 Championship amortisation cost as percentage of player costs

a small fraction of the cost of the players and therefore has a relatively smaller impact on profits and losses. Derby County have by far the lowest amortisation percentage in the division for 2016/17. Two years earlier, when their accounting policy was the same as for all other clubs, the figure was 29 per cent, much closer to the divisional average. If the figures are inverted it means that Derby are effectively amortising their player signings over nine years (1/11%).

A look at the accounting rules on the topic (Financial Reporting Standard FRS 102) per the Institute of Chartered Accountants in England and Wales shows the following:

> FRS 102.18.23 states that the residual value of an intangible asset must be nil unless either:
> - a third party has committed to purchase the asset at the end of its useful life; or
> - there is an active market for the asset from which the residual value can be determined and which is probable that such a market will be in existence at the end of the asset's useful life.

The rule would appear to suggest that Derby should not be using residual values for players unless:

(a) Derby have a third party committed to buying the player at the end of his useful life. This sounds reasonable, but surely at the end of a player's contract he is entitled to a Bosman transfer and so there would be no residual value, or;

(b) There is an active market for the asset. An active market is defined by accountants as "a market in which transactions for the asset take place with sufficient frequency and volume to provide pricing information on an ongoing basis".

The problem here is that when dealing with individual footballers, they are not being transferred on a frequent basis or at volume. There is, after all, as Derby fans occasionally sang, only one Bradley Johnson and as such there is not a set price for his registration. A football registration is not the same as the value of a barrel of oil or a taxi licence for a city where the value of the asset is identical. It would therefore appear that Derby's approach is inconsistent with the rules. This doesn't mean the club is wilfully doing something wrong, but the opportunity to reduce amortisation charges to comply with FFP limits is amplified.

So, what about the change in employee numbers? A few days after Derby County Football Club Limited submitted its accounts for 2016/17, SevCo 5112 Ltd did the same. SevCo 5112's accounts were for the 10 months to 30 June 2017. This appears logical as it ties in with the football club's year-end. SevCo's accounts showed that it now controlled a number of companies that had been set up to operate the different activities of the club (see Table 13.4).

Table 13.4 Subsidiary undertakings of SevCo 5112 Ltd

13. Fixed asset investments

Subsidiary undertakings

The following were subsidiary undertakings of the Company:

Name	Class of shares	Holding	Principal activity
SEVCO 5113 Limited	Ordinary	100%	Intermediate holding company
Global Derby (UK) Limited	Ordinary	100%	Intermediate holding company
Gellaw 101 Limited	Ordinary	100%	Intermediate holding company
Derby County Football Club Limited	Ordinary	100%	Playing activities of a professional football club
Club DCFC Limited	Ordinary	100%	Event and catering activities
Stadia DCFC Limited	Ordinary	100%	Sponsorship and broadcasting
The Derby County FC Academy Limited	Ordinary	100%	Playing activities of a professional football club
Derby County Stadium Limited	Ordinary	100%	Dormant
DCFC Limited	Ordinary	100%	Dormant

Source: SevCo 5112 Ltd

This too is common in relation to the way that club activities are split up. When it comes to wages and salaries, under accounting rules all subsidiary company results (where the parent owns more than 50%) are added to those of the parent. Whilst it is unusual to separate out the academy team activities from those of the first team, setting up a separate company to do this is perfectly legal and would give Derby's owners a better indication of the costs of running an academy.

It therefore appears, rather than Derby employing fewer staff than the previous year, as had been indicated by the Derby County Football Club Limited accounts (see Table 13.5), employee numbers overall had in fact increased in 2016/17.

As can be seen from Table 13.6, wage costs for SevCo 5112 fell by nearly 7 per cent to £33.2 million. This, however, only covers a ten-month accounting period. If the figures are pro-rated upwards by multiplying by 12/10 it gives £39.8 million, an increase of 12 per cent over the previous year, much higher than the 4 per cent figure shown in the press release. While Derby and SevCo 5112's activities are within the law, in terms of being open and transparent the approach is at best described as muddying the waters. Derby will no doubt claim there are legitimate business, operational and tax reasons for the new set up of companies within the group and if so, that is perfectly logical restructuring. What rests less comfortably is the nature of the press release at an earlier date that paints a rosier picture of the club finances than might otherwise be the case. The club can argue that they are under no obligation to make the life of an analyst easy, but being obtuse only makes anyone with a curious mind want to look a bit closer, although the majority of fans won't care an iota as long as the club is winning and compliant with FFP.

Table 13.5 SevCo 5112 monthly number of employees, 2017

The average monthly number of employees, including the directors, during the period was as follows:

	2017 No.	2016 No.
Players and apprentices	69	62
Management and coaching	77	75
Groundsmen, kitchen and cleaning	20	19
Administration and marketing	117	109
	283	265

In addition to the above the Group employs on average 252 (2016: 282) casual matchday staff at a total cost of £413,055 (2016: £455,935).

Source: SevCo 5112 annual report

Table 13.6 Staff costs, SevCo 5112 at 30 June 2017

7. Employees

Staff costs, including directors' remuneration, were as follows:

	Group 10 months ended 30 June 2017 £	Group As restated 12 months ended 31 August 2016 £
Wages and salaries	28,638,991	31,316,323
Social security costs	4,341,257	4,018,415
Cost of defined contribution scheme	175,117	170,486
	33,155,365	35,505,224

Source: SevCo 5112

The following season, Derby's results also caused concern as the parent SevCo 5112 Ltd produced the profit or loss account in Table 13.7. Initially a loss before interest of just over £1 million seems very modest by Championship standards, but a couple of lines above that figure is £39.9 million of "profit on disposal of tangible assets". Further investigation reveals that this was the sale of the club's stadium, Pride Park, to another company controlled by the club owner, Mel Morris. There is nothing illegal in such a transaction but without it the club may have almost certainly exceeded allowable Profitability and Sustainability loss limits and may have been subject to a points deduction the following season.

An understanding of the basics of a set of accounts is of benefit for anyone who wants to analyse the finances of an individual club or division in a league. Some clubs produce excellent summaries of financial data, with Juventus perhaps producing the most detailed

Table 13.7 Consolidated statement of income year ended 30 June 2018, SevCo

	Note	12 months ended 30 June 2018	10 months ended 30 June 2017
		£	£
Turnover	4	29,145,483	24,627,218
Direct operating costs		(52,576,437)	(37,761,339)
Gross loss		(23,430,754)	(13,134,121)
Administrative expenses		(16,692,022)	(10,210,544)
Amortisation of players registrations, levies and associated costs		16,540,038	(4,381,877)
Operating loss	5	(46,662,814)	(27,726,542)
Profit/loss on disposal of tangible assets		39,940,387	–
Profit on disposal of players, registrations, levies and associated costs		3,719,424	7,193,881
Management compensation		1,850,000	–
Loss on ordinary activities before interest		(1,153,003)	(20,532,661)

Source: SevCo 5112 Ltd

of any club in terms of information about players. It is, however, concerning that too many clubs use creative accounting, legal loopholes, delaying tactics and sleight of hand when reporting their financial affairs, as this only reinforces the view held by many fans that some club owners are acting in their own interests rather than for the long-term benefit of the fans and local community.

GLOSSARY OF ACCOUNTANCY TERMS

Account payable (trade creditor)   A sum owed to another business by the club. Many, but not all clubs, separate this out between amounts due on player transfers and sums owing to other suppliers.

Accounts receivable (trade debtor)   Money owed to the football club by customers. May be separated between sums due from other clubs for transfers and other debts due to the club.

Accrual   An expense that has been incurred but not recognized initially in the accounts. For example, a club may have used an agent to sell a player before its 30 June 2018 year-end but does not receive the invoice until August 2018. The club would therefore accrue for the agent fee in the accounts for the year ended 30 June 2018.

Acquisition   The process through which one company acquires another, can be used when buying a football club.

Amortisation   The method used to expense purchased football players in the profit or loss account. Amortisation is the player cost spread over the length of the contract signed.

Asset   An item controlled by the club that generates income or saves costs due to a past event with a known value. Assets are part of the balance sheet.

Authorised share capital   The maximum number of shares a club can issue to investors according to its constitution.

Balance sheet   A financial photograph of a club on a particular date, usually the last day of the financial year. It summarises the assets, liabilities and equity of the club.

Cash equivalents   Short-term investments which are nearly but not quite cash. Usually things such as short-term deposit accounts of less than three months majority.

Cash flow statements   A summary of the cash received and paid by the club during the year, split into three areas of the business, operating, investing and financing.

Consolidated accounts   The accounts of the parent/holding company and all its subsidiaries added together.

Contingent asset   A possible asset of the club, often a sell-on transfer fee in respect of a player the club had sold at an earlier date. It is shown in the footnotes to the accounts rather than the balance sheet.

Contingent liability   A possible liability of the club, often money potentially due to other clubs, agents or players if certain conditions are satisfied, such as number of appearances, international caps and so on.

Current asset   An asset that is cash or is expected to convert into cash in less than one year.

Current liabilities   A liability that is due to be paid in less than one year.

Depreciation   The same as amortisation, but used for tangible assets such as property, machinery and office equipment.

Deferred income   Money received by the club in advance of providing the customer with goods or services. Usually season tickets paid for the next season or monies paid in advance by sponsors or broadcasters.

EBIT   Earnings Before Interest and Tax. Operating profit adjusted for non-recurring costs and income, such as profits on player sales and redundancy payments to sacked managers

EBITDA   Earnings Before Interest Tax, Depreciation and Amortisation. EBIT plus the non-cash costs of depreciation and amortisation. Liked by analysts because it is a cash proxy for profit.

Equity (capital)   The amount that is owed by the club to the owners, consisting of invested equity (share capital) and reinvested equity (profits made since the club started trading)

Fixed asset (non-current asset)   An asset used in the business for at least one year.

Impairment   Reducing the value of an asset, usually a player, in the balance sheet, due to injury, poor performance or being Mario Balotelli.

Income statement   Summary of income, costs and profit.

Intangible asset   An asset that has no physical substance. For most clubs this is the amounts paid for player registrations. Only applies if the club has paid a fee for the players, so those who come through the academy route are excluded as they have no cost.

Inventories (stock)   Goods and merchandise for resale owned by the club at the year-end.

Liability   An amount owed by the club to a third party, such as another club for a transfer fee, a bank for a loan, a supplier or bonuses for players.

Net profit   Profit for the year after all costs have been paid, which belongs to the club owners.

Non-current asset   See fixed asset.

Off balance sheet finance   Money owed by the club that doesn't appear on the balance sheet due to the dark arts of accounting.

Operating lease   Rent costs paid by the club, can also often find the future rent costs in the footnotes.

Operating profit   Income of the club less day-to-day running costs.

Profit before tax   Operating profit less net finance costs to banks.

Post-balance sheet events   Footnotes that show financial implications of major events since the balance sheet date. Main ones that fans will be concerned about are transfers in and out.

Provision   A liability which contains a bit of guesswork and is uncertain as to how much it will be and when it will be payable. Main ones tend to be legal claims against the club.

Recognition criteria   The rules that have to be satisfied before something can appear in the accounts.

Related parties   Transactions by the club with fellow subsidiaries, owners and companies controlled or influenced by the owners or their close families. Shown in the footnotes to the accounts.

Revenue   Income earned by the club in the year, mainly from matchday, broadcasting and commercial sources.

Stocks   See inventories.

Substance over form   Ignoring the legal nature of a transaction and showing the economic nature of it instead.

Trade creditor   See accounts payable.

Useful economic life   Life of an asset for depreciation or amortisation purposes.

FURTHER READING

There are many great contributors in relation to the business of football, here are a selection of my favourites. Simon Kuper and Stefan Syzmanski's *Soccernomics* (London: HarperCollins, 2018) is the godfather of football business books, combining the research of Stefan Szymanski with the journalistic curiosity of Simon Kuper, which looks at the economic factors that make some countries successful at football and why others are likely to stay in the doldrums. If you want to know how a player transfer is conducted, Daniel Geey's *Done Deal* (London: Bloomsbury, 2019) is the book. As a lawyer who has represented all sides of the deal, Dan Geey lays bare the intricacies and challenges of football negotiations. Michael Calvin's *Living on the Volcano* (London: Century, 2015) looks at the day-to-day challenges of being a football manager and how so many people are attracted to a job where the average tenure is measured in months rather than years. The financial challenges facing managers, especially those at lower league clubs, are laid bare. Joshua Robinson and Jonathan Clegg's *The Club* (London: John Murray, 2019) is a history of the Premier League and the people and factors that made it the most popular sporting broadcasting product in the world. In *The Fall of the House of FIFA* (London: Yellow Jersey, 2017) *The Guardian*'s rottweiler-like investigative journalist David Conn turns his sights on FIFA and the impact that money has made on decision-making within football's governing body. Nick De Marco's *Football and the Law* (London: Bloomsbury, 2017) is a very thorough analysis of how law impacts upon football in terms of disputes and disagreements between clubs, governing bodies and individuals from one of the UK's leading barristers specializing in the sport. Ben Smith's *Journeyman* (London: Biteback, 2015) charts Ben's career at a series of clubs and the negotiations he has with managers and owners shows that football finances from an individual's perspective are very precarious.

A couple of magazines are worth mentioning too: *The Athletic* has forays into the finances of football on occasion, and *FourFourTwo* is always a good read for anyone wanting interviews and insight into club and international football.

Similarly, the following Twitter feeds are good sources of information. No one has more spreadsheets and charts on the game in Europe than Kieron O'Connor, the Swiss

Rambler, @SwissRamble. A lifetime working in finance plus being multilingual allows him to analyse clubs from all over the Continent. Excellent taste in music too. Sets the standards that others can only dream to achieve. If you like stats, then Ben Mayhew's Twitter feed @Experimental361 is heaven in 280 characters. And @NTT20Pod focuses outside of the top division and often looks as the precarious nature of finances in the EFL.

INDEX